THE

WOMAN

ADVOCATE

THE

WOMAN

ADVOCATE

Second Edition

Abbe F. Fletman and Evelyn R. Storch
Editors

AMERICAN BAR ASSOCIATION
Section of Litigation

Cover design by ABA Publishing.

Printed in the United States of America.

12 11 10   5 4 3 2

Library of Congress Cataloging-in-Publication Data

Cataloging-in-Publication. Data is on file.
ISBN: 978-1-60442-723-3

Discounts are available for books ordered in bulk. Special consideration is given to state bars, CLE programs, and other bar-related organizations. Inquire at Book Publishing, ABA Publishing, American Bar Association, 321 North Clark Street, Chicago, Illinois 60654-7598.

www.ababooks.org

To my spouse, Jane Hinkle, and our children, Ted and Liz, who put up with yet another extra-curricular activity, and to all the women advocates who came before us and on whose shoulders we stand.

Abbe Fletman

To Elliott, without whom I would not even be a lawyer and who inspires me every day, and to my sisters at the bar and bench who, against all odds, succeed every day in large ways and small.

Evelyn Storch

Contents

Editorial Board

Foreword

THE FIRST EDITION of *The Woman Advocate* was published in the 1995–1996 bar year, during the tenure of the American Bar Association's first woman President, Roberta Cooper Ramo. Since then, other distinguished women lawyers have earned the honor of leading our association: Martha Barnett in 2000–2001 and Karen Mathis in 2006–2007. I am proud to be the fourth woman to serve as ABA President this bar year.

All four of us can remember a time when women were not given a seat at the table. Our association and profession have made progress toward greater gender equality. Yet, as women lawyers across the country know all too well, we also have a long way to go before women lawyers will have the same opportunities as their male colleagues. Although women now make up about 45 percent of students entering law school, we comprise only about 30 percent of lawyers and roughly 15 percent of partners in large law firms or general counsels in Fortune 500 companies. Significantly, we have only two women justices on our Supreme Court and few in the most powerful positions in the leadership of our government.

This book is a resource for women lawyers striving for equal opportunities at their workplaces. Leading women lawyers from various practice settings offer their views of the distinct challenges women face in the profession, tips about how to overcome these challenges, and thoughts about what the future holds.

We all can relate to, learn from, and be inspired by the contributors to this important volume. Their stories will help us overcome adversity and demonstrate on the merits that women deserve parity in the legal profession. I wish through some of the inspirational stories that you will set a course professionally to become all you are capable of being.

Carolyn B. Lamm
President, American Bar Association

Acknowledgments

Thanks to the leadership of the American Bar Association Litigation Section, without whom this new edition would not have happened. In particular, Bob Rothman, immediate past chair of the Section, and Lorna Schofield, our current chair, deserve our gratitude, as does Janet Kole, the Book Publishing Board co-chair, who championed this new edition, read every word, kept us on the right track and gave us wise counsel. Likewise, we thank the Woman Advocate Committee of the Litigation Section, which inspired both editions of this book and provided us with a talented group of authors. We are also grateful to Tim Brandhorst, the ABA publications staffer who saw us through the editing process, and Lisa Maroccia, Abbe's assistant who kept track of every version and communication. Finally, and most expecially, thanks to the authors of this book, who devoted time and energy to sharing pathways to success and roads better not taken. May their stories inspire the next generations of women advocates.

Abbe F. Fletman and Evelyn R. Storch

PART I

Where We Are

Introduction 1

By Abbe F. Fletman

M<small>ORE THAN</small> 130 years ago, the United States Supreme Court admitted the first woman lawyer, Belva A. Lockwood, to practice before it. Her admission did not come without a fight. She had to petition President Grant, who also served as president of her law school, even to obtain her law diploma. The Supreme Court initially turned her away until she successfully lobbied Congress to pass special legislation allowing the admission of women. Her success "virtually opened the doors of all Federal courts in the country to the women of the land. . . ." Belva A. Lockwood, "My Efforts to Become a Lawyer," *Lippincott's Monthly Magazine*, February 1888, pp. 215–30.

Much, of course, has changed for the better since Lockwood first opened the federal court system to her sister lawyers. As of October 2009, women comprised 48 percent of the first- and second-year associates at law firms throughout the nation. Women now hold 26.3 percent of the judgeships on state courts of last resort, 19.2 percent of federal district court seats, 20.1 percent of federal appellate judgeships, and 22.2 percent of the United States Supreme Court.

But after at least two decades of near-gender parity in law school classes, fewer than 16 percent of the equity partners at law firms are women. Only six percent of law firm managing partners are women. And women lawyers earn less than men at every stage of their careers. What starts as a $2,000 annual gap between male and female associates accelerates to a $66,000 annual gap between male and female equity partners.

Women trial lawyers still confront the dilemma of whether judges, juries, clients and colleagues will perceive them as strong and confident or overly aggressive. The debate over women's courtroom attire recently has exploded anew, with judges complaining about short skirts and plunging necklines.

Sixteen years ago, the American Bar Association published the first edition of the Woman Advocate. Many of the topics of discussion among women litigators remain the same, and so, as before, you will find chapters on succeeding in a variety of settings, from academia to the bench to law firms big and small. As topical as ever is how juries view women lawyers and how to thrive in the profession as a woman of color or a lesbian. Yet much has changed since the last edition of this book in 1994. New in this edition, for example, are chapters on emotional intelligence, bridging the generational divide, using the Internet and winding down a law career. We even have a chapter on having fun.

All of the authors of this book and all of the chapters are entirely new. What they provide, most of all, are unique and individual voices addressing the timeliest and most pressing issues for women advocates. We hope they provide sound advice, provoke your thinking and inspire your continued development and contributions to our profession and nation.

We unfortunately cannot escape that we have yet to reach parity with our male counterparts. But we are on the front lines of changing social attitudes about women. And, to paraphrase Justice O'Connor, "Each and every one of us has an important role to play" to complete the work of creating a society—and a profession—in which "all persons, regardless of gender, have the opportunity to earn respect, responsibility, advancement, and remuneration based on ability." Let us celebrate the steps we have taken and rededicate ourselves to finish the task.

Women in the Courtroom Today | 2

By Tara Trask

SUCCESS

In our society, it is understood that to be a lawyer is to be successful. Even as children, we are not taught that success is being an investment banker or a private equity partner, but rather a doctor or a lawyer—a professional. Consequently, most jurors come into the box with very deep respect for the success of attorneys, despite commonly expressed derogation of the profession.

Add to that the fact that, historically, litigation has been a man's game. The images of Perry Mason and Atticus Finch have seeped into the national psyche. One of the first female lawyer to come along on TV was Ally McBeal, and she was a bumbling mess. On a subconscious level, jurors tend to assume that lawyers will be men. While such assumptions are changing, it is still true that many jurors—including young ones—view lawyering as an inherently masculine endeavor, where women rarely venture.

This bias translates into a heightened scrutiny of female attorneys. The tendency to judge them can certainly be found in the courtroom:

> "She seemed organized, and I think she knew what she was talking about, but I didn't like her suits and I know she believes in her case, but she just seemed a bit shrill at times."

Juror in a post-trial interview after a closing argument.

Anecdotes such as this abound, yet it is difficult to imagine a juror making similar comments about a male attorney. Almost everyone has some story about a judge, a juror, or a colleague applying a double standard to women and men, or simply being impossible to please. Research on these topics in the last few years is bringing scientific data to bear where, previously, there was only anecdotal (although very consistent) information available. Women attorneys have two main things working against them in the courtroom: they are perceived as successful in a man's profession, and some of the qualities they need to do their job effectively simply do not help them win favor with jurors.

WHY YOUR SUCCESS HURTS YOU

Recent research suggests that males and females alike "penalize" successful women by characterizing them as unlikeable or hostile.[1] Even more importantly, studies are starting to explain why this happens. Women are motivated to punish successful women in order to minimize the effects of comparing

---

1. Parks-Stamm, E. (2008). Motivated to Penalize: Women's Strategic Rejection of Successful Women Pers Soc Psychol Bull. 2008; 34:237-247.

themselves with high-achieving females. Whereas both male and female participants penalized successful women, when researchers withheld information that would allow the participants to view the successful women as unlikeable, overly aggressive and hostile, female participants reduced their self-ratings of competence, while their male counterparts did not make an attendant reduction.

It appears that these unconscious feelings are very deeply rooted and become internalized at a young age. In fact, the participants in this study were all undergraduate students at a prestigious college and presumably young and quite successful themselves.

These results suggest that the penalizing of successful women by other women serves to protect against threatening social comparisons. How does this apply in the courtroom when considering the stay-at-home mom on the jury? The natural inclination may be to attempt to connect with her by talking about your own children, but this research at least gives pause to that strategy.

As discouraging as this research may be, it does comport with what many female attorneys express anecdotally and what is reported repeatedly in pre-trial interviews. What is interesting about this study is that the very thing many female attorneys do to try to humanize themselves to the jury may actually backfire. Sharing personal information may be a mistake—a woman on the jury who perceives the female trial lawyer as more successful may cause her to feel worse about herself (*i.e.*, rate herself lower), especially if the female attorney is also married with children.

THE TRIAL LAWYER ARCHETYPE

Another significant problem for a female trial attorney is the fact that she is up against a very old archetype, that of trial lawyer. Because being a trial lawyer—tough, arrogant, strong, aggressive, and even bombastic—requires attributes traditionally associated with men, women trial lawyers can be rebuked for displaying these very same qualities.

On point, one study examined the effect of gender on jury decisions and found that aggressive attorneys were, overall, judged to be more successful than passive attorneys.[2] Women, however, did not gain the same advantages from an aggressive style as their male counterparts, placing them in a Catch-

---

2. Hahn, P. & Clayton, S. (1996). The effects of attorney presentation style, attorney gender and juror gender on juror decisions. Law and Human Behavior, Vol 20, No. 5, pp. 553-554.

22. To be successful at trial, one must be forceful, yet being too aggressive can negatively affect jurors' views of women litigators. Aggressiveness in men, by contrast, has come to be expected and respected. Because aggressiveness is perceived as inversely related to friendliness, and our society expects women to be friendly, female attorneys who are in a role that is necessarily direct, assertive, and adversarial may be viewed negatively.[3]

In some cases, however, differences in how women and men are perceived may produce an advantage. In a study on aggression, for example, a male witness was considered friendlier when he was interrogated by a female attorney, implying that in a mixed gender confrontation, the exchange seems less abrasive and unpleasant.[4]

Women face a similar dilemma when it comes to expressing anger. A series of studies showed that both men and women reached the same conclusions: Angry men deserve more status, should get a higher salary, and are expected to be better at a job than angry women. These effects were somewhat mitigated when the women explained why they were angry.[5]

THREADING THE NEEDLE

So, as a female trial lawyer, if you have ever felt you were fighting an uphill battle, the research suggests that indeed you are. But how can these studies be reconciled with the clear success that many female trial lawyers achieve? The answer is that those women thread the needle.

The female trial lawyer who threads the needle is effective, confident, composed and in control, and, yet, at the same time, feminine. Most very successful female litigators seem to share a quiet but commanding confidence, a feminine compassion, and a demeanor that denotes a calm, matriarchal quality only slightly eclipsed by dedicated professionalism. There is a sense that she has a family and friends, but that her work is her passion.

The successful female trial attorney is not shrill, and she is not aggressive, although she needs to be assertive. She is confident without being icy,

3. Newcombe, N. & Arnkoff, D. (1979). Effects of speech and style and sex of speaker on person perception. Journal of Personality and Social Psychology, 37(8), pp. 1293-1303.

4. Hahn, P. & Clayton, S. (1996). The effects of attorney presentation style, attorney gender and juror gender on juror decisions. Law and Human Behavior, Vol 20, No. 5, pp. 553-554.

5. Brescoll, V. & Uhlmann, E. (2008). Can an angry woman get ahead? Status conferral, gender, and expression of emotion in the workplace. *Psychological Science,* March, pp. 268-275.

but gives the impression that her warmth will evaporate quickly if crossed. She is a professional but clearly takes time with her appearance. She sends no sexual signals, because she means business—on her terms.

If this picture of a successful female attorney seems narrow, that's because it is. The threading the needle analogy describes where women are in the courtroom today. Experience indicates that truly successful trial lawyers—those who are beloved by juries—tend to share these qualities. The trick is to thread the needle.

THINGS TO KEEP IN MIND

- Aggression does not work for women in the courtroom. Assertiveness can, but not aggression.
- Women tend to have the advantage of superior emotional intelligence. This allows them to better read the terrain, and how others are perceiving things.
- Confidence is good. Arrogance is bad. This may seem obvious, but consider the audience and consider the possibility that what you perceive as confidence may be viewed as arrogance by the working class mom on the panel. Modulate.
- Understand appearance. In Malcolm Gladwell's book, *Blink*, he laid out the importance of first impressions. First impressions are influenced by expectations, so it's important to fit with jurors' expectations of what a lawyer is—meaning professional and pulled together.
- Measure your use of emotion carefully. The range of emotions afforded to female lawyers is simply narrower than that afforded to men.

In one of the studies previously described, the participants who held women to a different standard than men were all college students. This is discouraging and suggests that perhaps we've not come as far as we would like. But societal changes experienced by the youngest jurors cannot be ignored. The contributions of women in the workplace, increased diversity, and a focus on diversity in the media should all continue to affect these trends positively. Perhaps, over time, the eye of that needle will continue to widen.

Striking a Balance in Law and Life | 3

By Alana K. Bassin

A LAWYER COLLEAGUE tells the story of when someone asked her three-year-old son if he wanted to be a lawyer when he grew up. He said, "No, I am going to be a man."

He thought all lawyers were women.

Those of us in the trenches know that not all lawyers are women. In fact, the attrition rate for women private practice continues to be staggering, and the percentage of women in ownership and management positions is almost pitiful. According to the National Association of Women Lawyer's 2006 national survey on retention and promotion of women in law firms, 50% of law graduates have been women over the past 15 years, but only 15% are equity partners.

Women no doubt leave the legal workplace for various reasons: personal choice, philanthropic work, the "maternal wall," among others. A common theme for most, however, is the difficulty of managing a successful professional career with a rewarding personal life. Every entering lawyer class asks the same question: "How do you do it? How do you balance work and your personal life?" Whether it is exercising, volunteering, taking care of an aging parent, enjoying an active social life, or parenting, everyone wants to know the secret to a successful career and having a life outside work.

Some argue a work-life balance simply cannot exist. They say if you are going to do a job and do it well, you must accept the fact that your work is going to take precedence over your personal life. That means you will have to miss your children's soccer games and doctor appointments; you will have to forego book groups and marathon training. In other words, you have to choose.

I disagree. *At times*, it is true, you will have to choose. After all, as a lawyer, you have clients, deadlines, too much to do, and not enough time. You will, *at times*, miss events in your life that you want to attend. You will, *at times*, be sleep deprived. But this does not have to be your life *all the time*.

Maybe the concept of "balance" rings false because we are constantly prioritizing one thing over another. Thus, nothing may seem in balance on a particular day. But over the course of your career, you can achieve a balance and have both a successful law career and a satisfying life outside of law.

I write this chapter while being a partner at the law firm, Bowman and Brooke, and with three kids, ages five, three, and one. I had my first child as a sixth-year associate, one year before making partner, and I have had two children since making partner. Although I love my job, my national trial practice *at times* exacerbates my work-life balance struggle. It often means I go on the road defending my clients wherever they happen to be sued, possibly away from home for extended periods of time. The year my first daughter was born, not only did I have platinum status with the airlines, but I tried a case in Galveston, Texas—1,250 miles away from home.

So back to the original question: How do you do it? I'm not sure I, or any of us, has the answer, but I did pose the question to my female colleagues and friends to hear their thoughts. From their candid suggestions and input and reflection on my personal experience, I offer a few suggestions to make balancing your work-life with your life outside-of-work a little bit easier.

MAKE IT WORK AT WORK

There are a few concepts that are key to success in law: do good work, be accessible, and delegate. If you can embrace these three concepts in your practice, you can balance work and life in a manageable way.

Do Good Work

It seems like such an obvious concept. Yet, good work is hard to find. Many senior people in law firms will tell you that finding a superstar associate is like finding a pearl in an oyster. Be the person at your firm who consistently delivers good work. The rewards are incalculable.

If you do good work, people will want to work with you. Opportunities to develop as a lawyer will open to you. If you do good work, you will develop a good reputation, which over time will develop your referral network and help you land clients. If you do good work, people will reward you for doing a good job for them. You will move up the chain of command because your supervisors will want to help you; you helped them. And if you do good work, people will want you to continue to work with them, so they will bend over backwards to accommodate you. In short, if you do good work, people will make it work for you.

Be accessible

Accessibility goes hand-in-hand with doing good work. If you want to succeed in the legal profession, especially in litigation, you need to be accessible. Most jobs do not "make" you work after 5 p.m., but the fact of the matter is you will have to work at non-traditional hours to advance. But you knew that. You knew it before you went to law school.

Work outside of the 9-to-5 work day does not mean an end to life outside of work. Like many working parents, I try to make my children's extracurricular activities as often as possible. But unlike some parents, I check my BlackBerry; sometimes I take a phone call. I also worked through both my maternity leaves as a partner. Many of my friends gasp at this and insist that work should have boundaries. The firm did not make me work; I did not have to do it. But I did it because as a lawyer in a firm, I was part of a business with clients. Work needed to be done. If I did not do the work, someone else would, and I wanted those clients to work with me.

I worked during maternity leave, but I did not forgo being a new mother. I spent many hours writing briefs, reviewing documents, and taking conference calls, but I spent every minute with my babies at my side or in my arms. It wasn't perfect. There were times when I apologized about a crying baby in the background. And there were times when I held the phone between my shoulder and ear, taking notes with one hand, changing a diaper with the other, and muting and un-muting the phone when necessary. I may have envied other mothers who seemed to have more "play" time. But I liked my job, and I liked parenting; I decided to take a crack at doing both. And I managed; I multitask (show me a woman who cannot multitask).

Just because you are accessible, does not mean you cannot have boundaries. I have one colleague who has very defined rules about accessibility outside of the office. For people up the food chain, such as clients, she is available any time or any place. For others, she enforces what she terms as "predictable and acceptable limitations." In other words, she does not spend time on her BlackBerry at 10 p.m. responding to emails on matters that can be resolved the next morning. Accessibility is part of the job, but it can be managed.

The concept of accessibility brings me to what I consider to be a very positive side of the legal profession, and that is the flexibility it allows. If you do good work and show that you are accessible, even when you are out of the office, you will be rewarded with more freedom regarding the terms and conditions of your work. It will likely not be problematic if you need to come in late, leave early, or work from home here and there, because your colleagues will know and trust that you will make it work, and they will want to help you make it work. The key is being accessible so that other people's work is not interrupted by the fact that you are out of the office. Unless you need to be in court or in a meeting, work can often be done on the phone or by computer with remote access. Unless there is a deadline, often it does not matter if you are working on a brief, discovery, or client letter at 2 p.m. or 2 a.m. Thus, if you need to run out for a doctor's appointment or dance recital, you can. I celebrate that I have a career that allows me to leave the office to watch my kids' soccer games and still do my job.

But a flexible schedule and work environment will not benefit you unless you make the most of it. I was in trial when my first daughter was six months old, but I did not leave her at home. Instead, with nanny in tow, I brought her to trial. I went to court all day, stayed up late, and worked in the war room like everyone else, preparing witnesses, outlines, and motions. But unlike the others, I was often awake in the middle of the night or early in the morning to feed my daughter. The upside for me was that I saw her in the morning, after court, and in the middle of the night. Meanwhile, I was as effective as my colleagues in court. Because she was there, I was able to focus on my work and not be distracted by thoughts of missing her. If she had been at home, I would have been aching to be there. All I had to do was envision this unconventional solution.

Delegate

Beyond the goodwill you establish by doing good work and being accessible, the other means to survival in the legal profession for someone who wants a life outside of work is delegation. Just because you think you can do a task better does not mean it is the best use of your time. Whether it is researching and writing a brief, taking an out-of-town deposition, or covering a hearing, delegate if you can. There are things you have to cover because of your expertise, abilities, or client relationships, but you do not have to do everything yourself.

For many lawyers, delegation is hard. For example, it can be difficult to delegate the research and writing on a brief because you know the material the best. It can be hard to delegate a deposition because you are afraid your surrogate will not be as strong. But you can train your associates to be knowledgeable and formidable. The more senior you become, the more you are involved in client meetings and communications, strategy sessions, budgeting, court proceedings, and hearings. Delegation becomes essential because there is still an endless amount of substantive and administrative things that need to be done. Delegate those whenever possible.

When you delegate, you are giving access and opportunities to more junior people in the office. It allows you to work with younger women (and men) who you can mentor and develop. It allows you to feed the pipeline of future leaders.

One caveat: if you are early in your career, delegation may not be appropriate, so do so cautiously. A senior lawyer may have assigned you work because she wants you to learn how to do it. The most important thing for you in the early years of your career is to gain experience and build a good reputation. Thus, you may have to wait a while to delegate.

MAKE IT WORK AT HOME

I have one non-lawyer friend who told me that the view she has on the work-life balance is not that one needs to have a life outside of work, but that one needs to have a life and fit work into it. I am not sure many lawyers would agree. For me, the one constant in my adult life has been work. My life outside work has changed from running marathons and socializing as a single person to getting three kids five-and-under out the door in the morning. But I always had work, and that work was always demanding. Thus, regardless of how one views it—"fitting work into life" or "fitting life into work"—it is hard to change work to meet the changes in life.

For life outside of work, I have two words of advice: get help. You either need a significant other who is willing to share the chores at home—cleaning, cooking, grocery shopping, laundry, etc. Or, if you do not have help at home, hopefully your budget allows you to outsource some of these tasks. You have limited time at home. You should spend it doing quality things that add value to your life—whether it is volunteering, exercising, or spending quality time with your kids. You may not be at every PTA meeting, but at least your spare time allows you to spend quality time with your kids.

One of my colleagues hired a babysitter to drive her child to after-school activities. Another has a stay-at-home significant other. Others have nannies, cleaning services, or food-delivery services. You can choose whatever works for you, but if you want to manage both life and work, you need to apply a strategy that helps you manage life outside the office similar to inside the office. In other words, delegate.

WINNING THE BALANCE BATTLE

Even if you have simplified and streamlined your work and home lives as much as possible, you need to realize that achieving work-life balance is a constant battle, and the only way to win is to have the right attitude. You need to be able to "let some of it go." You cannot do everything. You may not be able to go to every dance recital, make home-made meals every night, or sign up your two-year-old for music appreciation, swimming, and gymnastics. Pick what is important, and let the rest go.

Sometimes, you will be the person who is late for meetings out of the office, or forgets that it is show-and-tell day at school. Or, you may be the mother who sends her children to school with breakfast on their faces and their hair unbrushed. Consequently, you may feel that people are judging you. Resist the temptation of internalizing these instances as failures. Again, let it go.

It is not easy to be comforted when we drop the ball or miss milestones in our lives because of work, but do not forget the big picture and how your job adds value to your life, as opposed to thinking of only how it detracts from it. For example, you may not be the primary caregiver at all times, but you may be the primary breadwinner. Providing for your family's financial needs is essential, particularly in these uncertain times.

Undoubtedly, there continues to be a gender gap in how society values a working woman. A man who works long hours and consequently misses parent-teacher meetings is not questioned on his commitment to his family. This is not always so for a working mother. If the child fails to return a library book or is struggling in school, a negative gender-bias stereotype often attaches to the mother—that the child's mishaps are directly correlated to the inattentiveness of the working mother. Some suggest that this gender-bias exists only in a working mother's mind. I do not know whether internal or external forces create feelings of inadequacy, but the truth is that you, as a parent, are no more responsible for a child's successes or missteps than any other parent. Moreover, you contribute to your children's development in a different but equally important way. In addition to providing financial support, you act as a role model for your boys and girls to see that it is possible for a woman to have both a career and a family.

Guilt and feelings of inadequacy can also haunt you at work. Unlike life before children, you may not be the first person in the office in the morning or the last person out. I usually walk into the office in the morning after most others have already arrived. I used to find it hard to get from the reception desk to my office—walking by everyone who was already working. But eventually I learned to follow my own advice: I let it go. Unlike many others, I realized that I had put in the equivalent of almost an entire day before I even stepped foot in the office. And when someone wants to note my absence or tardiness, I try not to get defensive. Sometimes, I use humor and crack a self-deprecating joke. Other times, when a serious explanation is due, I subtly note that I had to get three kids dressed, fed, and dropped off at school. But most of the time, I ignore it and get to work.

Perhaps I am stating the obvious when I say that you need a support system, and not just a back-up driver to pick up your kids from school when your mediation runs late. It is essential that you connect with women who are going through the same thing. It is not that misery loves company, but company makes you less miserable. I am not saying that you should be drowning in your tears—after all, managing work and an active life means you have a lot to celebrate—but, frankly, whether it is through email, phone calls, or a monthly dinner, it feels good to vent with others similarly situated once in a while.

Finally, I leave you with an important concept: think of the higher cause. When things are hard, I always think of why it is important to work. And I do not mean that it is important to work to make money or use my brain (although these are admittedly important factors), but because it is important to have strong women in the work force. Our foremothers worked on improving equal pay rights, breaking the glass ceiling, enacting sexual harassment laws and maternity leave policies, along with many other issues. We need to continue to advance, achieve management positions and leadership roles, and prevent female attrition, to help those who come after us.

I close quoting my dear friend from law school, Lisa Ridgedale—mother of two, past president of the Vancouver Bar Association, and senior litigation counsel at the BC Securities Commission in Vancouver, British Columbia—who made the following remarks at a Women in the Law Conference in Canada on October 11, 2007:

> As much as we'd like, we really can't have it all, all of the time. Some weeks we lose the fight to achieve balance and some weeks we fly so high we wonder what everyone else is complaining about, but the reality is there will always be something that will have to give. One day it will be your family, the next it will be your work and sometimes it will be you and on bad days everything feels like it is about to collapse. If we just accept that there will be sacrifices across the board, that we can't be perfect and that doing our best is as good as it gets, then there is more of a chance that we might feel balanced at least some of the time. This is a lot to ask of most professional women since we seem to be perfectionist and competitive by nature, but the more we congratulate ourselves for what we have done rather than beat ourselves up for our shortcomings, the more we can focus on winning the balancing act or at least tipping the scale to work in our favor—one day at a time.

Staying in the Game 4

By Paulette Brown

AT THIS STAGE of my career, after practicing for more than 30 years, I am often asked about what motivates me to continue to do so, *and* as a litigator. To understand why I have stayed in the game, you need to know how I got here. It has been an interesting and somewhat non-traditional journey, and the challenges were many. In fact, there are very few women of color who have been litigating for more than 30 years.

When I went to college, it was not my intent to become a lawyer. There are no lawyers in my family, and I did not know any lawyers personally. But my parents told me there was nothing I could not do. They set high expectations for me. My mother believed that anything short of excellence was unacceptable. My father, a true renaissance man, drilled into my mind this credo: There are no girl jobs and no boy jobs. I went to college believing I would be a social worker, an honorable profession dedicated to helping others. I came to understand while in college, however, that law was my true calling.

I went to law school during a time when there were no diversity initiatives, and very few students of color enrolled. In my class of 1976, there were eight African Americans who graduated and no Hispanic/Latinos, Asian or Pacific Islanders, no Native Americans, and no openly gay or lesbian students. Career counselors at my law school did not give the African American students the proverbial "time of day." African American students were discouraged from applying or not told about opportunities for employment with law firms, the prosecutor's office, or judicial clerkships. To the extent there was any encouragement to apply for employment at all, it was with Legal Aid or the public defender. But as a result of being ignored, I learned to stand on my own and withstand the bumps and bruises.

My first paid position as an attorney was with Legal Aid, where I immediately started trying cases. I could tell you stories about being mistaken for a criminal defendant, court reporter, client, any one but a lawyer. But working at Legal Aid was a tremendous learning experience. As a Legal Aid attorney, I was compelled to learn quickly the rules of court, the idiosyncrasies of judges, and how to meet the needs of my clients. During this time, I took every CLE course available, read every applicable court rule and relevant law, and observed and consulted with attorneys more experienced than I. I learned there is no skill greater than being prepared. Thus, when I appeared at a deposition or in court, I believed that I would provide the best possible representation to my client. In thirty-three years, my commitment to my clients has not waivered. There is nothing better than sharing a moment with a satisfied client. Practicing as a Legal Aid attorney was something I thoroughly enjoyed, and it gave me the opportunity to help others.

After working for Legal Aid, I did stints in-house for several corporations. But it was not for me. I did not feel like an advocate, did not feel really connected with a client or with a cause, which is one of the primary reasons I went to law school. I did not come to understand until much later in my career that I had been relegated to handling routine matters and not the more complex cases handled by my counterparts who are not of color.

But opportunities did come. After about five years, I decided to go back to litigation full time and opened my own law firm with a former law school classmate. I started to become involved in various bar associations, which transformed my career.

At bar association events, I networked with attorneys from around the country who were outside my limited circle. My participation in these events caused me to understand that there is nothing wrong with a person of color representing corporations, seeking to handle more complex matters, and stepping out of the traditional personal injury practice, seemingly reserved for the small office practitioner, and, most particularly, for African American attorneys. Thus, my involvement in bar associations has enhanced my practice, and, with the help of others, I came to recognize that I belong everywhere, that I did not belong in a particular box, and that I was not being disloyal to any demographic or constituency.

Becoming involved with bar associations also helped me to hone my leadership skills. Those leadership skills, along with being prepared, led me to my first corporate client referral from a member of the National Bar Association who worked in-house. He recognized, through the committee work I did, that I was committed to excellence and service and would provide the same zeal in representing his company. That initial business propelled me into position to work for other corporations.

So, 33 years as a litigator . . . how did I get here? Belief in myself. A passion to help others. An unquenchable thirst to keep developing myself and my craft. Always striving to do my best to represent my clients' interests and satisfaction from success in doing so. And the qualities that got me here are also the reasons I stay in the game.

But the game has changed since I began practicing. It is not possible to engage in the pure practice of law. It is now more the business of law. Thus, it is necessary to develop a business plan. It is never too early to have a business plan, even if your business plan only tells you to learn how to be a lawyer and the steps necessary to becoming a great one. Your business plan should include the training you will need and benchmarks for each year in your career. A business plan can include such simple functions as calling upon former law school friends on a quarterly basis, just to check in. Many of them will at some point go in-house and become your potential clients. The plan can also include the journals you will read on a regular basis and articles you will write. A comprehensive business plan should be done on an annual basis with updates made during the course of the year. A business plan is not something that is swirling around in your head. It must be in writing with the tasks necessary to achieve the goals set forth in the business plan. Dates must be assigned for every task. Those dates include communications with existing clients, your expectations from them, and further assignments you can get from them for yourself and others in your firm. The business plan should include targets. It is necessary to be nimble with respect to the content of the business plan, as events will not always occur as expected. The primary purpose is to have focus and direction, so that the possibility will exist to stay in the game for 30, 40 or even 50 years.

What stokes my fire for the practice of law is my curiosity for uncovering the truth as it relates to social justice, the ability to do intellectually stimulating work, and the honor of being respected by my peers for doing what I love—helping others. I do not define success in pure monetary terms, although I would not be honest if I did not admit money helps. Instead, I define success as engaging in conversation with a young lawyer sitting alone in the corner and coming away with her in tow, willing to meet everyone else in the room. Success is handling a case pro bono and achieving a just result. Success is serving as a mentor to a young female attorney or several of them. Success is being able to sleep peacefully at night.

Helping others is not limited to individuals, but also to my corporate clients. I stay in the game for them as well. So often people view corporations as the enemy. I recall early in my litigation career, I came upon a former law school classmate at the weekly trial call. He inquired about the name of the case that brought me to court that day. I gave him the name of the case without telling him the name of my client. When he found out I was representing Ford Motor Company, he was stunned and expressed disappointment. In his view, I had crossed over to the "dark side." I think he thought that because I am African American, I should not represent corporations, and instead should always represent the plaintiff, the presumed underdog. I am passionate about the work I do for my corporate clients. They, too, can be the underdog.

The theory of my former classmate is a driving force for me representing corporations or defendants in civil litigation. They too, have a right to have excellent representation when frivolous lawsuits are filed against them. Not only that, but the representation of the corporate client has provided me with an opportunity to counsel the corporation when its policies and procedures are out of sync with a true sense of justice. Fortunately, I have not had the occasion to have a client disagree with me on this type of issue. I am indeed fortunate. Thus, in the end, best interests of all are well served.

My work as a lawyer is consistent with my values and beliefs and who I am when I am not practicing law. Simply put, the reason why I have stayed in the legal game is that I still want to do the work—for myself, my clients, my peers, and the young lawyers who will eventually succeed me. I need to give back some of what has been given to me.

Succeeding As A Woman of Color 5

By Kimberly M. Talley

THE VAST MAJORITY of articles written about women of color in the legal profession tend to emphasize the difficulties that we face on a day-to-day basis because of our gender and race. The statistics in nearly every survey that has been published about how women of color are faring in the legal profession are even more disappointing. Nevertheless, as I look around today at the advancements women of color have made in the legal profession, I am not discouraged. Despite the constant reminder of the challenges we confront in an already demanding field, I believe that we have chosen to face these challenges head-on rather than let them deter us from our chosen profession.

Routinely, I come into contact with women of color who have achieved great success in their legal careers. These women are prominent trial attorneys, managing partners, general counsel, and high-ranking public officials and public servants. Whether it is in the judiciary, private practice, government service, or academia, women of color in the legal profession are, in fact, making their way to the top.

The remarkable women profiled in this chapter, four of whom were my classmates at Harvard Law School and one of whom is a former colleague, exemplify the many outstanding women of color who have achieved phenomenal success in the practice of law and related fields. They are women of varying ethnic backgrounds who have all risen to positions of influence and power. To recognize their accomplishments is not to ignore the significant work that needs to be done to ensure that opportunities for success remain available to all women of color. Rather, it is to demonstrate that, when opportunities are made available to us, we soar to the highest heights in our profession based on merit, talent and drive. It is also to inspire other women of color, including those just entering the profession, by showing them that the opportunities for success are limitless.

PREETA BANSAL: TRAILBLAZING ADVISOR TO THE PRESIDENT AND WORLD LEADERS

I first met Preeta Bansal at Harvard Law School in 1986. We were both in Section No. 2—one of the four sections of the first-year class. She did not say much in class, but whenever she spoke, the entire class listened intently because we knew what she said would be profound. I remember hearing a rumor that Preeta had become ill during the break to study for first-year exams and still managed to get all As. Recently, I was able to speak with Preeta and confirm whether this rumor was, in fact, true. As with most rumors, the story was slightly wrong. Preeta had taken ill during an actual examination but ended up making all A+s, a mark that is rarely given to any student at Harvard Law School. This year is our twentieth-year reunion from HLS and, during this time, Preeta, who is now a high level public official in the White House Administration, has accomplished more than one could ever imagine.

My admiration of Preeta's accomplishments is not just the praise of a former classmate. In 2008, Preeta was named one of the 50 Most Influential Minority Lawyers in America by the National Law Journal. The New York Times profiled her and called her a "legal superstar." The New York Law Journal referred to Preeta "as one of the most gifted lawyers of her generation, who combines a brilliant analytical mind with solid, mature judgment."

Preeta's accomplishments are particularly noteworthy given that she had no role models of her own national origin (Indian-American), male or female, to emulate in charting her path. Indeed, while the number of African-American attorneys was not overwhelming, we still had role models in people such as Supreme Court Justice Thurgood Marshall, John M. Langston and Constance Baker-Motley, to name a few. Moreover, because of the civil rights movement, studying law was considered a noble and elite profession for young African-American men and women.

In contrast, at the time Preeta entered college, most Indian-American students went to school to become doctors or engineers or to pursue careers in scientific or mathematical fields. Choosing not to take the route of many Indian-American professionals, Preeta became a legal pioneer in her community—the first Indian-American in many categories in the field of law—rising to become the highest-ranking Indian-American and South Asian lawyer in the United States.

Given her path-breaking success, it is no surprise that President Barack Obama has tapped Preeta to be the General Counsel and Senior Policy Advisor to the Office of Management and Budget (OMB), In other words, when charged with the monumental task of fixing the budget during one of the most difficult economic times our country has faced, President Obama chose Preeta to be included in the team of national advisors who would help him get the country through this economic crisis.

Preeta's credentials are some of the most impressive of any attorney practicing law anywhere in the world. At the age of 16, she entered Harvard University, graduating *magna cum laude* and Phi Beta Kappa. She then attended Harvard Law School, where she served as Supervising Editor of the prestigious Harvard Law Review, graduating *magna cum laude* in 1989. Following law school, she received a coveted court of appeals clerkship. She went on to serve as a United States Supreme Court law clerk to Justice John Paul Stevens.

Before Preeta reached her thirtieth birthday, she had served in the Clinton Administration as Counselor in the U.S. Department of Justice and as Special Counsel in the White House, where she was tasked with guiding President Clinton's judicial nominees through the Senate confirmation process.

By her mid-30s, Preeta already had assumed significant public and private sector responsibilities. In 1999, she became Solicitor General of the State of New York, where she helped manage the 600 lawyers of the New York Attorney General's office and directly supervised the heavy appellate docket for the State of New York. While many attorneys dream of appearing before the U.S. Supreme Court at least once in their career, Preeta had the opportunity to represent the State of New York multiple times in the Supreme Court.

In addition to her stellar oral advocacy skills, Preeta won the "Best United States Supreme Court Brief" Award from the National Association of Attorneys General every single year that she served as the New York Solicitor General. She also was widely credited by the legal and judicial communities in New York for her path-breaking leadership in raising the profile and quality of the New York Solicitor General's office.

Before President Obama appointed her as the OMB general counsel, Preeta headed the appellate litigation and complex issues practice department at the prominent law firm Skadden, Arps, Slate, Meagher & Flom LLP. With over 2000 attorneys firm-wide, Skadden ranks as the largest law firm in the State of New York, the fifth largest law firm in the United States and the eighth largest law firm in the world. Skadden also is considered one of the most prestigious law firms in the world.

Preeta was the go-to attorney for some of Skadden's most significant and high-profile litigation. In 2006, for example, Preeta and another partner successfully represented Merrill Lynch before the U.S. Supreme Court in *Merrill Lynch v. Dabit*, an important case involving the extent to which Securities Litigation Uniform Standard Act of 1998 preempts state-law securities fraud class-action claims. The Supreme Court, in a unanimous decision, ruled in favor of Merrill Lynch. Preeta also successfully represented the Empire State Development Corporation in a significant appeal involving interpretation of the "Takings Clause" of the U.S. Constitution.

Moreover, Preeta has become a leader in national and worldwide affairs. Her influence has been felt around the globe. In 2003, Preeta was appointed by then-Senate Leader Thomas Daschle to the U.S. Commission on International Religious Freedom (USCIRF), a bipartisan federal commission. The USCIRF was created by the International Religious Freedom Act of 1998

(IRFA) to "monitor violation of the right to freedom of thought, conscience and religious belief abroad, as defined in the IRFA, and set forth in the Universal Declarations of Human Rights and related international instruments." 2008 Annual Report of the U.S. Commission on International Religious Freedom. According to the 2008 Annual Report of the U.S. Commission on International Religious Freedom, the commission is "the first government commission in the world with the sole mission of reviewing and making policy recommendations on the facts of violations of religious freedom globally." Id.

Preeta became the first person not of Judeo-Christian heritage and the second woman ever elected to chair the commission, serving during the 2004–2005 term. During her tenure as chair, Preeta presided over the congressionally approved study on the Department of Homeland Security's procedure relating to the expedited removal of asylum seekers. Asylum seekers are people who have fled to the United States seeking refuge from persecution they have suffered in their homeland on the basis of religion, race, nationality or political conviction. The study has received national and international acclaim.

President Obama is not the first President that Preeta has advised on world affairs. She met with former President George W. Bush and senior members of his administration to discuss the commission's findings and recommendations on a number of issues of world significance. She also met with Secretaries of State Colin Powell and Condoleezza Rice to discuss issues pertaining to freedom of religion in Iraq, including the plight of religious minorities in that country.

Indeed, when the Afghanistan and Iraqi constitutions were being drafted, the world community listened to Preeta's opinions and expertise on the sufficiency of these documents to ensure human rights and freedom of religion and belief. In addition to traveling to Afghanistan and Iraq, she has participated in U.S. diplomatic missions to Syria, Jordan, Uzbekistan, China, Russia, Turkey, Hong Kong, Saudi Arabia, Vietnam, Sri Lanka and Bangladesh to advance U.S. foreign policy.

While Preeta's professional accomplishments are clearly extraordinary, it is also her character that makes her stand out as such a remarkable woman of color. Indeed, what is most impressive to me about Preeta is that she is a very humble and unassuming person who exudes humility, compassion and integrity. She has been described as a rare lawyer who combines creative brilliance with solid judgment and excellence with integrity and commitment.

Unlike many accomplished people, Preeta does not ascribe her success to a career plan that guided her every step. While acknowledging that hard work was partly responsible for her success, she believes that her fast-track career was, in fact, serendipitous. She describes herself simply as a "nice girl from the Midwest" who never aimed to be a superstar. Everyone who knows her would agree that Preeta's success has not been achieved because of pure ambition and drive but, rather, because of her natural gifts and talents and a calm grace.

Preeta has blazed a trail, not only for young Indian-American women and Indian-American lawyers, but for women of all ages and ethnic backgrounds. What is most exciting about Preeta's career is that we can expect many more amazing things from her in the future.

SHERYLL CASHIN: LEGAL SCHOLAR AND DISTINGUISHED AUTHOR

Sheryll Cashin was in my Apellate Advocacy class at Harvard Law School. She joined our class as a second-year student after beginning her legal studies in the United Kingdom. During our first year of law school, Sheryll, who had been selected as an elite Marshall Scholar, was attending Oxford University. By the end of the year, she would graduate from the prestigious school with honors, holding a masters' degree in English Law.

By our third year, Sheryll already had established a reputation for brilliance and drive. She was an editor of the Harvard Law Review and was selected to clerk for Judge Abner Mikva on the U.S. Court of Appeals for the D.C. Circuit. Sheryll next clerked for one of my heroes and a hero of many, the late U.S. Supreme Court Justice Thurgood Marshall. Following her graduation from Harvard Law School with honors and her judicial clerkships, Sheryll worked for President Bill Clinton and Vice-President Al Gore at the White House as an advisor on urban and economic policy.

Because I was a great admirer of Sheryll, I followed her career and wondered what she would do next. There were few African-American females in the United States with qualifications as exceptional as Sheryll's. In addition to her graduate degrees from Oxford University and Harvard Law School, she is a *summa cum laude* graduate of Vanderbilt University with a bachelor's degree in electrical engineering. With her superb credentials, she could rise to partnership at any premier law firm in the country, become a successful politician or write her own ticket in whatever legal field she chose. I soon learned that Sheryll had become a law professor at Georgetown University School of Law in Washington, D.C.

Sheryll's decision to become a law professor is significant not only to the world of academics, but also to the African-American community in ways that people probably have never considered. While at law school, I, along with many students—black, white, Latino and other races—staged a sit-in at Harvard Law School, because there was not a single African-American female professor in the entire law school. The late Dean James Vorenberg took our demands seriously and acknowledged that Harvard Law School was not the only academic institution that was lacking in diversity.

The Administration's claim, however, was that there were no African-American women with the credentials to teach at Harvard Law School. Another one of my heroes, Professor Derrick Bell, disagreed with the Administration's assessment and, in 1992, resigned from the school to protest the institution's failure to tenure an African-American female professor.

Six years later, Lani Guinier joined the faculty at Harvard Law School and eventually became the first tenured African-American female in the history of the institution. Unfortunately, since Professor Guinier's admission to tenureship at HLS, the percentage of tenured African-American female professors has not increased dramatically.

Sheryll's decision to enter academia is truly a gift, not only to the field of legal educators, but also to the world in general. She has one of the most brilliant legal minds in the country and her contributions to the nation's dialogue about race, poverty, segregation, inequality and other important legal and public policy issues have been significant.

While the courtroom is the stage for most lawyers to defend their cause, Sheryll's advocacy is done through her research and scholarship. She writes primarily about race relations and inequality and is most passionate about the plight of the inner-city poor. After writing a series of influential law review articles that helped her to earn tenure and the rank of full professor within five years, she decided that she needed to write not just for academics but also for civil rights and policy advocates and the reading public.

Her first book, *The Failures of Integration: How Race and Class are Undermining the American Dream* (Public Affairs, 2004), was written to coincide with the 50th year anniversary of *Brown v. The Board of Education*. It is a thought-provoking work, backed up by meticulous research and statistical data, about how segregation by race and class status is continuing to affect American democracy.

Hundreds of law review and other scholarly articles have cited *The Failures of Integration*, and the book has received critical acclaim from a number of national publications. David Garrow, in a review for the *Chicago Tribune*, described *The Failures of Integration* as "superbly erudite and enormously thoughtful . . . any who wants to celebrate *Brown*'s 50th anniversary . . . will draw practical inspiration from Cashin." Sheryll received similar praise for her literary scholarship by *The New York Times.* Samuel G. Freedman, a professor of Journalism at Columbia University wrote: "Cashin . . . asks the difficult but necessary questions about why public schools in affluent black suburbs of Washington perform worse than those of neighboring, whiter communities."

The Failures of Integration was a finalist for the 2005 Hurston/Wright award for nonfiction and an Editor's Choice in *The New York Times Book Review.*

In her most recent book, *The Agitator's Daughter: A Memoir of Four Generations of One Extraordinary African-American Family (Public Affairs, 2008)*, Sheryll chronicles her family's history through the slavery, Reconstruction, Jim Crow, civil rights and post-civil rights eras. Originally from Huntsville, Alabama, Sheryll comes from a long line of political activists, her father and grandfather being the most notable. She was arrested at the age of four months along with her mother, Joan, at a sit-in at a segregated lunch counter, and she was an active pre-teen volunteer in her father's political party, The National Democratic Party of Alabama. It is well known that the NDP helped bring an end to white supremacy politics in the state.

As a renowned professor, Sheryll has continued this fight by writing about social injustice and by offering intelligent, thought-provoking solutions for change in America. In addition to her books, Sheryll is a frequent guest lecturer and speaker and an active member on four non-profit boards. She also somehow manages, along with her lawyer husband Marque Chambliss, to raise toddler twins, Logan and Langston.

ANGELA J. REDDOCK: MOVER, SHAKER AND RAINMAKER

I interviewed Angela Reddock for her first legal position out of law school. I knew then that Angela, a gifted African-American attorney, was destined for great things. As a first-year associate at Gartner & Young, APC, she insisted on taking plaintiff depositions, writing motions for summary judgment, appearing in court and having one-on-one contact with the firm's clients—many tasks that were reserved for partners or associates who had been out of law school for several years. What was more impressive, however, is that she was able to perform these tasks at the same level as her more senior colleagues.

Since graduating from UCLA School of Law, Angela has appeared on numerous "rising star" and "people to watch under 40" lists. She has always been a go-getter: a mover and a shaker. Even as a young associate, she was out developing business for the firm, recognizing that it is never too early to develop business contacts.

When the larger firms did not afford Angela the time and opportunity to pursue her public service goals, she was undeterred. She left the security of large law firm practice and opened up her own law firm, the Reddock Law Group, where she now represents corporations and high-level executives in all areas related to labor and employment law. While her private practice takes up a significant amount of her time, she wakes up at 5:30 a.m. every morning so she has time to pursue her other passions: community service and politics.

At the earliest age she can remember, Angela was involved in community activism and local politics. She even recalls attending post-civil-rights demonstrations at a very young age with her grandmother in Birmingham, Alabama. One of the earliest demonstrations Angela remembers involved a labor dispute with a nurses' union. It is probably during that time when she acquired her passion for both the law and public service. The *Los Angeles Sentinel*, a local newspaper, has stated the following about her: "During a time when community leadership sometimes seems uncertain, Los Angeles Attorney Angela J. Reddock is a ray a hope for all who live to make a difference."

And that is what she has done: made a difference in her community. In addition to her public service, Angela also is the chair of two very important organizations. The first is the Los Angeles African-American Women's Public Policy Institute, an organization that trains women to pursue careers and opportunities in public policy and public affairs. The second organization, Ability First, is a non-profit organization that provides programs and services to children and adults with physical and developmental disabilities. Angela also has been appointed to various state and local boards. Currently, she serves as a commissioner on the Los Angeles County Local Government Services Reform Commission and the Los Angeles City Transportation Commission.

Angela's confidence in her abilities was instilled in her at a very young age. When she was nine years old, her family moved from Birmingham, Alabama to Compton, California. She attended public school in Compton until she reached high school. Angela's mother, a single working mother, learned of a scholarship program being offered by a prestigious private school in Brentwood, California. Believing that it would help her daughter acquire even greater confidence and the skills to thrive in college, the family submitted an application, and Angela was accepted into the program.

Brentwood School is an academically demanding private school located in one of the most affluent neighborhoods in Los Angeles. Today, the annual tuition for kindergarten is $25,000 and nearly $30,000 for high school. Admission to the school is highly competitive, and the school is extremely selective in choosing its students. At Brentwood, Angela was surrounded by students who not only were from very wealthy and influential families but also were academically advanced because they had attended Brentwood School for years before high school. This new environment, with its increased academic and social challenges, did not hinder Angela. Despite being one of only a handful of minority students in each of her classes, she thrived and excelled in her new surroundings. In addition to her stellar academic performance, Angela's natural leadership and speaking abilities blossomed. By the time Angela graduated from Brentwood School, she had been accepted to Amherst College, one of the top liberal arts colleges in the country.

Angela's confidence in her abilities is only part of what has made her such a successful attorney and politician. She is a fearless advocate for justice. When a community leader asked her to take on a criminal appeal of a young boy, she easily could have said that her area of legal expertise was employment law, not criminal law. However, instead of walking away from what she knew would be an uphill and complicated legal battle, Angela met with the parents and agreed to undertake the representation.

Greg Harris, her then 14-year-old client, had been convicted of second-degree murder after he struck and killed another boy with a baseball bat after a Pony League game. Witnesses had testified at trial that the other boy had shoved and taunted Harris before the fatal incident. After months of preparation, research and learning an entirely new area of law, Angela successfully argued before the California Court of Appeal that her young client had not intended to murder the other boy, but had acted out of passion in the heat of the moment. The Court of Appeal agreed with Angela's well reasoned arguments and declared Harris guilty of a lesser offense—voluntary manslaughter. Other criminal attorneys and legal experts following the case considered the victory just short of miraculous. Today, the 17-year old is a free young man because of Angela's outstanding legal work.

Harris's case was not the first high-profile case handled by Angela. While a partner at Collins, Mesereau, Reddock & Yu, LLP, Angela served as lead counsel in a sorority hazing case that garnered national attention. In that case, Angela represented the young child of a woman who had drowned at the beach during a college sorority hazing incident. Angela was able to negotiate a substantial settlement to be held in trust for her client.

In her current practice, Angela has successfully defended corporations and executives in high-stakes litigation involving labor and employment matters. While this type of litigation traditionally has been reserved for larger law firms, Angela has proven that she has the expertise and experience to handle such matters. Before opening her own law firm, Angela served as co-chair of the Employment Litigation and Counseling Group at Carroll, Burdick & McDonough, a prominent California firm. She also has worked at other leading labor and employment firms, including the national firm, Jackson Lewis. In addition to her legal work and public service, Angela is a legal commentator and has published numerous articles and books. If that is not impressive enough, she still has time to sing in the church choir.

As Angela, there are many outstanding women of color who deliberately have chosen not to stay at traditional law firms—not because they have not been successful at these firms, but because they want to pursue other professional interest and goals. Such career choices have been very fulfilling and equally financially rewarding. Angela's advice to all those coming after her is to "pursue your passion" and the professional fulfillment and financial rewards will follow.

ANA MARIA SALAZAR SLACKER: NATIONAL SECURITY EXPERT AND INTERNATIONAL DIPLOMAT

The drug trafficking problem in Mexico has reached a new level of crisis. Indeed, when people talk about the "war on drugs" in Mexico, the scene of hand-to-hand combat actually comes to my mind. Retaliation in the form of murder and torture, against public officials, judges, or anyone standing in the way of these violent drug lords is not uncommon. According to published accounts, the U.S. military has been deployed to assist the Mexican government in fighting drug traffickers in the country because the situation has become so dire.

Among the dedicated and exceptional public servants who have devoted their careers and professional expertise to tackling this international crisis is Ana Maria Salazar Slacker. Anna Maria is a Latina woman, president of her own consulting firm, host of *Imagen News,* and author of the *Mexico Today* blog, along with other publications and books.

I always knew that Ana Maria would utilize her Harvard Law School degree to serve the public in some fashion. I recall Ana Maria speaking knowledgeably and passionately in our advanced criminal law and procedure class with Professor Susan Estrich.

Since graduating from Harvard Law School in 1986, Ana Maria has become widely recognized as an expert in national security and international law. World leaders have turned to her for advice in confronting the war on drugs and similar issues affecting national security in the United States, Mexico and other third world countries. As a result of her accomplishments, Ana Maria was recognized by *Hispanic Business Magazine* as one of the "100 Most Influential Hispanic Americans in the United States."

As my other classmates and colleagues, Ana Maria's numerous and impressive credentials are chronicled in the many biographical materials that have been written about her. Between 1998 and 2001, Ana Maria served at the Pentagon as Deputy Assistant Secretary of Defense for Drug Enforcement Policy and Support. Before joining the Pentagon, she worked at the White House as a policy advisor for President Clinton's Special Envoy for the Americas and in the U.S. State Department's Bureau of International Narcotics and Law Enforcement Affairs.

In those positions, Ana Maria was responsible for formulating policies to assist in advancing President Bill Clinton's agenda for Latin America and the Caribbean in areas relating to law enforcement, national security, human rights and international trade.

Earlier, Ana Maria served at the U.S. State Department's Bureau of International Narcotics and Law Enforcement Affairs; she advised the assistant secretary of defense regarding issues pertaining to international criminal organizations, counter-narcotics, and efforts to counter money laundering.

Ana Maria's work frequently has taken her abroad. She currently lives in Mexico City. She also has worked in Colombia, South America as the Judicial Attaché at the US Embassy in Bogotá, where she coordinated evidence and information requests for the prosecution of drug kingpins.

Ana Maria has received numerous honors and commendations, including several from high ranking public officials and world leaders. For example, she received the "Medal for Outstanding Public Service" and the "Joint Meritorious Award" from the U.S. Secretary of Defense, the "Medalla Militar-Ministerio de Defensa" from the president of Colombia, and the "Orden Naval Almirante Padilla" from the Colombian navy. In 2006, Oklahoma State University honored Ana Maria as a Henry G. Bennett Fellow.

DEIRDRE STANLEY: STRATEGIC THINKER AND NATURAL BORN LEADER

In 2008, media giant Thomson Reuters generated nearly $13.4 billion in revenue. With nearly 50,000 employees in 93 countries worldwide, it is the largest international multimedia news agency in the entire world. The directory that lists the corporate leadership of the company includes the names of five men and one woman. The sole woman is an African-American woman and my former classmate, Deirdre Stanley. As the general counsel and an executive vice-president of Thomson Reuters, Deirdre is the person tasked with overseeing all aspects of the legal affairs of this international corporation, from its day-to-day operations to its billion dollar acquisitions and divestitures.

Deirdre's reign as chief legal advisor began three years before her fortieth birthday when she was asked to transform the legal department of Thomson Reuters' predecessor, the Thomson Corporation, into a more strategic business partner. While this seems like a task for someone with an MBA from Harvard Business School, Deirdre was able to accomplish this goal in virtually no time at all. Among her initial achievements included overseeing several teams of lawyers involved in the divestitures of NETg Inc. for $285 million dollars and Thomas Learning Centers Inc. and Nelson Canada together for $7.8 billion dollars. By 2006, Deirdre's team of lawyers also had completed 119 acquisitions totaling $1.8 billion dollars. In 2008, she demonstrated her true leadership genius by overseeing multiple law firms in the United States and Europe in the acquisition of Reuters Group Ltd. for $17.2 billion dollars. As a result of her accomplishments, this year she was named by the National Law Journal as one of the 20 Most Influential General Counsels in the entire country.

Deirdre's business acumen is not simply the product of her years as an M&A lawyer at Cravath, Swaine and Moore LLP, an elite Wall Street firm, or her training at the London School of Economics following her graduation with honors from Harvard Law School. Rather, it is a culmination of her life experience, as well as natural leadership skills and intelligence that were passed on to her by her parents, a business man and an English professor. They instilled in her a strong work ethic and the mind-set that excellence begets excellence.

And excellence is the standard on which Deirdre has built her legal career. After matriculating from Harvard Law School, where Deirdre served on the prestigious Harvard Law Review, she received a year fellowship at the London School of Economics and Politics. Deirdre then joined Cravath, Swaine & Moore LLP, where she developed her interest in corporate law. Established in 1819, Cravath is the second oldest law firm in the country, and is ranked number one in terms of prestige by Vault.com. Chambers, an esteemed publication itself, has ranked Cravath at the top for, among other things, Banking and Finance, Capital Markets, Corporate and Mergers & Acquisitions. In 2008, the average profits per partner exceeded over $3 million dollars.

Landing a position at Cravath is a feat that only an elite few law students accomplish. A noted online information source put it this way: "Entry to the firm is highly selective, generally open to only the most academically successful students from the most elite law schools in the United States and Canada. As with many top law firms, employee turnover is exceedingly high, with many attorneys departing the firm following a relatively brief tenure. As a rule of thumb, half of an entering class departs by the end of their second year, and three quarters depart by the end of their fourth year."

Deirdre, who worked at both the New York and London offices of Cravath, defied these statistics, excelling at the firm during her eight-year tenure. Deirdre recalls being only one of two African-American attorneys in the entire corporate department at Cravath when she was a young associate. Although her associate assignment rotations at Cravath exposed her to project finance, international finance, securities law and banking law, it was her rotations on merger and acquisition projects that captured her interest.

After leaving Cravath, Deirdre took her M&A experience to GTE Corporation, where she headed the mergers and acquisition practice group as an Associate General Counsel. In 1999, she joined USA Networks as Deputy General Counsel, and later served as an Executive Vice-President of Business Development and Strategy for the Electronics Commerce Solutions Division of USA Networks, now USA Interactive Inc. In addition to serving as Thomson Reuters General Counsel, Deirdre is also a member of the Thomson Reuters executive committee, which consists of the eight most senior executives of the company.

In 2003, Crain's New York business publication named Deirdre as one of the 100 Most Powerful Minority Business Leaders. Deirdre also has been recognized as one of the most powerful women in publishing. She is often called upon as a featured speaker at conferences around the country, particularly those relating to minority, women and leadership issues.

I recall Deirdre Stanley telling me that if she could have written her life story in advance, she never would have foreseen that her professional and personal life would have turned out to be so incredibly amazing. In addition to her remarkable career, she has an accomplished husband, Dr. Shaun Massiah, and a two-year old son, Maxwell. In fact, Deirdre was pregnant with Maxwell during one of Thompson's biggest divestiture deals.

Despite all of Deirdre's significant responsibilities, she still makes time to stay active in such causes as the National Kidney Foundation and the Girl Scouts Council of Greater New York.

SOARING TO NEW HEIGHTS

The group of women profiled in this article is but a small sample of women of color who have risen to influential and powerful positions. Space constraints do not allow me to address fully such impressive women as Laurie Nicole Robinson, vice president and assistant general counsel of CBS Corporation. Laurie, who is African-American, is the founder and CEO of Corporate Counsel Women of Color®, a non-profit organization of over 2,300 women attorneys of color who work predominately for Fortune 1000 and Forbes 2000 legal departments. The organization has received national acclaim for promoting diversity in the legal profession.

Another extraordinary women of color on the rise to national prominence is Kamala D. Harris, who in 2003 beat her former boss, a two-term incumbent, in an election to become the first District Attorney of San Francisco of African-American and Indian-American descent. She was overwhelmingly re-elected to office for a second term in 2007, and recently announced her candidacy for Attorney General for the State of California. In an article published by the *New York Times* entitled "She Just Might Be President Someday," Ms. Harris was one of 17 women identified in the article to likely be the first female to hold the highest office in the United States.

Across the country, Cassandra Butts, another Harvard Law School alumna, was appointed by President Obama as Deputy White House Counsel. Leecia Eve, an African-American woman, served as senior policy advisor to Secretary of State Hillary Clinton, then a senator.

Even in organizations where you do not expect to see women in high ranking positions, we are there. Tatia L. Williams, an African-American woman and a Harvard Law School alumna, is vice-president of business affairs for the National Basketball Association.

Brilliant Associate Professor of Law Olatunde Johnson is making her mark in the field of academics at Columbia School of Law. Olati is a graduate of Yale University and Stanford School of Law. She joined the Columbia faculty in 2006 following her two years there as a distinguished Kellis Parker Research Fellow.

Kimberly Crenshaw and Tonya Brito too have contributed greatly to the field of academic scholarship as renowned law professors at Columbia University and the University of Wisconsin.

In my own professional career, I continuously have been exposed to highly successful, powerful and influential women of color. After meeting

Karen Randall, an African-American woman and member of her firm's executive committee, I decided to accept my first law firm position at Wyman, Bautzer, Kuchel and Silbert, then the 13th largest law firm in California.

At age 42, Karen became managing partner of Wyman's successor firm, Katten, Muchin, Zavis and Weitzman. As well as being one of Wyman's leading rainmakers, she was also an outstanding trial attorney. She was a role model to me and my colleague, Anne Haley Brown, when we were both young African-American associates at the firm. After leaving private practice, Karen became senior vice-president and general counsel for MCA, Inc.

Twenty years later Anne herself became the Managing Assistant City Attorney for the Outside Counsel Oversight Division, responsible for selecting all outside counsel for the City of Los Angeles.

Naomi Young, initially my boss and later my partner at Baker & Hostetler LLP, was voted One of America's Top Black Lawyers by Black Enterprise Magazine based upon her distinguished career in the field of labor and employment law. After managing her own successful law firm for many years, she joined Baker and Hostetler LLP as co-chair of the Labor and Employment Group. As my mentor for over 15 years, I watched her successfully run a nationally known labor and employment boutique, bring in seven-figure books of business on an annual basis and successfully litigate cases through trial.

In fact, while I worked at Baker, 50 percent of the women in the Labor and Employment Group in the Los Angeles office were women of color and 70 percent were minority attorneys. Angela Agrusa, who was recently voted one of the Top 100 Attorneys in Southern California by Los Angeles Magazine, headed the Litigation Department at Baker.

Helen Kim, an Asian woman, who holds degrees from Juilliard School of Music in addition to Harvard-Radcliffe College and Yale Law School, became Angela Agrusa's successor after she left the firm. Helen is now a highly successful partner at Katten Muchin Rosenman LLP where she handles high stakes securities and class action matters. In 2007, she was named to the *Daily Journal's* list of the 75 Top Women Lawyers in California.

At Mitchell Silberberg & Knupp, Emma Luevano is one of several talented women of color. In 2006, she became the first Latina partner ever in the history of the 100-year-old firm.

These women are but a few of the women of color who continue to inspire me. It is because of them, and many others like them, that I will continue to remain optimistic about the future of women of color in the practice of law.

Inside and Out 6

By Laura W. Brill

LUCKING OUT

We are at dinner at a posh New York restaurant that my mother loves. My mother and I are with two of her friends. My mother's friend, Ira, has two gay sons, one recently out of college, and he worries that they will face discrimination as they make their way in the world. My mother knows Ira and his wife, Joanna, through volunteer work at PFLAG (Parents, Families and Friends of Lesbians and Gays), and we have been trying to find a time for the four of us to get together.

Ira and Joanna know the things about me that a proud PFLAG mother would tell her friends: that I am a partner in a Los Angeles law firm, that I went to Columbia Law School and clerked on the Supreme Court, that I have been "out" as a lesbian since college, that I was married this past summer, following the decision of the California Supreme Court recognizing the right of same-sex couples to marry, and that my wife, Ellen, and I have two children and have been together for more than 20 years.

Soon after the entrees arrive, Ira leans over and asks the question that must have been on his mind all evening: "So, have you ever faced serious discrimination because you are gay, or do you just live a charmed life?"

The restaurant is lively, in an Upper East Side sort of way. The glazed duck that I ordered sits in front of me. The answer is pretty clear, if uncomfortable to say aloud for anyone with an ounce of superstition: charmed life.

The full story, of course, is more complicated. Many things have happened because of sheer luck, starting with being born in Manhattan in the mid-1960s to open-minded Jewish physician parents. Some incalculable nature-nurture combination gave me a strong work ethic. I met Ellen, who sat at my side quizzing me from flashcards on the archanae of diversity jurisdiction as I studied for the bar exam and has supported me for more than two decades in ways that are countless and immeasurable.

But there is more than luck. By the time I reached adulthood, the American Psychiatric Association had long since taken homosexuality out of its diagnostic manual, and being gay had begun losing its stigma in some parts of the country. Tireless work by others had established some legal protection in some parts of the country. Everyone wants a measure of stability, and Ellen and I made a lot of choices that took advantage of these gains. Like skaters on a recently frozen pond, trying to stay where the ice is thickest, we've lived in places like San Francisco, New York, and West Hollywood, where legal protections and acceptance for gay and lesbian people and same-sex couples are strongest. We had children after the legal framework for second parent adoptions in California had become reasonably secure. I chose to work at a law firm widely praised as among the most welcoming to gay and lesbian people. Skating out where the ice is thinner would no doubt have exposed us to more adversity.

I came out at a lucky time and in a lucky place. It was the mid-1980s, and I was a sophomore at Brown University. This was well before kids routinely came out in high school, but college was a time of self-discovery, and while many gay and lesbian students remained closeted, others were out and un-apologetic about their sexual orientation. Gay and lesbian students were a visible and sizeable presence on campus. At Brown, as at other schools, we fought to persuade the university administration to add sexual orientation to the school's anti-discrimination policy, a fight that, despite Brown's liberal reputation, did not end until 1990, after every other Ivy League school had already adopted such policies. Ellen and I met at Brown, and we have been together ever since.

I started law school in 1991, and began looking for my first law firm summer position in 1992. Not all New York law firms were welcoming places for openly gay and lesbian attorneys at that time, but Ellen and I had already been together for five years, and I wasn't about to hide our relationship or to work somewhere that would feel uncomfortable. It was easy enough to find out which firms had good reputations for being open, and giving out plum work assignments without regard to sexual orientation. Gay and lesbian associates would compare notes, and gay law students tended to gravitate to these firms. At the firm I spent my second year summer, six of us out of a class of 50 were openly gay or lesbian.

Friendly though such firms were, they still did not offer health or related benefits that would cover the same-sex partners of attorneys or other employees. Gay and lesbian attorneys had already begun asking for benefits for their domestic partners, and, as summer associates, we wrote to the firm that we felt such benefits should be provided. Within a year, that firm had updated its policies to offer equal benefits. Others quickly followed suit. By 1993, the questions among progressive New York firms, as far I could tell, were not whether to do it at all, but how it would be done. All steps on the road to equality should be so smooth.

WORKING OUT

By 1997, when I began looking for a permanent law firm job following my clerkships, many firms had already realized the recruiting value of gay-friendly policies. All of the firms I interviewed with had equal benefits policies in effect, openly gay and lesbian partners and associates, and a warm welcome for Ellen and me in social recruiting events. This allowed me to make a choice among solid firms based on factors like the strength of the intellectual property and appellate practices, opportunities for associates, and issues of firm structure, rather than the need to avoid bigotry.

After I had been at the firm for a few years, Ellen and I started trying to have children. We decided she would carry our first child. After a few visits to the doctor's office, we received notice from our health plan that they were denying reimbursement for her fertility treatments. According to the Texas-based plan administrator, although our plan covered fertility treatments, we were not entitled to benefits because they did not believe that Ellen could not get pregnant in "the natural way." I asked if they required the wives of infertile husbands to visit a singles' bar and try to find a new mate before they would provide benefits to them, a question the plan administrator was unable to answer except by mumbling defensively that she was not discriminating. When the dialogue reached an impasse, the benefits director at my firm stepped in to get the matter resolved in our favor.

When our daughter was born in 2001, I received the same paid leave that the firm offered for fathers or straight adoptive parents. When I gave birth to our son in 2003, I received full maternity benefits. As far as firsts in my life, I'm proud to be not just the first openly lesbian partner at my firm, but also the first person to have received both paternity and maternity benefits!

As far as I know, being out at work has had no negative consequences for me, and it has had plenty of positives. Aside from the obvious benefit of living an honest life, it has led to wonderful pro bono opportunities that have been among the most gratifying of my career.

Several years ago, I had the opportunity to work with a team at my firm, Lambda Legal, and People for the American Way Foundation, to represent high school students in Orange, California, when their high school would not let them form a "Gay-Straight Alliance" club at their school. The mission of the club was to talk about and raise awareness of issues like discrimination, bullying, and equal rights relating to sexual orientation. The school had a juggling club, a Christian club, a glee club, and many other non-curricular student groups, but school administrators feared they would lose their jobs if they allowed the Gay-Straight Alliance to meet. We obtained the first ever preliminary injunction requiring a public high school to allow a Gay-Straight Alliance to meet on the same terms as other non-curricular student groups.

Years later, at an annual gay pride parade, rows of high school students marching under a Gay-Straight Alliance banner stretched along wide Santa

Monica Boulevard in the heart of West Hollywood. Each of them was likely aware that the suicide and attempted suicide rates for gay teens is estimated to be three times higher than for straight youth and that their rights are not yet secure. Yet the strength and pride in their gazes made it clear that they felt fully entitled to lead a charmed life. And they were certain that the ice under their skates would grow stronger day by day.

LOOKING OUT

We are fortunate that law schools and the legal profession, in the quest for talent, have become increasingly open to gay men and lesbians, as well as other previously excluded groups. And although we have had the opportunity to construct our lives to take advantage of the patches of protections, indignities and obstacles abound.

There was the time we were seeking to re-enter the United States from a vacation abroad with our two children. After a long flight, and long wait on line at immigration control, the U.S. Customs official refused to allow us to present ourselves as a family. We were faced with a split-second choice. Either we make a fuss, and the children clue into the fact that this official is refusing to recognize us as a family, or we go quietly along. One of us must wait behind the red line while the others proceed through. All around us, families stream through together. Welcome home.

Then there is the voir dire at jury service. If there is no state recognition for civil marriage, when the judge asks you to state under oath "what is your marital status and what is the occupation of your spouse?" what is the "domestic partner" to do? I faced this dilemma a few years ago. Ellen and I had been married in Oregon in 2004, but that marriage had been declared invalid by the Oregon Supreme Court. We were registered domestic partners in California, which did not yet recognize the right of same-sex couples to marry. Either I must declare myself "single," or "unmarried," which I counted as betrayal and which does not address the purpose of the question designed to elicit information about possible bias, or else I must come out to the judge, prosecutor, defense attorney, venire panel, criminal defendant and assorted witnesses and observers to accurately explain my status, which is what I did. While I'm open about my sexual orientation, requiring such disclosure in the context of jury service, as this questioning did, felt needlessly intrusive.

Obviously, there are bigger problems as well. I cannot deduct health insurance expenses for Ellen. We cannot file a joint federal tax return. If one of us dies, the other will be treated as a stranger for federal estate tax purposes and social security. These are just some of the many problems created by the federal "Defense of Marriage Act."

In California, we are at a crossroads. In May 2008, the California Supreme Court recognized a right to marry that extends to same sex couples. Ellen and I were married a few months later, as were thousands of others. Then in November 2008, as a result of a brutal and deceptive initiative campaign, a bare 52 percent of voters elected to amend the constitution to provide that only marriage between a man and a woman is valid and recognized in California.

The California Supreme Court is now poised to consider whether such a sweeping change—eliminating a fundamental right only for members of a suspect class—can be enacted by simple majority vote under our constitution. If the initiative was procedurally proper, which of our rights will be targeted next? The right to own property? To practice law? To raise children? Which other unpopular groups will have their rights stripped away? For many other groups the threat is not so severe since the protections of the federal constitution are reasonably secure. For us, with the current U.S. Supreme Court, state constitutions and courts are our main source of protection.

What will happen to marriages, like ours, entered before November, 2008? Our state supreme court will also decide whether the amendment invalidates existing marriages. Ken Starr, who is of counsel at Kirkland & Ellis and the Dean of Peperdine Law School, has filed a brief stating that our marriages must no longer be recognized.

Even if our marriage remains valid as a matter of state law, what will happen to us as we travel from state to state? At the time I write this, no states other than Massachusetts and Connecticut recognize the right to marry. While several others recognize marriages contracted in other states, 45 states define us as outsiders by prohibiting recognition of same-sex marriages altogether. As we travel from state to state, our marriage may be deemed meaningless by government officials and others, even in emergency.

The problems are not hypothetical. A same-sex couple from Washington State was in Florida recently for vacation with their children. One of the women suffered a heart aneurysm, and although the other was able to produce valid powers of attorney, the hospital refused to let her see or make medical decisions for her life-partner. Hospital staff said the reason was that Florida is an anti-gay state. The woman who suffered the aneurysm died in that hospital. Every time I travel to states like Texas, Arizona, South Carolina, Virginia, Georgia, and Idaho, in which gay and lesbian people are most vulnerable, I am painfully aware that the same could happen to me.

Although one state court after another has been considering the issue of equal marriage rights for more than a decade, the ABA (American Bar Association), with its mission of equal justice, has planted itself firmly on the sidelines and still has not embraced full equality for gay and lesbian people. It was not until 2007—nearly four decades after the 1969 Stonewall riots—that the ABA affirmed as one of its goals the full and equal participation in the legal profession by "persons of differing sexual orientations and gender identities."

Even today, the ABA has not adopted a policy calling for an end to laws prohibiting same-sex couples from marrying. The most the ABA has been willing to say on this subject is that the federal government should defer to the states on the question of marriage rights, a policy that would leave undisturbed laws that discriminate based on sexual orientation, as well as those that do not. While a policy statement of this kind may be pragmatic, it does little to help the Washington couple denied the right to visit and participate in health care decisions in a hospital in Florida. Decades from now, when the history of our nation's struggle for equal marriage rights is written, absent a swift change in policy, the ABA will be written off as irrelevant.

But the possibilities for change are all around. There is now some hope of passing federal legislation that will protect us from the most blatant forms of discrimination in employment, housing, public accommodations, and education. There is a chance that the military's Don't-Ask-Don't-Tell policy, which keeps thousands of qualified people from serving our country in a time of great need, may be repealed. More states will consider whether their own laws restricting same-sex marriage are constitutional.

Will we remain a country in which protections are scattered, families headed by same-sex couples are stigmatized, and our rights can be stripped away by popular vote guided by ignorance and fear? Will career success require a charmed life, carefully constructed on patchwork protections, cobbled together in a handful of states? Or will we be a unified country in which a family's rights cannot dissolve upon crossing state lines? The answer—and the possibility for real success—really depends on us.

PART II

How We Got There

Using Emotional Intelligence | 7

Ellen Ostrow, Ph.D.

"PLEASE DON'T SAY anything 'touchy-feely,'" a woman litigator and the director of professional development admonished me before my first large law firm presentation. In a decade of consulting with lawyers and law firms, I have yet to get a clear definition of "touchy-feely," but that it is always uttered with a mix of anxiety and contempt says a great deal to me about the norms of the legal profession.

For the most part, the legal system values technical competence above all else. Law schools select students based on grade point averages and LSAT scores. Law firms try to hire the smartest law school graduates in spite of evidence that grades are not necessarily good predictors of success in legal practice.

Prohibitions against expressing emotion at work are not unique to law. Physicians preserve the appearance of invulnerability and maintain emotional distance from the suffering of their patients. The belief that the workplace is no place for the expression of emotions is relatively widespread. Consider the extent to which you agree with the following statements:

- Lawyers should put their personal feelings aside at work.
- It is important for an attorney to control her emotions.
- Overly emotional people do not make good lawyers.
- Decisions should be made based on logic and rational analysis.

Even if you believe these statements, scientific research demonstrates that emotions are not just important for effective decision-making; they are absolutely necessary. Emotional responses are triggered in every human action and are important elements of almost any phenomenon with legal relevance. Rather than trying to eradicate them, a litigator can learn to recognize them, analyze how they may be affecting her own or another's behavior as well as their relationship, and respond appropriately. This is the essence of emotional intelligence.

Human reasoning and decision-making depend on many levels of brain processes, some of which are conscious and overtly cognitive and some of which are implicit, emotional and non-conscious. In fact, observations of patients with lesions in the emotion centers of the brain led neuroscientist Antonio Damasio[1] to conclude that defects in emotion and feeling play an important role in impaired decision making. The emotion centers of the brain

---

1. Damasio, A. R. (1994) <u>Descartes Error: Emotion, Reason and the Human Brain.</u> New York: Putman.

are not relegated to a secondary place in our reasoning. Rather, they are an integral part of what it means to think, reason and be intelligent.[2]

Most litigators, particularly trial lawyers, are aware that the emotions of jurors significantly influence decisions and work to influence these reactions. In some instances the legal system explicitly addresses emotional phenomena, for example, in considering mitigating circumstances in criminal law and emotional injury in tort law. What may be more challenging, however, is for an attorney to accept the influence of emotions in her own "rational" decision-making—and in almost everything else she does as a lawyer. Emotions play a significant role in advocacy, negotiation, client counseling, persuasion, influence, communication, business development and leadership. Thus, the issue is not whether to allow emotions to influence your work, but rather how you can optimally utilize them to enable you to succeed.

WHAT IS EMOTIONAL INTELLIGENCE

In 1990, Yale psychologists, John D. Mayer and Peter Salovey, introduced the concept of emotional intelligence.[3] They defined it as including four hierarchically[4] arranged sets of skills. The four competencies are:

1. accurately perceiving and identifying emotions in oneself and others;
2. using emotions to facilitate thinking;
3. understanding emotions in order to be able to predict emotional reactions; and
4. managing emotions and effectively incorporating them into thinking, problem-solving, judgment and behavior.

Before moving to a more detailed explanation of emotional intelligence and its use in litigation practice, it is important to be clear about what emotional intelligence is not. It is not "being nice." This is particularly important to emphasize to women advocates. Gender role stereotypes describe women

---

2. Goleman, D. (2006) <u>Social Intelligence: The New Science of Human Relationships.</u> New York: Bantam Books.

3. Salovey, P. & Mayer, J. D. (1990) "Emotional Intelligence." *Imagination, Cognition and Personality, 9*, 185-211.

4. Salovey and Mayer call these EI skills "hierarchical" because deficiencies in basic skills like emotion perception will interfere with the development and implementation of more complex skills like emotion regulation.

as "warm" and "nurturing," among other qualities. Women advocates who behave in ways that violate this stereotype are vulnerable to accusations that they are not "emotionally intelligent." A truly emotionally intelligent woman litigator would be able to accurately assess how she is feeling, in what ways these emotions were affecting her behavior, and the impact of her behavior on others; she then would determine whether she is accomplishing her goals in that particular situation. Sometimes she will decide to behave in a nurturing fashion regardless of whether she is feeling the impulse to care for others. At other times she may conclude that her goals would be better served by behaving more assertively. Emotional intelligence always requires taking gender stereotypes and other culturally determined emotional-display rules into account. That the emotional display rules of the "typical" litigator are in conflict with feminine gender stereotypes presents special challenges for women advocates. This topic will be addressed more fully later in the chapter.

Emotional intelligence is also not "intelligence" in the way that term is conventionally used. It is not a measure of cognitive/verbal/academic competence. Nature-nurture arguments about the causes of intelligence not withstanding, IQ tends to be stable after childhood. In contrast, emotional intelligence competencies can be taught, practiced and learned.

EMOTION

Objections to the acceptance of emotion in the workplace are invariably a response to its disruptive effects. One woman family lawyer confided to me that her all time worst work experience was the day her eyes filled with tears while being addressed by a judge in a courtroom. Her humiliation was certainly understandable. What was more disturbing to me was that the judge was shouting at her in a harsh, belittling, contemptuous manner—and his behavior was not considered nearly as inappropriate as was hers.

There is a long-standing view that emotions are disorganizing influences on cognitive activity. Because they are seen to disrupt effective thinking they must be minimized or controlled. In contrast, emotional intelligence theorists view emotions as organizing processes that enable individuals to think and behave adaptively. Emotions augment rather than interfere with other cognitive capacities. Emotions have signaling functions that provide significant survival advantages both for the species and for individuals. They are also the primary source of motivation—they arouse, sustain, and direct human attention and action. Furthermore, our own emotional experiences provide us with important information about our environment and situation.[5]

Emotional reactions occur automatically in response to some change in the world around us. They produce rapid physiological changes that shift our attention and prepare us for action. "Emotions are a signal, and if you pay attention to what an emotion is signaling, chances are the emotion is going to help you out of a tough situation, prevent something bad from happening, or help bring about a positive outcome."[6]

Emotions have critical survival value. The ability to detect danger, respond to an emergency, explore the environment, create and maintain bonds with others, fight back against attack, and provide care determine which species and individuals will survive. Even when survival is not at stake, the intelligent use of emotions enables us to behave adaptively. Anger may lead us to fight against being treated unjustly; worry and fear may motivate us to prepare to avoid negative consequences in the future.

Our emotional reactions often communicate important interpersonal information to others. A smile of happiness telegraphs that we are approachable, while an angry expression signals that others should leave us alone. In fact, the social nature of emotion has the most important implications for the woman advocate. Recent research in cognitive neuroscience demonstrates that our brains are social—we are wired to connect. Mirror neurons in our brains sense the emotions of others from nonverbal emotional signals like facial expressions and stimulate those same feelings within us. Mirror neurons activate what we observe. The activity in your brain triggers parallel circuitry in the other person's brain. This process takes place at an automatic level outside our awareness and at immense speed. This give-and-take of feeling accompanies every human encounter. "When it comes to emotions we cannot *not* communicate."[7]

Mirror neurons are responsible for emotions' contagious nature.[8] People at work "catch" feelings from one another. You have undoubtedly had the ex-

---

5. Salovey, P., Detweiler-Bedell, B. T., Detweiler-Bedell, J.B. & Mayer, J. D. (2008) "Emotional Intelligence." In Lewis, M., Haviland-Jones, J. & B & Barrett, L. F. (eds.) Handbook of Emotions, 3rd. ed. New York: The Guilford Press.

6. Caruso, D. A. & Salovey P. (2004) The Emotionally Intelligent Manager: How To Develop and Use the Four Key Emotional Skills of Leadership. San Francisco: Jossey-Bass.

7. Goleman, D. (2006) Social Intelligence *Ibid.*

8. Iacoboni, M. (2008) Mirroring People: The New Science of How We Connect with Others. New York: Farrar, Straus & Giroux.

perience of arriving at the office in a good mood only to feel it sour after a conversation with a particularly obnoxious opposing counsel. Even if he did not take or threaten any adverse action, just his tone of voice can jolt you out of your positive frame of mind. Emotional contagion has important implications for you as a leader whether you are leading a law firm, a practice group or a litigation team. The absence of emotional intelligence in a leader can result in disastrous consequences.

When we distrust emotions, we typically try to banish or ignore them, but this is ineffective. Emotional suppression requires energy. When people try not to feel their emotions, they wind up diminishing their ability to learn and recall information.[9] There is no realistic alternative except to welcome emotions, understand them, and learn how to put them to good use.

EMOTIONAL INTELLIGENCE SKILL 1: ACCURATELY IDENTIFYING YOUR OWN AND OTHER'S EMOTIONS

The ability to recognize emotions accurately is the most basic EI skill. Obviously, we cannot manage feelings of which we are unaware. How well can you discriminate your frustration from fatigue? It matters since you will have a tough time overcoming an obstacle if what you really need is sleep. How able are you to read other people? The ability to read facial expressions and identify emotions expressed nonverbally is a core EI skill.

Consider how important this competence is for your legal practice. Clients—particularly those outside of a corporate legal setting—typically seek legal help for very emotion-laden concerns. The client seeking assistance with tax problems, responding to being served with divorce papers, on the verge of bankruptcy, or facing criminal charges is likely to bring a host of intense emotions related specifically to his or her legal situation. This is often compounded by feeling intimidated by the size and/or formality of a legal office. Educational, social class and cross-cultural differences between you and the client add to the emotional mix. Accurately perceiving these emotions allows you to approach the situation with finesse.[10]

In part, some of the negative public perception of lawyers comes from their failure to notice and react to their clients' emotions. Too many lawyers

---

9. Baumaister, R. F. & Tice, D. M. (2000) "Ego Depletion: A Resource Model of Volition, Self Regulation and Controlled Processing." *Social Cognition, 18,* 130-150.

10. Silver, M. S. (2007) "Emotional Competence and the Lawyer's Journey," in Silver, M. A. (ed.), The Affective Assistance of Counsel: Practicing Law as Healing Profession. Durham, NC: Carolina Academic Press.

respond to the client's legal problem rather than to the client. Increasing your emotional intelligence does not require you to get a degree in psychology. Instead, consider the benefits of re-writing your job description to include detecting and processing your own and your client's emotional states and deciding how to respond.

The attorneys I coach often ask me what is "the best" way to communicate with a client/prospect/supervising attorney/junior member of the trial team. Publishing "Best Practices" is commonplace in the legal profession. Unfortunately, if you are looking for a set of rules, there is none. Emotional Intelligence is your best guide.

The negotiation context may be a good one for understanding this point. At the beginning of a negotiation, both parties present their positions. But there is always more at stake than just what is being addressed explicitly. The other party's interests, his or her sense of legitimacy, pride, and many other emotion-laden variables are likely to be operating. To be most effective, you need to track the other party's nonverbal emotional signals. Did your last offer seem to evoke more tension? If that is not your goal, you need to adjust your approach. Emotional intelligence requires attending to the "how" of the interaction, not just what is said. You will be most effective if you track the effects of your words, manner and emotional signals on the other person, and make adjustments to steer things in your desired direction.

The ability to identify emotions accurately provides you with core data necessary for making and taking emotionally intelligent decisions and actions. Consider the consequences of failing to note the increasing impatience of a judge. Which attorney is more likely to be hired by corporate counsel—the one who senses how much is at stake in the case or the one who waxes on about all the services that her firm can provide? Nonverbal emotional signals inform all social interactions. Accurately reading facial expressions and body language is crucial for success.

Correctly perceiving your own emotional state is vital for preventing the unintentional explosion of emotion that can spread through your team or organization. It is a paradoxical fact of life in law firms that although emotion is officially rejected, explosions of anger are implicitly accepted all the time. This lack of emotional intelligence can result in a toxic work environment.

Proficiency in accurately reading other people's emotional states is invaluable. How much more empowered would a young woman attorney be if she detected the anxiety behind her supervising partner's impatience and micro-management? Too many young lawyers fear asking questions. They read the reactions to their inquiries as indications of their stupidity and inappropriateness. Far more often, their queries simply trigger the anxiety of overworked partners who fear that the question opens the door to yet one more problem that must be addressed. Enormous amounts of time and energy are lost, because partners are unaware of their own emotions, and associates are blind to their supervisors' emotional states.

In these days of overloaded legal practices and multi-tasking, our emotional intelligence is impaired. The urgent focus on tasks interferes with taking the time to reflect on your own emotional state. Communicating by email makes it impossible to access the cues required to perceive other's emotions. If you are looking at your BlackBerry or answering the phone during client meetings, you cannot possibly be attending to important emotional information from your clients or yourself.

Many claim that they are too busy to stop and pay attention to what they and others are feeling. If you make this claim, you need to understand that you will be depriving yourself of data that may be crucial for an effective alliance with your client, for obtaining information necessary for your case, for bringing in new business and for managing your own behavior.

Moreover, one of the most common ethics complaints from clients about their lawyers is inadequate communication. Imagine a woman client going through a difficult divorce. Her husband makes wild threats about winning custody of the children and denying financial support. Panicked, she calls you, her attorney. You are away from your office, so she leaves a voicemail. If you listen carefully, you will hear the fear in her voice. Simply hearing from you would calm her somewhat. Having you explain her legal rights and the limits of his would make a world of difference. As a former psychotherapist, I have heard this story more times than I can count. And each time, the attorney failed to return the client's call. Often, as the client's anxiety mounted, her calls became more frequent. Her attorney likely began to experience her as a nuisance. In most cases, the client subsequently fired her attorney and hired another, more emotionally intelligent one. Think of the difference a few moments of focused attention and a brief phone call could have made.

As noted by Harvard law professor Todd Rakoff[11]:

The general public perception is that lawyers are more unfeeling than they ought to be. Maybe we don't teach enough about the relationship

11. Harvard law professor Todd Rakoff quoted by Lambert, C. (1998) "The Emotional Path to Success." *Harvard Magazine, Sept.-Oct.* available at http://harvardmagazine.com/1998/09/path.html

between lawyer and client. The attorney may overemphasize legal reme-dies; sometimes lawyers may be tone-deaf when it comes to what a client really wants.

EMOTIONAL INTELLIGENCE SKILL 2: USING EMOTIONS TO GUIDE THINKING

Although you may take pride in thinking of yourself as a rational, analytical thinker, the best decisions depend on the interplay of emotions and thought. On an intuitive level, you know which emotions are helpful in different situations. You probably do not discuss your compensation with a partner on the compensation committee when he is in a foul mood.

Psychologist Alice Isen's research[12] demonstrates that positive emotion facilitates problem solving, especially when tasks are complex. Positive affect leads people to be more flexible thinkers and decision-makers. When experiencing positive emotion, we are more able to see things in new ways, to consider multiple aspects of situations, to switch our attention among them and, thereby, to respond more effectively to complex or changing circumstances. As new facts are revealed, a litigator needs this kind of cognitive flexibility to developing a theory of a case. Your ability to access positive emotions will enable you to be more creative in this endeavor.

On the other hand, negative emotions narrow our focus. Fear brings our attention to the source of threat and prepares us to attack or flee. Negative affect helps an attorney focus on details and detect errors. Since so much of a lawyer's work concerns anticipating, preventing and detecting problems, negative emotion can be an ally. However, it is important to use these emotions intelligently. The ability to shift your emotions in a positive direction when prudent focus on problems is no longer needed is a very important skill. Positive emotions are crucial for building social bonds and broadening thinking. They promote mental and physical health and build cognitive and emotional resources.[13]

---

12. Isen, Alice M. (2008) "Some Ways in Which Positive Affect Influences Decision Making and Problem Solving." In Lewis, M., Haviland-Jones, J. M & Barrett, L F. (eds.) Handbook of Emotions, 3rd ed. *Ibid.*

13. Fredrickson, B. J. (1998) "What Good are Positive Emotions" *Review of General Psychology, 2*, 300-319.; Fredrickson, B. J. (2001) "The Role of Positive Emotions in Positive Psychology: The Broaden-and-Build Theory of Positive Emotions." *American Psychologist, 56*, 218-226; Fredrickson, B. J. & Branigan, C. (2005) "Positive Emotions Broaden Thought-Action Repertoires: Evidence for the Broaden-and-Build Model." *Cognition and Emotion, 19*, 313-332.

Your emotional state also affects your ability to remember. Memory is affect-dependent. The closer the match between the mood you experienced during learning and the mood you are in when trying to remember what you have learned, the better able you are to remember. Many supervising attorneys have complained to me about the failure of young attorneys to remember important negative feedback. In spite of how it seems, the young lawyers are not selectively remembering. It is far more likely that their failure to recall is due to their improved mood.

Emotional effects on memory are particularly important to keep in mind as you prepare witnesses and speak to juries. Seasoned trial attorneys know this, at least intuitively, when they embed the facts of a case in a particularly emotion-filled narrative.

One of the most important and often neglected uses of emotional intelligence is empathy. The ability to see things from another person's perspective is not just a cognitive task. When we put ourselves in someone else's shoes, we position ourselves to feel with them. Empathy is essential for trust. A client in distress wants to know that you can genuinely relate to her situation. Even if your practice is corporate, emotions play a far greater role than you may imagine. There are always at least two lawyers with equal expertise, experience and "smarts." Once the client has narrowed down the field to a small handful, the decision about whom to hire becomes emotional. As David Maister has so often pointed out,[14] ultimately hiring a law firm is about confidence and trust. It is an emotional decision.

Empathizing with others is critical to building a successful work environment, an effective team and quality relationships. How often has an upset client left your office having heard something completely different from what you tried to communicate? Your capacity to empathize enables you to know when a client is able to hear you. Often your expression of empathic concern will calm a client and increase his receptiveness to your input. In a very fundamental way, lawyering is not just about the legal issue—it is about the relationship between the lawyer and her client. As noted by law professor Martha Minow:

> *Lawyers I know say they don't want to hire anybody who can't talk to a client. By that, they mean understanding a client's concerns and motivations, helping clients sort through their own tangle of priorities and*

---

14. Maister, D., Green, C. & Galford, R. (2000). <u>The Trusted Advisor.</u> New York: The Free Press; Maister, D. (2008) <u>Strategy and the Fat Smoker.</u> Boston: The Spangle Press.

feelings. You need these skills not just in family law but in corporate law, takeovers, complex tax issues.[15]

EMOTIONAL INTELLIGENCE COMPETENCE 3: UNDERSTANDING EMOTIONS

This is the most cognitive of the EI skills. It involves understanding why people feel as they do, appreciating an emotion's probable trend over time, and knowing under what circumstances emotional intensity increases and decreases. For example, understanding that a sense of injustice typically leads to angry feelings allows you to predict how the associates at your firm will react upon discovering that their bonuses were half those of their colleagues at a peer firm. Unless they understand the financial rationale for the decision and believe that the burden was equitably shared by all members of the firm, you can predict their state of mind and their vulnerability to being recruited away. Appreciating the causes of emotions provides you with insight into the solutions for problems.

Understanding emotions also includes recognizing that most emotions exist on a continuum of intensity. A small irritation can progress to frustration which, if unaddressed, can intensify into anger and finally build up into rage. Recognizing this enables you to make predictions about your own and others' reactions and behavior. You know how people are likely to feel if events unfold in a particular way.

Having a rich emotion vocabulary also facilitates your reasoning about emotion. Being able to discriminate shades of difference among emotions provides you with more precision and sophistication in your understanding. Your emotional vocabulary enables you to communicate more effectively with others. You are more likely to ensure that your client recognizes that you empathize with her if you are able to articulate how you imagine she feels.

Consultant Ronda Muir[16] surveyed the emotional intelligence of lawyers using the Mayer Salovey Caruso Emotional Intelligence Test (MSCEIT.) Her sample scored a standard deviation below the average for the general population. Their scores on the third EI competence (understanding emotions) were higher than those on the first two competencies (accurately per-

---

15. Harvard law professor Martha Minow quoted by Lambert, C. (1998) "The Emotional Path to Success." *Harvard Magazine, Sept.-Oct.* available at http://harvardmagazine.com/1998/09/path.html

16. Muir, Ronda (11/8/2007) available at http://www.lawpeopleblog.com

ceiving emotions and being able to use them in reasoning.) However, the capacity to analyze emotions logically without being able to perceive them correctly is not very useful. Muir's study of a sample of lawyers selected from the Best Lawyers in America revealed that these highly rated attorneys performed 20 percent higher on average than her sample of lawyers in general. But these lawyers, too, scored highest in understanding emotions and lowest in perceiving emotions.[17]

This is further evidence of the tendency among attorneys to over-rely on their cognitive-analytical abilities. Taking the time to focus attention on your own emotional experience and to listen actively to others would strengthen these EI competencies. Active listening involves not just attending to the other person's words but also taking careful notice of their facial expressions and body language. Your excellent debating skills may hinder your ability to dialogue effectively. In dialogue, parties endeavor to listen, to understand one another rather than refute the other's argument. Being absorbed in your own thoughts or preparing your response will only interfere with your ability to perceive emotional information accurately. Although it requires a commitment to practice and ultimately change a habit, it would enable you to make far better use of your ability to understand cognitively how emotions work.

EMOTIONAL INTELLIGENCE COMPETENCE 4: MANAGING EMOTIONS

Can you inspire your team? Can you help an upset client to calm down? Can you psych yourself up in preparation for arguing a motion? When someone does something that angers you, can you compose yourself before discussing it rather than being pushed to react by the intensity of your emotion? Are you skillful at detecting your own stress level early to enable you to take steps to disengage and relax, or does your stress seem to mount until it overwhelms you? These are the kind of emotional intelligence skills involved in managing emotions.

This competence is the keystone of emotional intelligence. People who excel at affect management can be very emotional and passionate. However, they have good emotional self-control. They reflect frequently on what they are feeling so that they catch themselves before emotions build to high pitch. When experiencing strong feelings, they can temper them so they can think clearly.

---

17. Muir, Ronda (12/20/206) available at http://www.lawpeopleblog.com

You are probably all too familiar with people who are unskilled at managing their emotions. They seem impulsive and take their feelings out on others. Or they may be coldly rational, attending only to the facts as they see them. Such individuals appear lacking in sensitivity to, or compassion for, others.

There are a variety of means by which we can manage our emotions.[18] We can choose to be in a situation that we know will affect our mood, for example, going to lunch with a supportive friend. Emotionally intelligent individuals know that sharing their emotional experiences is an efficient means of organizing and thus regulating their emotions.

Re-directing our attention away from whatever is eliciting our emotion to something that changes our mood is another emotion regulation strategy. Among the most advanced EI tools is engaging in a positive emotion generating activity. This enables us to recover more quickly from negative events without avoiding or denying their effects altogether.

Changing how we think about a situation or coming up with an alternative interpretation of whatever triggered the feeling enables emotion management. For example, if I am initially upset by a colleague's brusqueness, because I have taken her behavior personally, I can consider the possibility that she had a fight with her significant other or is developing a migraine or just found out she had lost a case.

Efforts to suppress feelings entirely are not effective means for managing emotion. Trying not to react emotionally to an event is likely to interfere with your ability to recall the event. It also takes considerable energy not to feel, which robs you of the energy you need to solve problems and make decisions effectively. Suppressing feelings also blinds you to the information they contain.

Sometimes you simply have to accept a feeling even if it is uncomfortable or unwelcome. Emotions are short-lived. They linger and become moods only when we ruminate about them or the situation that triggered them.

Emotions have an action component or tendency. They motivate behavior. We can use emotions to inspire ourselves and others to act. Great leadership works through emotions. The best leaders are those who have found ways to understand and improve the way they handle their own and other people's emotions. As the focus of attention and the one to whom others look for meaning and direction, the leader's emotions tend to be the most conta-

---

18. Gross, J. J. (2008) "Emotion Regulation." In Lewis, M., Haviland-Jones, J. M & Barrett, L F. (eds.) <u>Handbook of Emotions</u>, 3rd ed. *Ibid.*

gious. Because of this, a leader's most fundamental competence is knowing and managing her own emotions.

Many litigators tend to be more skillful at influencing the feelings of others, particularly juries, than managing their own emotions. It is impossible to manage your own emotions without being aware of them. All too often the trial attorney takes more time to think through her closing argument than how she feels about an inadequate work product from a junior attorney and the most effective way of addressing this problem. Giving yourself the psychological space to recognize your feeling: consider its source, its intensity, what information it's telling you; the extent to which it is influencing your thinking at the moment; the likely consequences of acting on it now and the benefits of detaching from it for the moment and returning to it later is what it means to integrate cognition and affect to generate effective solutions. This is emotional intelligence.

WHAT ABOUT GENDER?

The stereotype of women as more emotional than men is pervasive across cultures. Although gender differences have been widely documented, emotionality depends upon personality, social, cultural and situational variables. Stereotypes typically elicit self-confirmatory behavior and women's own gender-stereotype beliefs may influence their reports of emotional experience. However, gender differences do emerge using measures other than self-reports. For example, women refer to both positive and negative emotions more often than men in both conversations and writing samples. Female physicians engage their patients in more feeling-related talk. Women tend to be more facially expressive and score higher than men in identifying the meaning of nonverbal cues of emotion.[19]

The results of research about gender and emotional intelligence have been mixed. On the MSCEIT, women have been found to exceed men in their ability to use emotion to facilitate thought, to understand emotion and to manage emotions. There is a large body of data indicating women's advantage in perceiving nonverbally communicated emotions.[20]

Women advocates face particular challenges presented by stereotypes of lawyers in general, and litigators in particular. In general, the male gender stereotype is more consistent with people's ideas about lawyers: assertive, ag-

---

19. Brody, L. R. & Hall, J. A. (2008) "Gender and Emotion in Context." In Lewis, M., Haviland-Jones, J.M. & Barrett, L. F. (eds.) Handbook of Emotions, 3rd ed. *Ibid.*

20. Brody, L. R. & Hall, J. A. (2008) *Ibid.*

gressive, unemotional, competitive, achievement-oriented, etc. Women lawyers in general are permitted a narrow band of behavior beyond which they are likely to suffer negative consequences. What is assertive for a man is aggressive for a woman; what is pride for a man is self-aggrandizing for a woman.

Sociologist Arlie Hochschild[21] coined the term "emotional labor" to refer to occupational requirements to conceal some emotions while intentionally displaying others. The prototypical example has been the requisite smiling face of the airline hostess. Surface acting, i.e., intentionally showing an emotion different from what you actually feel, has been linked to burnout and job turnover.

Many women trial lawyers find the masculine arena of the courtroom to require significant emotional labor. Sociologist Jennifer Pierce[22] systematically observed courtroom behavior at The National Institute of Trial Advocacy training and described hyper-masculine behavioral norms. Concepts like "Rambo litigators," and "scorched-earth" and "take-no-prisoners" tactics do not evoke feminine gender stereotypes. If these are required for "zealous advocacy" of one's client, what's an emotionally intelligent woman advocate to do? Women trial lawyers often describe walking a fine line in the courtroom: judges and juries are frequently more accepting of Rambo-litigation tactics from male than female attorneys.

Your emotional intelligence should guide you in these situations. Paying close attention to the reactions of jurors and judges as you question a witness should provide vital information for how best to proceed. Emotional display rules require women to conceal angry feelings more so than men. It seems a reasonable hypothesis that much more emotional intelligence is required for women advocates to succeed, as compared to men.

In her interviews with women lawyers, Mona Harrington was told by many that they best represent their clients by listening, observing and reading opponents rather than by being aggressive and confrontational. They reported getting better results in depositions by approaching witnesses sympathetically rather than antagonistically, so that the witnesses forgot that an attorney was deposing them.[23]

---

21. Hochschild, A. R. (1983) *The Managed Heart: Commercialization of Human Feeling.* Berkeley: University of California Press.

22. Pierce, J. (2004) "Rambo Litigators: Emotional Labor in a Male-Dominated Occupation." In Sachs, N & Marrone, C. (eds,) <u>Gender and Work in Today's World.</u> Westview Press.

23. Harrington, M (1995) <u>Women Lawyers: Rewriting the Rules.</u> New York: Penguin.

Besides becoming exhausting, emotional labor is often unsuccessful. It is impossible to fake the facial muscles involved in genuine emotions.[24] Because emotional intelligence is useful in every aspect of life, not only work, invest your energy in developing these skills. Higher emotional intelligence is associated with better stress management, coping more effectively with negative experiences, being a more successful leader, creating a positive work environment, and being viewed as interpersonally sensitive and easier to deal with than people with less EI.[25] It seems like a sure win.

24. Eckman, P. (2003) <u>Emotions Revealed.</u> New York: Henry Holt.
25. Mayer, J. D., Salovey, P. & Caruso, D. R. (2008) "Emotional Intelligence: New Ability or Eclectic Trait?" *American Psychologist, 6.*

Battling Bias: Managing the Difficult Adversary

8

By Evelyn R. Storch

"HI, YA, SWEETIE. How's tricks?" In five tasteless words, my adversary has attempted to degrade, disparage, and marginalize me. He has objectified me, he has quite literally called me a hooker, and he has tried to exalt his own status at my expense. But he has picked the wrong "Sweetie" this time. "Not bad, Honey. How's it hangin'?" I retort to recalibrate the dialogue to equilibrium.

This is a coarse exchange to be sure. But Mr. Adversary's challenge—and make no mistake, a challenge it is—must be met with strength and a force that will repel any notion of repetition. As a women litigator, you are frequently called upon to level the playing field—to overcome the gender bias your adversaries feel and/or seek to exploit. To be effective advocates for your clients, you simply cannot allow men to have the upper hand, especially just because they are men. You must make certain that you seize the initiative wherever possible so that you (and, hence, your client's cause) will get serious consideration.

There are a myriad of ways your adversaries seek to undermine you, and you must be on your guard against all of them. The use of demeaning pet names is a frequent tool. It is easy to ignore the quick jab a passing "honey" or "dear" represents. But, in my view, letting it pass lets the camel's nose under the tent and invites ever-escalating challenges. I believe a response in kind each and every time you are so addressed is both appropriate and necessary. You needn't be vulgar, as in my opening example, but you do need to show your counterpart that two can play that little game. Any nickname will do, but terms of endearment that encompass his appearance, such as "cutie" or "handsome" or "big guy," are generally more effective to knock your adversary off-kilter. Don't forget, he's far less accustomed to that approach than you, which gives you an automatic advantage.

Sometimes, however, ignoring adverse counsel is a very effective means of handling his attempt to undercut you. I had an adversary once who made little speeches after many questions at the depositions at which my client was present. These speeches were designed to demonstrate his supposedly superior knowledge. If I were being honest, I would have to concede that his "mini-lessons" were truly annoying, but you'd never have known it at the depositions. I never looked at him when he was speaking—I stared straight at the witness—and whenever he was finished, no matter how long it took, I simply said to the deponent, "You may answer." At the breaks, I would explain to my client what a fool my adversary was making of himself since his antics had no effect on the answers I was getting to my questions. I was quick to point out any substantive mistakes counsel had made as well. Since his tactic was completely ineffective, it was I who had gained the upper hand. And, incidentally, when we tried the case, our all-women team (inside and outside counsel and the expert), crushed Mr. Speechify.

Another ploy some male counterparts use is to treat us as if we are china dolls. They assume a frailty few women litigators possess, and they "cater" to our supposed weaknesses. The smart ones do so with feigned courtesy, such as offering (almost invariably only when others are around) to move a box of documents for us or racing to pick up a pen we dropped. Others are clumsier in their effort to undermine us, such as using sports terminology or analogies and then "explaining" the terms used upon the "realization" that we might not understand them. Do not be fooled, whether smooth or clumsy, neither move is chivalry. It is an attempt to exercise superiority over the "weaker sex."

Dealing with these maneuvers requires an analysis of your audience and the effect your adversary's tactic has had on that audience. Sometimes, although you will have noticed what Mr. Faux-Chivalry has done, your audience will not. In such cases, discretion is the better part of valor and, even if it is irksome, you should ignore it.

But if the judge/jury/client/adverse party/other audience seems to have reacted, action is in order. If the reaction is favorable, i.e., if your audience is reacting as you are, an appropriate response might be an exaggerated one that serves to mock your adversary. For example, to the box-toter, you might say, "Oh thank you, kind sir, whatever would I have done without you?" A slight curtsey or a subtle batting of your eyelashes might put the finishing touch on your response. The anticipated laughter will now be at your adversary's expense, not yours, and he will have been stripped of his chivalrous veneer.

If, on the other hand, Mr. Faux-Chivalry has hit his mark, you must respond with strength and immediately dispel the notion of weakness. You might call him out expressly, such as stating, "I know you are trying to portray me as weak, but it will not work this time." If he tries to deny his intent to enfeeble you, you might retort, "Thank you for your unsolicited assistance, but, in the current posture of this case, it is your client's cause that needs help, not I." Whether you take a humorous approach, a direct confrontation or something different that fits your style, you must not allow your audience to perceive you as weak for your client's interests inevitably will suffer.

One note of caution is in order. There has been substantial research demonstrating that both men and women object to aggressive women. You must find the balance that permits you to present yourself as strong and assertive, but not aggressive. It is the Catch-22 we all face and the tightrope you must walk. Would that there were a one-size-fits-all answer to this dilemma. But there is not. It is something you must learn by trial and error to discover what works for you.

The learning process must take into account all of the stereotypes and outmoded views of women generally and women advocates in particular. Surely, you have arrived at your adversary's office and have been asked by the receptionist, "Are you one of the lawyers?" How many of your male counterparts do you think have encountered that question? How many have been mistaken for the court reporter as you have? It is these preconceived notions that weaken you and against which you must fight in large ways and in small.

My secretary, not quite a feminist but close, used to answer my partner's phone, "Mr. So and So's office." But when she answered my phone, she would say, "Evelyn Storch's office." When I asked her why she did that, she had no explanation. I explained to her that it was sexism even if she hadn't intended it to be; that she was granting greater respect to my male partner than she was according me. She was horrified at her subconscious gender bias. While this is truly a small matter, it underscores the need to be on constant guard against being diminished simply because you are a woman.

Whether or not it is true in any particular case, most people believe that women, by nature, are more nurturing and empathetic than men. This can benefit the woman advocate. As a woman, you can often coax a witness into giving you answers to questions that men would be hard-pressed to obtain. Because both men and women are likely to find you less intimidating, they are more relaxed and, hence, more likely to fall into a rhythm of favorable responses. An empathetic tone can further lull a witness into "spilling his guts" to your willing ear. These tools, while available, do not come easily to men.

Once again, however, there is a fine line to walk between acting as a nurturer to obtain information and displaying weakness. The former will serve your client well. The latter can be your undoing (and, hence, your client's). Your adversary may seek to exploit what he perceives as your "weakness" as a nurturer by attempting to bully you. While this can work to your advantage with the witness, who might identify with you, bullying is never a tactic with which you can afford to allow your adversary to succeed. Repond firmly. I prefer a blunt challenge, such as "I know what you're trying to do, and it won't work. I will ask the questions and get the answers to which I'm entitled even if you misbehave as you just did." You might prefer a less direct retort, but it can be no less strong in the face of a bully.

Another preconception with which you have to deal as a woman advocate is that you are emotional and, therefore, incapable of evaluating the situation objectively. There will be times, in front of a jury, when that notion will work to your advantage, and you can use emotion to prove a point. Most of the time, however, it simply casts you as the weaker, less capable litigator, and you must push back. In the midst of a disagreement over discovery, for example, have you had your adversary ask you if you always get "this emotional" about things or, worse, if it is "your time of the month"? This, in my opinion, is not the time for anger. That sort of challenge calls for an icy reply that returns the conversation to the topic at hand. Your cool demeanor can make the nasty sarcasm of your adversary backfire, showing him to be the fool and enhancing your own stature.

The battle of the sexes often heats up when you enter the courtroom or the judge's chambers. In general, women are far less apt to toot their own horn. Mr. Adversary often uses that to his advantage if you let him. In conferences in chambers, for example, the braggadocio will begin swiftly, and your adversary will attempt to mesmerize the judge with tales of his courtroom prowess. You have such stories too—and now is the time to put them on display. I'm not suggesting you get into a battle of "Can You Top This?" I am suggesting, however, that you cannot let the judge and Mr. Adversary roll merrily along in a conversation in which you have played no part, or they may form a bond that will be hard to break through when the discussion turns to the merits of your case.

Although the situation is improving, judges, too, will undercut your position, sometimes deliberately, oftentimes (and perhaps more dangerously) unconsciously. Perhaps you've had the experience of hearing the judge greet a room full of lawyers by saying, "Good morning, counsel; good morning, ladies." Or you've been in court when the judge calls you or another woman advocate "Little Lady"? Naturally, you want to avoid provoking the judge, but turning it into your opening remark, if you have the opportunity, is a way to let the judge know you don't appreciate the put-down while still keeping him focused on the merits. Once when I was called, "Little Lady," I opened by stating, "This Little Lady has a mighty big problem—Mr. Defense Attorney thinks he can play the Big Man On Campus and stonewall on discovery." And then I launched into my argument. Needless to say, I got the discovery I needed.

As advocates, we are taught to marshal the facts and the law and to plead our case forcefully and with conviction. As women, we are taught to seek common ground and foster understanding. As women advocates, we must meld the two roles. We must use our nurturing skills to our advantage while being ever-prepared so as to enhance our power. We must recognize that gender bias is a reality that requires us to prove our strength at every turn. But we must also realize that if we can neutralize that bias with techniques such as described here and others we develop to suit our own styles, the very fact that we have had to work harder and smarter puts us (and, therefore, our clients) way ahead of the game.

Making Rain 9

By Linda A. Monica, Esq.

RAINMAKING

Rainmaking is hard. Reports, data, and anecdotal evidence from a variety of sources demonstrate that far too few women attorneys achieve a high level of success when it comes to bringing in new business. The purpose of this chapter is to provide practical suggestions and steps that women litigators can take to overcome obstacles to marketing, whatever their origin, and to become more effective in developing new business.

DETERMINE AND COMMUNICATE YOUR PROFESSIONAL GOALS

You must begin with an assessment of your professional goals. Your goals will vary over time and will be influenced by many personal and professional factors. This is particular true for women lawyers who find that the balance between their work life and professional life regularly requires assessment and adjustment. Whether your goal is to become a partner, to make the jump from income to equity partner, or to pursue business development while working part-time, your goals will directly affect the direction and extent of your marketing activities. Embrace your personal goals and recognize that you can attain them over time in a way that is consistent with your personal and professional lives. Set realistic objectives for years one, three, and five and write them down. Refer to them often as you develop your specific action plans for getting new business.

It is important to communicate your professional goals to the lawyers in your firm. You want to ensure that your business development goals are aligned with the firm's overall marketing strategy and that you understand what the firm expects of you in terms of both billable hours and marketing efforts. Let's be honest—the pressure of billable hours and the demands of a litigation practice make it difficult to dedicate the number of hours that are required to be successful at marketing. Don't be afraid to consider modifying the balance between your billable hours and business development time. A reduced billable hour requirement will enable you to make an increased commitment to your business development plan. While there may be short term ramifications to this approach, the long term benefits of having your own book of business may more than make up for it.

Know what you can expect from your firm support of your business development activities. Learn how the firm allocates its marketing budget so that you can be prepared to submit requests for support of your marketing strategies. Provide regular reports and feedback about your business development efforts. When making partnership decisions, firms consider not only the results of an associate's business development, but also the associate's level of effort and determination that indicates she "gets it" when it comes to marketing.

Finally, learn the rules of the game and understand that many are not written down anywhere. Know how the firm deals with "credit" for new clients. Is credit divided among all the lawyers who play a role in bringing in this business? If so, who decides how? How does the firm recognize efforts to enhance work from existing clients? If the firm allocates varying levels of credit to "originating attorneys" versus "managing attorneys," what does that mean in terms of your compensation level and recognition of your business development efforts? Understand the rules so you won't be surprised as you start down the road of building your book of business.

DEVELOP AND MAINTAIN A POSITIVE ATTITUDE

Attitude counts when it comes to business development; and having a positive attitude really counts. Developing your professional reputation and building your network of contacts take considerable time. Not every business development effort will be successful, and not every contact will turn into a viable referral source. This is especially true for woman litigators who are trying to assess how, why, and where the next wave of litigation may arise. It would be easy to become discouraged, so it is important to understand how important your attitude is.

In a recent survey of more than 400 women attorneys, the Legal Sales & Services Organization (LSSO) (www.lsso.org) distilled four factors that were key to the successful development of business—and the first was having a positive attitude and the ability to evaluate and learn from marketing efforts. Successful women rainmakers do not view unsuccessful attempts as rejection or failure. Rather, they understand that building a book of business takes time and not every marketing effort will pay off in the manner or within the time period anticipated. They fill their minds with "positive" talk and readily acknowledge their successes. They are optimistic, resilient, and persistent.

Women lawyers who viewed their business development successes and failure in an evaluative manner were significantly more successful than those who had a negative attitude. The LSSO survey provided quantitative results to back up these findings. Women lawyers who utilized an "Evaluative Approach" to their business development efforts had origination fees twice that of women who had a negative response to their setbacks. Those who viewed their efforts from an "Educational" point of view had origination fees that were 50% higher than those women who had "no response" to their success or failures.

So stay positive and remember that persistence will pay off. Understand that it will take time for you to define and refine your marketing messages and strategies. With the right attitude, you are ready to identify your target market and focus your business development efforts.

FIND YOUR NICHE AND TARGET YOUR EFFORTS

The LSSO survey also found that successful marketers invest their time wisely in efforts that are focused, targeted, and consistent. Because of the broad range of matters that constitute "litigation," it is especially important for women litigators to find a niche that allows them to target their marketing for two important reasons. First, your time for marketing is limited, especially given the pressures of the practice of law and the demands of your personal life. You simply cannot afford to take a shotgun approach or engage in activities that may have only limited potential from a marketing standpoint. Instead, you must identify a specific niche so that your efforts can be focused as you gain credibility, visibility, and contacts.

Second, it is important that your niche be focused so that you are able to articulate how your specific skills can meet the needs of potential clients. In other words, you need to describe what you do in a short and concise way that captures the interest of others and informs them how you can help them or others. Potential clients are more likely to remember you if your niche is distinctive, as opposed to being broad and general litigation services.

How you describe what you do can either lead to the opening of a door or its abrupt slamming. For example, some lawyers introduce themselves by saying: "I am a litigator. I represent people who get sued." The typical response to that introduction runs along the lines of "I hope I never need your services." Saying you are "a litigator" neither describes a niche nor expresses in a meaningful way how you help people. Instead, describe how you help to solve problems. If you handle employment litigation matters, describe your practice by saying, "I help companies develop and implement fair and effective employment policies so they avoid problems with their employees, and I help companies resolve any problems that do arise." Think about what you do in terms of the needs your services satisfy or problems you help solve.

Don't be hesitant to find a niche. Some lawyers are afraid this will limit them either in their marketing efforts or in the scope of legal work they do.

Neither is the case. First, having a niche does not limit the number of people to whom you can market. Having a niche makes marketing more effective and targeted, because it allows you to stand out as being an expert in a specific area and best suited to meet a client's need when it comes to those specific problems. Second, the fact that your marketing efforts are honed in on a specific niche does not mean that you cannot handle cases or matters that are outside of your marketing niche. You can aim your efforts directly at your target markets so that you are getting the most out of your marketing.

It is important as a litigator to think about a niche that will get you a seat "at the front of the bus." That means you should consider the first thing a potential client may do when faced with a lawsuit. For example, if you want to represent engineers and architects in professional negligence claims, think about the first thing they will do when served with a complaint. It is likely they will consult their insurance policy. So become an expert on the types of insurance policies offered to these professionals. Work with insurance brokers, claims adjusters, and others to understand the different types of policies and the pros and cons of each. Now you are in a position to offer valuable services to these professionals by helping them determine and obtain the insurance best suited to their business and legal needs. If you are the one who has helped them with insurance coverage issues, it is likely that you will get a call when suit is brought.

Perhaps your niche is the representation of nursing care facilities in negligence cases. If a complaint is brought alleging inadequate care, a nursing home will turn to its policies and procedures to see if they complied or whether their procedures are lacking. Get to the front of that bus by researching and developing a "Best Practices" model for nursing homes that includes policies for complete documentation of care, for clear articulation to residents and family members of the specific level of care and services provided, and for explicit criteria for incident reporting. Offer to present your "Best Practices" to nursing homes and their staff. Help to update written polices and manuals. Write articles and speak to their associations about these issues. Activities that are focused in your niche area and on your targeted clients will make it more likely that you will be among the first contacted when there is a problem.

You will reap many benefits from focusing your marketing efforts. Your marketing time will be well spent and directed to efforts likely to have the greatest potential for new clients. You will be perceived as an expert and confident in your niche area because you have spent time and effort to become an expert. Clients will be more willing to pay for your expertise. You will have an advantage over other lawyers who are more "generalists" and are not experts in your area. Finally, it is more likely that potential clients will remember you because of your defined niche.

RECOGNIZE THE IMPORTANCE OF CLIENT SERVICE

It goes without saying that the foundation of your entire marketing effort is your excellence as an attorney. You must do the highest quality work every step of the way. Demonstrate enthusiasm for your work and interest in your clients, their cases, and their overall business. Outstanding client service is one of the most import aspects of your marketing efforts. Successful women rainmakers recognize the value of "Client Service" as a key component of their marketing strategy as demonstrated by the LSSO survey. Women attorneys who viewed "Client Service" as their primary business development strategy had origination fees that were 50% higher than those who thought it had no impact.

As a litigator, consider how to demonstrate a higher level of client service that goes beyond your work on a specific case. Learn about your client. If you are handling a discrete litigation matter for a company, find out more about its overall business. Go to the company's website, read its brochures and public filings, and learn more about the industry. All of this will enable you to talk meaningfully with your client about matters of concern to them and will demonstrate your interest in the client beyond this one case. Set up a "Google Alert" for the client and its industry so that you will be among the first to know of new and relevant developments. Forward the information to your client along with related articles or other information that will be of interest to them. Continually try to think of ways that you can take the extra step to offer exceptional client service.

If you are an associate or junior partner, recognize that the other lawyers in the firm who give you work are also your "clients" and you should treat them that way. Do excellent work and keep them well-informed. Get to know all of your colleagues in the firm and their areas of practice and make sure they know the same about you. Some of your best business development opportunities are likely to include selling the services of others in your firm. You will be more effective at this if you know the areas in which your colleagues practice and also have specific details regarding the clients with whom they work and successes they have had. Similarly, other lawyers will be in a better position to refer matters to you or bring you into cases if they know your niche practice area.

BECOME CREDIBLE AND VISIBLE

Developing credibility and visibility in your niche area is key to your success. Clients and referral sources are looking for the short list of lawyers who are associated with a particular area of expertise. Although your expertise can be developed in a number of ways, pick those positioning activities that will be most effective given your objectives. Whether a particular activity is one that will work for you will depend on a number of factors, including your niche area, your target market, how effective you are at the activity, and how much time is required. Each way of "getting your name out there" needs to be assessed in terms of these criteria.

Speaking, writing, and becoming involved in organizations are three of the best ways to get yourself known. But evaluate each to ensure it is the most effective use of your marketing time and is an activity that you are comfortable doing. For example, while speaking is the way many lawyers establish credibility, be sure you have developed the skills to be a compelling and engaging speaker. If not, take the time to get some training as you will do more harm giving a poor presentation than not giving one at all.

There are many opportunities to speak before lawyers and prospective clients and to write articles. You want to ensure, however, that you will be before your target audience and speaking on a topic that is relevant and interesting with the potential to lead to further inquiries about your services. When you give a presentation or write an article, you want it to enhance the perception of you as an expert and cause potential clients to remember you and your niche practice area. Tie your presentation or article as directly as possible to your niche area. For example, if you accept an invitation to speak before lawyers about discovery rules, then talk about the rules in the context of cases brought against architects and engineers, if that's your target market. It will reinforce in the minds of your peers that this is your litigation niche. Later, you can present this information in an effective manner to relevant industry groups.

After you have identified a target forum, follow a strategy for becoming a speaker or writer. For example, if you want to present at a CLE litigation seminar sponsored by your local bar association, become involved and find out who plans the seminars. Make your interest in speaking known and volunteer to help plan the program. If your goal is to speak at a national seminar, first go as an attendee. Meet those in charge of the program and talk about how speakers are chosen. Some seminar companies keep a data base of attorneys with an interest in speaking and their topics. Make sure your information is on file. For some national seminars, speakers are chosen by the conference chairs selected by the seminar company. Find out well in advance who they are and contact them. Express your interest in being a speaker and demonstrate why you are an appropriate choice. Tell them if you have tried cases involving the same issues or if you have written an article on the subject. Prepare an outline of a topic or an abstract of your presentation. Give them a reason to want you.

Once you have been asked to speak, you <u>must</u> deliver an outstanding presentation. Both your written materials and your presentation must demonstrate your expertise and the fact that you put considerable effort into providing the audience with valuable information. Lawyers tend to do an excellent job preparing their materials, but often forget that more than half the impact a speaker makes on her audience is determined by body language. Look confident and connect with your audience. Make eye contact; demonstrate your interest in the topic; and keep your audience engaged.

Joining professional and industry organizations is another way to enhance your visibility. When it comes to organizations one fact is crystal clear—it is far better to be actively involved in one organization than simply a member of many where you are nothing more than a name on a membership list. Determine the organizations most relevant to your niche, prioritize them in terms of the greatest likelihood of enhancing your business development efforts, and join only the ones in which you have the time to become active.

Leadership roles in the business community provide the opportunity to demonstrate your expertise, to make contacts, and to develop referral sources. The LSSO survey identified "Taking Leadership Roles" as another key characteristic of successful women rainmakers. Whether you were a partner or an associate, women who held leadership roles had significantly higher origination fees than those who did not. Women equity partners in leadership roles had origination fees 35% higher than their female counterparts. Similarly, income partners and associates who were in leadership positions had origination fees that were 45% higher than their colleagues. So the bottom line is join and lead.

LEVERAGE YOUR TIME AND
BUSINESS DEVELOPMENT EFFORTS

Lack of time is the number one obstacle that women attorneys give when it comes to business development. Therefore, you must make every marketing minute count. There are a number of effective ways to leverage your business development efforts.

Clone the Event

Developing and maintaining contacts underlies all your rainmaking efforts. Since you can't be in two places at once, expand your contacts at any single event. For example, you will want to connect with other lawyers, especially litigators, to ensure that they know about your expertise in your niche practice area. Other lawyers can be referral sources, references, or evaluators asked to rate you as attorney. But don't connect with other attorneys one at a time. Take the time, for example, to coordinate a lunch with three or four lawyers, not just one. One lunch . . . one hour invested . . . three or four other lawyers updated on your practice area, expertise, and interest in developing business.

Use this same strategy as you work to become more effective at cross-marketing with the lawyers in your firm. Organize groups of three or four lawyers from the firm to go to lunch for the express purpose of sharing information about each other's practice areas. End the lunch by brainstorming ways to cross-market to each other.

Find three or four business people who share a similar interest or problem. You get the idea. Take the time to think about how you make any event have a broader impact. The extra time you spend in arranging the event will come back to you many times.

Do Your Homework Before and After Attending A Seminar

We all attend seminars that are perfect places to work on business development. First of all, you have the opportunity to make new and significant contacts. While you may not know in advance who is attending the seminar, you will know the speakers. They already are recognized for their expertise. These lawyers and business people are worthy of your attention and are the kind of contacts you want to make. Research their backgrounds. Read their biographical material on the internet and learn about their practice areas. Identify three or four speakers whom you would like to meet. Perhaps one speaker has written an article directly related to your niche practice area or maybe she is the head of an ABA Committee you are interested in joining or perhaps he is associated with a social cause that you too support. One of the speakers may be the corporate counsel for a company you would like to work for. Research her background, look at the company's website, and understand its challenges so you are prepared to engage in a meaningful discussion. During breaks, at lunch, or at the reception, seek out these people and expand your network while you learn.

Leverage the materials and information you gain at the seminar. While listening to the presentations, consider developing an article from this information and your own research on how your jurisdiction or clients might be affected by any new developments. Consider whether this information could be included in a client newsletter or think about emailing your clients about something of interest that you learned at the seminar. Don't do what most lawyers do—put the materials on a bookshelf in your office never to be looked at again.

Take the Initiative

Don't hesitate to take the initiative at a seminar to organize your own networking events. For example, some seminars now include "Women Networking" events as part of their programs. If you don't see one listed in the brochure, call the seminar sponsor and ask if they could arrange one. Other times, seminar companies post sign-up sheets to organize groups for dinner. Sign up and go. You are at the seminar, so make the most of your time.

Set up your own networking event if one isn't offered. It isn't hard to organize a dinner. You will be hosting an enjoyable evening that will benefit all those attending who will also have a reason to remember you. Most importantly, you will have effectively utilized your time by bringing people together to talk about issues related to your business development activities.

Leverage Your Lunch Hour

When you are thinking about time, don't let the lunch hour go to waste. There are many ways you can leverage that hour. Set up a monthly brown bag lunch with other women litigators. Make it substantive and add regular discussion topics, including discussions regarding business development. The benefits from this are multiple. You will be increasing your contacts with lawyers, developing strong relationships with other women attorneys, strategizing about personal and professional issues, and enjoying yourself all at the same time.

Arrange a monthly lunch with litigators in your substantive area. At your lunch, discuss new legal developments and network. If you have taken a leadership role in your section of the bar, use the time to develop ideas for future CLE programs or other events.

Consider putting on a lunch time seminar for your clients. You will be able to interact with clients and to demonstrate your expertise. Be sure to invite lawyers from your firm to enhance their ability to cross-market your expertise. And don't forget to leverage the materials you prepare for the seminar by sending them out as a newsletter to clients or to other business people.

Contact your local Chamber of Commerce about putting on a lunch time seminar. This will provide you with a much bigger audience of business people in your community. Turn this into a monthly series where you bring in other speakers and act as moderator. In that way, you will significantly expand your contacts and put yourself in front of business people every month.

Embrace Modern Technologies

There was a time when it was very costly to have a presence on the internet. No more. It is now possible to have a professional website for a reasonable cost and expand your reach further than ever before. Given the extent to which we all now use the internet, a website is an indication of your credibility and expertise. The ways in which this leverages your exposure to potential clients is obvious.

Don't overlook new on-line professional networks. There are over 25 million professionals who already have their profiles on LinkedIn. Your profile includes your biographical information as well as groups to which you belong and interests that you have. From that point on, you can invite colleagues to be linked to you and accept the invitation of others. You can be introduced to a new contact through an existing contact and be part of on-line discussions. These professional networks are relatively new but have the potential to be a very powerful way to open the door to contacts.

Work with Strategic Partners

You can significantly leverage your business development efforts by identifying others with whom you can partner on marketing. Four women attorneys in a small New England law firm used this strategy to interact on a regular basis with the other businesswomen in their community. They partnered with women in other companies—real estate, accounting, personnel services to name a few—and formed a group called the "W.E.B.," "Women for Excellence in Business." They combined their lists of contacts and invited more than 150 businesswomen to a monthly meeting that featured a continental breakfast, time for networking, and a presentation on a current business issue of interest to women. The first speaker was the city's female mayor and the next speaker was their state's female United States Senator. The W.E.B. accomplished its goals—the women attorneys interacted with many other women in business on a monthly basis with the investment of only a few hours of their time.

Partnering with others does not have to be limited to networking events. Another small firm wanted to put on the first seminar dealing with the legal and business issues surrounding the "Year 2000" computer problem. The largest accounting firm in the city agreed to partner with them. Once again, they combined mailing lists and put on a joint daylong seminar that was well-attended and received considerable press, because it was the first of its kind. At this one-day seminar, the lawyers had the opportunity not only to be in front of their own clients, but also the accounting firm's clients—potential new clients for the firm. They invested time in preparing presentations and then leveraged them by writing follow-up articles and sending out a newsletter to their clients.

PARTING THOUGHTS

Remember, developing business takes time and isn't easy. You must be consistent, persistent, and optimistic. Try the strategies outlined in this chapter, modify them to fit your practice, and develop new ones for your own style. If you do, you will see it start to rain.

How To Be A Good Lawyer and A Good Boss (They're Not Mutually Exclusive)

10

By Lucia E. Coyoca
Partner, Mitchell Silberberg & Knupp LLP

WHY IS IT IMPORTANT TO BE A GOOD BOSS?

For many of us, being a good lawyer takes precedence over being a good boss. When we were new to the profession, we were so busy learning how to write good briefs and argue articulately in the courtroom, that we never focused on learning the skills necessary to manage people in the office effectively. Managing people is definitely not a skill taught in law school. For some of us, we never learned *how* to communicate what we need from others in a manner that would motivate them to help us with our jobs.

In addition, lawyers are notorious for needing a high degree of autonomy. Typically, a litigator who values her independence does not accede easily to being "managed" by others. Therefore, many of us simply never learned what differentiates a good boss from "the boss from hell."

ARE LAWYERS INHERENTLY BAD BOSSES

In an insightful article, "Are Law Firms Manageable?" David Maister examined the reasons why it is so difficult for good lawyers to be good managers. (*The American Lawyer,* April 2006). As Maister pointed out, the legal analysis skills and litigation behaviors that help lawyers do well in the legal profession act as impediments when lawyers use those same attributes to manage the people who work with them. The very models of thinking that are encouraged in law school create barriers when employed in managing the relationships we have with our assistants and colleagues. For example, Maister noted four personality traits typically associated with lawyers that keep lawyers from functioning effectively in groups:

- Problems with trust
- Difficulties with dogmatic ideology, values, and principles
- Professional detachment
- Unusual approaches to decision making

A "typical" successful Type A litigator has a high desire for autonomy in how she runs her practice. Generally speaking, she does not want to be told how to do things and questions whenever she is told that things must be done a certain way. She exercises complete control over every aspect of the case and does not trust that anyone will handle a task as well as she could. And she is capable of complete emotional detachment from the fray of the battle, keeping a cynical objective dispassionate view of issues as they unfold. Is it any wonder that this particular personality type has difficulties managing others? She does not want to delegate work to others, because she does not trust that it will be done properly. When given an answer about something, she does not trust that it has been properly analyzed. She is emotionally dispassionate and does not relate well to complaints that feelings have been hurt or egos bruised. She just wants the work done. Do you recognize this individual?

Learning to develop the right skill-set to manage others is just as important as learning the intricacies of the civil procedure code or the various exceptions to the hearsay rule. In particular, your assistant can really make or break you in the law firm when you are a junior associate. If he likes and respects you, then he will help you to succeed and make you look good inside and outside of the firm. If he dislikes you, there are a myriad of ways that he can subtly undermine or sabotage you, and your job becomes that much harder.

This chapter will help you understand the things you need to know to be able to communicate effectively with the people that you rely on to do your job well—your assistant, the paralegal assigned to your case, the office support staff, the law firm librarian, and, someday, the junior lawyers who will be working for you on matters that you will be supervising.

Through many missteps and trial and error, over the course of my practice, I learned that the following five practices were critically important to having a successful relationship with assistants, staff, paralegals and the associate lawyers with whom I have worked. If you can incorporate these "best practices" into *your* practice, you will soon reap the benefits of having a smooth, coordinated team of individuals who are jointly focused on serving your clients' interests as their highest priority.

1. Convey Your Expectations Clearly.

Lesson No. 1: Always think ahead about each detail of the task you are assigning and convey precisely and clearly what you want done.

The single most important thing about working with others? Let them know *exactly* what it is that you want them to do without leaving any room for ambiguity, doubt or confusion. I learned this lesson the hard way as a young associate in a large law firm. I was working with an inexperienced assistant, and I was an equally inexperienced lawyer. She was nervous and wanted to do things *exactly* right. When left with any task that called for her to exercise a modicum of judgment, she was so afraid she would make the wrong decision, that she would not do anything. While we were working together, a third party witness canceled his deposition late in the day before the deposition. I was out of the office for another case that afternoon, so I told my assistant to call and "let everyone know" that we would reschedule. She canceled the court reporter, called opposing counsel, told the partner on the case and so on. She did all of this, but did not call the client (who was planning to attend the deposition), because she was unsure whether *she* should be calling the client, who had been somewhat brusque with her in prior phone calls.

This incident happened in the days before cell phones and email, and, sure enough, the next morning, the client appeared in my office for the deposition. He was not pleased that the deposition had been canceled and that he had not been told about it, and he certainly let me (and the partner I was working for) know about his displeasure. I should have (and could have) avoided the problem by clearly telling my assistant exactly whom to call to let them know about the change in schedule, but in the rush of the day's events, I simply assumed she knew to call the client.

Too often, I have heard lawyers explain that the reason something was not done is because they "assumed" their assistant would take care of it. Well, why did they make that assumption? We convey to our assistants that every bit of detail, nuance, and minutia about a case is important. Your assistant rightfully assumes that if you do not expressly direct her to do something, you do not want her to do it, and so it is not done.

This same advice applies equally in situations when you are assigning a junior associate a legal research or other task in a litigation matter. A common criticism leveled by partners at junior associates is that he or she "lacks judgment" or "doesn't seem to get the overall picture." My response is always to probe the situation a bit more carefully: Did the reviewing partner really think out what it is that he or she wanted the associate to do? Did the reviewing partner have a clear understanding of the issue that needed to be researched? In my practice, I've learned that I need to first organize my thoughts and analysis, before I can begin delegating work to others to perform. If I do not understand the significance of a legal issue to the case because I have not taken the time to review the documents and facts in play, then how can I ask a lawyer ten years my junior to figure out the right legal strategy?

2. *Provide the Information Necessary to Get the Job Done.*
Lesson No. 2: Don't Hoard Information—
Communicate, Communicate, Communicate.

I worked for a time in a law firm that had associates evaluate partners. The input that the associates provided (anonymously, of course) was invaluable. The key lesson that I learned from that process was the importance of keeping everyone on the litigation team up to speed as to the facts and communications with the client, opposing counsel, and the court. Lawyers often complain that they do not have the time to explain everything to everyone who works on the case and just want "the work done, with no questions asked." Well, that is a good way to guarantee that the work product that you receive from the associate will not be what is needed for the particular situation.

Every person working on a case should know exactly what is going on in the case. If motions are noticed, but you agree to grant opposing counsel an extension to submit an opposition and move the hearing date, then your assistant and the other lawyers working with you on the case need to know the motion has been rescheduled. On the other hand, if the case is to be fought at every step, and continuances will not be granted for any reason, then your team needs to know that information as well, and why that strategy is being employed.

It is difficult to work in a vacuum. Your assistant is dealing with filing deadlines, court clerks, court reporters, messengers, clients' assistants, and a myriad of other people who are also trying to do their jobs. Let people know why they are doing something. It is only meaningful to them when they are able to put the work that they are doing into the greater context of the case overall.

On the other hand, this does not mean that you need to take the tone that you are communicating with a three-year-old or assume your assistant or associate has a pre-kindergarten level of competence. Your instructions should be specific and clear but not condescending or off-putting. It also helps to make it known to your assistant or the associate that you are working with that you recognize that he or she has expertise in certain areas that you do not know and that you are relying on that expertise to get it right. If you tell your assistant that the judge has issued a standing order giving special procedures as to how he or she wants to receive filings in the case, then you need to provide a copy of that standing order to your assistant, and make it clear that you expect your assistant to review the order and take responsibility for complying with it.

I once mentored a young summer associate who was very bright, wrote well, and had impeccable academic credentials. Let's call him "Sam." Sam was assigned to work with a seasoned litigator ("Harry"), who had been practicing for more than four decades. Harry was a very good lawyer but very difficult to reach, because he was always in court, depositions, or meetings with clients. Harry called Sam into his office early in the summer and gave him the following task: "Give me an overview of the law as to when covenants not to compete are enforceable." That was it. Harry did not provide any further information, no explanation as to which jurisdiction(s) were in play, whether our client was trying to enforce or invalidate a covenant not to compete, or the facts or players that gave rise to the question.

Sam came to me, and we talked through the list of questions that Harry needed to answer before the research and analysis could be done. But, throughout the summer Sam could not pin Harry down. Even when Sam managed to corner Harry at a cocktail party and ask some more questions, he was short and not very communicative about the facts that were involved. Sam labored as best he could, putting together a compendium of information summarizing the status of the law on covenants not to compete, trying to take into account the differences as to how particular jurisdictions viewed covenants not to compete, whether there was a difference if the competitor was a former employee, whether a confidentiality agreement had been signed, how long the covenant was expected to be enforced, etc.

At summer's end, Harry gave Sam a negative review, complaining that the work was useless and could never be billed to the client, because Sam had written a "law review" article, rather than a cogent analysis of the law in light of the client's particular set of facts. Sam quickly responded that he could not analyze anything, since he'd never been given the facts. Harry was faced with a huge write-off, and Sam had a negative review on his record. Who lost in that situation, Sam or Harry? You might say Sam lost the most, but I say both—Sam received an unfair negative review, but Harry lost too. He lost an opportunity to have the work done for the client in an efficient and competent manner and the opportunity to work with a clearly intellectually capable associate. If Harry had made the initial investment in time to communicate with Sam about what he wanted done and to train him as to how he should work up the issue, Sam would have been able to handle tasks for Harry that would free Harry up to spend more time developing business or attending to other matters.

3. Learn the Right Way to Give Constructive Feedback and Criticism.

Lesson No. 3: When Managing a Mistake, Focus on Fixing the Problem, Not Laying Blame.

No one is perfect. Perfection, however, is what most law firms strive for. Mistakes happen. What matters most is how you respond to and manage the mistake. If you want your assistant to really *listen* to you when you are trying to manage a mistake that has been made, the worst thing you can do is to blame, berate, or harshly criticize your assistant for the error. As human beings, we dislike being criticized. When attacked, we attack back. Focus on fixing the problem rather than venting your frustration or anger.

When an assistant or an associate working for you makes a mistake in a case that you are responsible for handling, your first inclination may be to blame them for the error to protect yourself and your own reputation. But, if you have the self-control and presence of mind to put aside the needs of your own ego and calmly say, "We need to talk about what happened to make sure that it does not happen again," you are setting the stage for a constructive dialogue. Rather than delivering a monologue of blame and laying out a series of doomsday repercussions, try to get at the root of what caused the mistake. Fixing a problem, rather than blaming your assistant for the problem, is the best way to ensure that a one-time mistake does not turn into an ongoing situation.

On the other hand, do not avoid talking to a poor performer. Avoidance of a difficult conversation is everyone's first instinct. Most of us do not want to confront a colleague or deliver bad news to a subordinate. But, avoiding the conversation is not good for anyone—silence when a mistake occurs hurts your assistant, you, and ultimately the law firm, if the problem is not addressed and resolved. Moreover, in discussing a problematic situation, focus on results, not personalities. If a client complains that your assistant was rude on the telephone, explain to your assistant the importance of the client relationship to the firm, listen to any excuse your assistant may proffer as to why the client may have had the (mistaken) impression that he was being rude, but politely and firmly bring the conversation back to the importance of the client relationship to the firm and the economics of the firm. Along those same lines, it is important to review work as soon as it is completed to provide current and relevant feedback, rather than waiting until a project is completely over and has been dormant for several months.

4. Treat Others As You Would Like To Be Treated.
Lesson No. 4: The Golden Rule Still Applies.

"Social exchange" theorists posit that all human relationships are formed by the use of a subjective cost-benefit analysis and the comparison of alternatives. In other words, if you are trying to motivate someone to do something for you, their initial response may be to try to figure out what is in it for them. A cynical point of view? Perhaps, but the fact of human nature is that even if you are paying someone for their services, the only way to get

100% dedication and commitment from them is if you first invest in the re-lationship. So before you need something from your assistant or an associate working with you on a case, try to get to know them without first making any demands or issuing a directive or order.

I am by no means advocating invading your assistant's right of privacy or injecting yourself into their personal life, but I do think it is important to con-vey that you value the relationship on an individual level, and that you value the individual as a person. Be sincerely interested in the people working for and with you. If the only time your assistant hears from you is when you want something done, he will form a kind of resistance to your efforts to control the relationship.

You will only truly have the ability to motivate an individual if she thinks you are sincerely invested in her. The most influential managers are those who convince others that they care about them as people. You cannot fake this interest. To be a good manager, you sincerely have to be interested in people, not just your own success or the success of your case or the matter you are working on. If you are not interested in people, that does not mean that you are a bad person, but it does mean that you are going to have to work doubly hard to overcome that limitation if you want to be a successful manager.

The best managers are catalysts for action. They recognize that, individ-ually, they cannot accomplish as much as they can with the combined efforts of others. A good manager does not see herself as the "boss," but rather as the leader of a cohesive team of autonomous and competent individuals. Treat the people with whom you work as you would like to be treated. Give them the respect and autonomy that you would like for yourself.

It is also important to try to help your assistant and associates with whom you work in setting goals for their own professional advancement. This type of informal mentoring and relationship building occurred more frequently when I started practicing more than twenty years ago than today. Perhaps due in part to the inordinate pressure placed on partners and associates alike to bill more and more hours, experienced lawyers seem to spend less and less time with associates outside of the cases on which they work.

I've also noticed that lawyers starting out in practice today are much more likely to solicit feedback and honest evaluation from the senior lawyers for whom they work and are much more savvy about the importance of de-veloping skills at the appropriate career milestones. Unlike past generations, young lawyers today know that it is unlikely that they will stay in the same firm for decades, and each job is an opportunity to learn and grow. You should try to meet on a regular basis with your assistant and those associates who work with you on cases, even if that time cannot be billed to the client. Are such meetings onerous and time consuming? Yes, but regular "development discussions" with each of your colleagues in which you discuss how the individual may grow professionally and how you and the firm may be able to support them yields long term benefits to you in terms of increased loyalty, more skilled performance, and satisfied associates and staff.

Low morale is often a result of fear or insecurity. When you communicate your expectations and standards with those with whom you work, you are helping to allay concerns about job security and impermanence. In addition to pointing out when things have not gone well, are you also giving credit or praise when a task is properly handled? Balance negative comments with more frequent positive comments. Let the people with whom you work know you are there to help them be successful in their jobs, not to embarrass, demean or harass them.

5. *Recognize the Importance of Process.*

Lesson No. 5: Figuring out How to Handle a Problem is 90% of the Solution to Fix the Problem.

The one thing that I wish I had known when I first started out practicing law is how important process is to getting things done. What I mean by this is that for some individuals, it is truly more important to them that they be given a voice as to the manner in which a problem is to be addressed, and their suggestions as to process are considered and adopted (if possible), than actually solving the problem. For these individuals, the process by which tasks are assigned, carried out, and evaluated, can be more important than the actual result of the work. Do not rush through that step of figuring out how to manage the work that needs to be done. Take the time needed to truly understand what your assistant or associate is saying to you when they raise a procedural or process concern about a task or legal issue that you want them to handle.

In addition, when assigning or delegating work to others, you need to recognize your own weaknesses in project planning. When I am approaching trial or have several legal balls in the air, I have a tendency to become intensely focused on the legal issue at hand and non-communicative with anyone or anything but my computer. I may lose sight of the need to organize the logistics of the battlefield. When that happens, I become anxious and revert to my innate tendency to try to exert control over every small detail and rely almost exclusively on the barking out of orders to get things accomplished. My personal goal is to be mindful about that shortcoming and avoid reverting to that style the next time trial rolls around. But easier said than done.

Moreover, even if the disorganization caused by the press of trial activities does not cause you anxiety, the General Patton style of managing litigation will surely not be appreciated by those who are working with you. It is important to help those that work with you develop a sense of autonomy as to their work. It encourages a sense of professional independence if you make it a practice to have those working with you develop their own plan of action as to how to handle tasks and then give you a detailed explanation as to how they will go about accomplishing what needs to be done. If the individuals that work with you recognize the importance of accountability when they are working on projects or tasks that you have assigned, your job will become that much easier. The best way to develop that sense of accountability is to permit others to have as much control and autonomy as the requirements of the task or project permits.

There are several ways to adopt this objective as part of the management of your practice. Let people know that *you know* they can do it. When following up on a particular project, ask questions creatively so the action to be taken is suggested by the person who is to take it, rather than you directing that the action be taken. Ask others for their estimate of how long it will take to do a project. When possible, agree and hold them accountable for that goal. Share ideas and responsibility with others rather than just assigning someone to do it for you or doing it yourself.

Finally, recognize you are not the only one who can do a job right. Trust others to do things for you. When you are given accolades or credit for a job well done, be sure that credit is (publicly) shared with all who were involved. This will nurture your relationships and will motivate others to support you in the future. Above all, let others know that you recognize their contributions and their importance to you, your practice, your clients, and the firm.

Teaching and Learning From Others | **11**

By Dinita L. James

MY IDEAL CONCEPTION of the perfect teacher comes from a relatively obscure literary source, the first volume of Mary Stewart's Merlin Trilogy, *The Crystal Cave* (1970). Her version of the Arthurian Legend starts with the boy Merlin, a bastard child in a royal Welsh household, who wanders in the woods beyond his castle. He stumbles upon a hermit who teaches him magic and the healing arts, along with the geographic and political map of his time. These tools are the foundation he will use to serve as King Arthur's wizard.

Stewart's description, in Merlin's voice, of the hermit Galapas' methods and Merlin's experience training by them capture in a magical way the love of learning that brings joy to my law practice.

> He was a good teacher, and I was quick, but in fact I hardly thought of my time with him as lessons. . . . [W]ith Galapas to begin with it was only like listening to a story teller. He had traveled when young . . . , and seen and learned strange things. He taught me practical things, too.

Among the practicalities Galapas passed on to Merlin were how to read maps and stars, who ruled which lands, and how to travel the world using the streams and stars as guides. Very few of us are lucky enough to have such a teacher to guide us in the political geography of practicing law in our communities and firms or legal departments.

Successful women advocates find the teachers they need for whatever the task at hand. One of the pleasures of a litigation practice is the variety of the factual circumstances presented by the cases. Regardless of the subject matter, a dispute is about a particular set of factual circumstances, and to be an effective advocate we need to understand the disputants' business or personal affairs at a sufficiently intimate level to explain the dispute to six or twelve complete strangers, including why the facts interrelate as they do. Regardless of the size of our individual caseloads (which astoundingly can reach to three digits for some government lawyers), as a rule, we learn and digest fact patterns quickly. To be successful advocates, we need to understand how others—the fact-finders—will react to our cases. Our own reactions are not reliable predictors of how our judges and juries will respond to facts.

Learning extends to many other areas of our practices. For example, we need to understand the interests and wishes of our clients. We need to work collaboratively with our colleagues and staff to serve our clients. We need to function well and fit within our practice setting, so that we harmonize our personal and professional goals. We need to learn constantly about our professional world and the worlds of our clients. We need to stay current on the substantive and procedural law that governs the disputes we handle.

Most of the people from whom we need to learn are willing to impart their knowledge. It is the rarer case—the adverse witness, the obstructive opposing counsel, the corrupt or embittered public servant, the deceptive "friend" or family member—from whom we must extract information. Mastery as an advocate lies in finding the optimal way to obtain needed information and using it effectively to persuade.

THE PERFECT MENTOR

By the time this essay is published in *The Woman Advocate*, 2nd edition, I will have passed the half-century mark, a big, round birthday that is looming large as the days of my life speed by. In all those years, I have never had a woman who considered herself my mentor in the dictionary definition sense of that word. I have been very fortunate, however, to have had a male mentor.

Mentor was an older friend of Odysseus in Homer's *Odyssey*. When Odysseus went off to the Trojan War, he entrusted Mentor with his palace and the education of his infant son, Telemachus. Mentor raised a "splendid" (as Homer calls him) son to young adulthood. Then the goddess Athena disguised herself as Mentor and counseled Telemachus to stand up to his mother Penelope's suitors and leave home in search of his father, launching a key character into Homer's adventure epic.

There is only one lawyer who would describe himself as my mentor, Marvin Barkin, a founding partner of the law firm where I spent a summer as a law clerk and practiced for the first eleven years of my legal career. I believe Marvin would accept the appellation mentor, because I have introduced him as such to ABA colleagues. I'm sad to say that I only see Marvin at ABA meetings these days, as we live and practice more than 2,000 miles apart.

For a beginning commercial litigator like me at what, in those days, was a big firm by Tampa, Florida standards, Marvin was the perfect mentor. During my eight to ten weeks as a summer associate, I had a handful of assignments from him and from other attorneys who were working on his cases. The specifics elude me, but I spent considerable time in one of the two comfy chairs in front of his plank-like desk in his corner office 26 stories above the point where the Hillsborough River pours into the bay. I know he took a personal interest in me, as our wide-ranging discussions included his disarming but very effective questioning about my background, interests, and other assignments I was working on that summer.

When I returned to the firm as a beginning associate, Marvin immediately put me to work on some of his cases, often in a third-chair role. Again, a lot of my early billable hours were spent blissfully in that comfy chair as he painted for me the big picture of the cases to which my work related. He wanted initial oral reports, and we had thoroughly enjoyable conversations about how my narrow slice of expertise—the cases, laws, rules or such that I had found in my research—affected the strategy or merits of the matter. He shared with me his insights about the motivation of the litigants and the strengths and weakness of the opposing counsel. Most keen was his assessment of the judges and how best to persuade them.

While I sat in his office for our discussions, Marvin did the juggling a senior litigator did in those days. Other attorneys stuck their heads in for quick questions or updates. His assistant would call him by intercom or step into his office to tell him of incoming calls, approaching appointments, or to bring the dreaded faxes that were the litigation weapon of choice in those days before email and electronic filing.

I sat while he took calls from clients, opposing counsel, family members, or colleagues who were reporting from hearings, depositions, or meetings. Occasionally, he would pick up the dictating machine behind his desk and dictate a short note, letter, or memorandum based on the latest interruption. Although it may sound like I was wasting a lot of time sitting there waiting to resume our discussions, I actually was getting a chance to observe an excellent trial lawyer and law firm leader as he interacted with all of the important people in his practice. I was being mentored in the finest sense of the word.

I learned much from our work preparing briefs together. Marvin toned me down when I was too strident and aggressive in my arguments. He edited me so that our work product was concise and precise and did not waste the time of judicial officers. He also taught me not to pull my punches but to drive my point home with a short, well-crafted sentence that made it clear why our client should prevail.

One of Marvin's passions has been his work on behalf of the Florida Judicial Qualifications Commission, which investigated allegations of wrongdoing and prosecuted judges when necessary before the Florida Supreme Court. I had the privilege of being second chair to him as we made new law on how and when a judge can be suspended after indictment for federal crimes involving judicial corruption in the Operation Court Broom scandal in Miami in 1991. I was at counsel table as we argued the emergency matter before the Florida Supreme Court. It was exciting and important work, and I grew tremendously as an advocate because he shared it with me.

We would go to lunch once a week or so, usually grabbing a bite because we were together when the noon hour hit. We'd talk politics, sports, or world events. He would explain the workings and history of the firm, including the relationships among the partners. I watched as he gracefully handed things over to his younger partners, when others of his colleagues who founded the firm (they called themselves the Young Turks, eight lawyers—all men, of course—who left a large, established Tampa firm in 1970 to form the upstart practice) struggled to accept the inevitable and necessary process of succession.

The firm started an attorney lunchroom, putting out cold cuts and sandwich bread, or a hot entrée now and then, and reserving a conference room for any attorneys in the office to grab lunch and spend down time together, socializing and sharing information. Marvin was a regular in the lunchroom, getting to know everyone, gently passing along the firm culture and sharing his insights on the practice of law.

He was also gently teaching me the art of our profession. I started to handle hearings and discovery matters on my own, getting my marching orders and reporting my results to Marvin. Soon I was drafting his correspondence, preparing him and, with him, his witnesses for depositions. The progression continued gradually and without us remarking on it. We'd get to the deposition and he'd suggest I conduct the examination. Then I was just scheduling myself to take and defend the depositions.

When we were together in public, whether grabbing a quick lunch during a workday or traveling around Florida for a conference, deposition, or hearing, he introduced me enthusiastically to his many acquaintances. I took great pride in how he often introduced me as "his lawyer."

As I became a partner and handled my own matters, I sought his guidance and ran things by him. He handed important and complex matters over to me to run day-to-day, awaiting my regular status reports and calls for assistance. Even when we did not spend nearly as much time working together, we still found time to talk about politics—in the firm and in the larger world. He always wanted to know what I was working on and how things were going. He always had an encouraging word.

Thus was I blessed with a perfect lawyer mentor. I know how fortunate I am. But these archetypal mentors are not easy to come by. For generations of women lawyers, there were no women among the available mentors. Even after women entered the practice in significant numbers, many were too busy fighting for their own success to devote much attention to bringing others along. My generation, which succeeded these pioneers, can resent or forgive them, but in large part that was the reality. There were, of course, notable exceptions. I always am inspired by the stories of the Margaret Brent Award winners told in video at the ABA Annual Meeting awards luncheon. Invariably, the honorees draw praise for their role in mentoring other women advocates.

The fact remains, however, that most women who have been practicing 20 years or so and who had mentors had male mentors. The path behind our cohort is littered with shared memories of successful senior women who, having fought their way to success, dismissed us struggling behind them with an "I paid my dues, now you do it" attitude, and declined to lend a hand.

I believe that my generation of women lawyers is doing a better job mentoring young lawyers, male and female. We talk about mentoring and advocate its importance in the professional development of lawyers. We push and assist our firms and legal departments in developing formal mentoring programs. We join bar associations that foster mentoring and assign mentoring pairs to interact in person, by telephone, and email. Whether because we struggled without mentors or benifited from their guidance, we recognize mentoring as a requisite for success.

DON'T WAIT AROUND FOR THE PERFECT MENTOR

While I encourage seeking the perfect mentor, as its blessings are abundant, none of us can wait around until we find him or, thankfully more often now, her. From our personal lives and fairy tales we know that sometimes you have to kiss a lot of frogs to find your prince or princess.

So my main endorsement is the pursuit of any and all opportunities to obtain the help of another person in the lifelong effort to become an excellent woman advocate. Many women advocates do this instinctively. Therefore, I offer the following non-exclusive list of opportunities to learn from others, not as some kind of revelation, but as a reaffirmation that just about everything we encounter in life can teach us and help us grow if we are open to the possibilities.

1. Other lawyers at your firm or legal department

You may be lucky enough to find your perfect mentor in your own law firm, as I did. Count yourself among the fortunate few, if you do. From all indications, it is even more unlikely that beginning women lawyers today will enjoy the attention of the kind of mentor Marvin Barkin was to me.

Among the reasons the small odds have lengthened further?

- **Lawyer mobility:** Including my time as a summer associate, my experience working in Marvin's firm endured for a dozen years. Most beginning lawyers today change jobs within their first three years.
- **Client resistance:** Marvin came of age when lawyers sent bills to their clients that stated in full: "For professional services rendered"—and the dollar amount; and the clients paid by return mail. Among my generation, we always have accounted for our professional lives in six-minute increments; but when I started practicing, there was much less scrutiny by clients of how their lawyers managed the legal work. Today, Fortune 1,000 general counsel send letters to all outside attorneys prohibiting the use of first-year attorneys on their matters. Attendance of more than one lawyer at a deposition is a risk if undertaken without prior client approval. I remain amazed at how many clients refuse to pay for in-house attorney conferences, despite the reality that a senior attorney can deliver much more cost-effective supervision through a quick discussion with a junior attorney than in an exchange of emails or memoranda. If attorneys cannot talk to their more junior colleagues about a matter or allow them to learn by observation, how can they possibly train them to practice law?
- **Drain on firm profitability:** The only way for law firms or legal departments to train attorneys in the most effective and time-honored tradition of our profession—working together on a matter—is to make a huge financial commitment to do so. The AmLaw 100 pressure for profits per partner and the recent (although reversing) trend of steep escalation in associate salaries mean that a firm needs to make profits from junior associates. Yet it is very hard to achieve profitability from a junior attorney when there is client resistance to allowing on-the-job training on their matters. More confounding, the point at which profitability can be reached realistically is also the point when most young attorneys make their first job change. Corporate legal departments have given up on training beginning lawyers. They hire only experienced attorneys and thus are part of the reason young attorneys are leaving firms at just about the point they could become profitable.
- **The billable hour:** Count me among those who believe that the private practice of law must move to an economic model that does not depend upon the billable hour. A practical and effective economic model for law firms would make it more financially rewarding to increase effi-

ciency. The current model actually punishes efficiency; an attorney who accomplishes a task in two hours gets a lower fee than the one who accomplishes the same task in three, assuming equivalent rates. Likewise, the current economic model is detrimental to training and developing junior attorneys. The billable hour pressures provide a disincentive to stop billing and teach. In contrast, an economic model that financially rewards those lawyers who resolve disputes successfully and deliver quality work product in the quickest, most effective way necessarily will have a side benefit on the way the legal profession trains beginning lawyers. So here's a tip: Learn everything you can from lawyers and clients who are coming up with alternative billing arrangements that align the interests of the client with those of the lawyer. I'm betting that the way of the future (even though it may be a distant future) will look a lot more like the past.

These examples of barriers to finding the perfect mentor reinforce the need to grab every opportunity for learning. Even though you may not find your perfect mentor within your own firm, that does not mean you cannot have rich learning experiences there. There are many ways you can learn and grow from your lawyer colleagues in your office.

While they may not be the perfect mentor, there likely will be lawyers with more experience than you who are willing to share what they know. Just keep your eyes open and you will notice what senior attorney's door gets the most pop-in visitors. Don't be shy. Pop your own head in next time you would like a sounding board. If it was a productive visit, make more of them.

Use your firm's email system to pose a general question. Then make it easy on those who respond. Don't bombard the responder with more emails. Walk down the hall, if possible, and, if not, pick up your phone and call the responder with your follow-up questions. Ask if this would be a good time to talk and, if not, schedule a time that would be. Express your appreciation. Express it not only at the moment, but at the appropriate time report back on how you benefitted from the shared knowledge. Before you know it, you may have a very supportive mentoring relationship.

This tactic works not just with senior attorneys but also with your peers and even more junior attorneys who have expertise from which you can benefit. I'm not revealing any great mystery here. This is common sense and probably to some degree an instinctive lawyer survival mechanism. Nevertheless, I have been surprised over the years at how many of my colleagues, junior and senior, did not take advantage of the collective wisdom and experience of their colleagues within the firm or legal department.

2. Co-counsel and counsel for aligned parties

As a beginning lawyer, I was assigned to drudge work in discovery in multi-party actions that involved counsel from top firms across the country. One was an environmental case involving a chemical plant in Pensacola, Florida, and we had several week-long document reviews in the plant basement, where the various plant owners had stashed every piece of paper dating back to the 1920s! There were eight or so of us junior associates, and we had the benefit of working under a joint defense agreement enabling us to share information and work together to determine what was relevant from among all the boxes and boxes of documents in that basement. Together, we unearthed the historical record of the contaminated plant site.

We spent our days in the plant basement, but our evenings were spent dining together and sharing our experiences at our various firms around the country. The case went on for several years, and we were fortunate that the associate group remained intact. We progressed to deposition practice and then discovery hearings and briefings. The group broke up eventually as various parties settled out, but not before I learned a great deal from working with those other attorneys. The subject-matter of my education included not just civil discovery practice. I learned about the life of associates in big law firms, the commonalities and the variables. I tried, and watched other young lawyers try new strategies and techniques, sometimes successfully and sometimes not.

The opportunity to observe and learn from other lawyers while working on the same litigation matter presents itself more often in some practices than others. You may be fortunate, like I was, to have several cases that involve attorneys from multiple firms representing the same client or aligned clients. That is as close a substitute as you can get to that most perfect model of attorney training—junior and senior attorneys working together on a matter. You may be local counsel for an out-of-state attorney or be the non-resident attorney appearing with a pre-eminent local attorney. Take full advantage of the opportunity to learn from these professional relationships in which you can be completely open about strategy, the many ways to serve the client's interests, develop the factual record, and prove your case.

3. Opposing counsel

You can learn from your adversaries, just not in the same way as when you are representing common interests and have the freedom to confer and collaborate without waiver of any privilege or immunity. Sometimes the learning experience can be painful, if your opposing counsel out-lawyers you at trial, gets a pivotal admission from your client at deposition, or uses the authorities you cited against you in a responsive brief. Those experiences are nevertheless valuable.

Even better, however, are the occasions when you can represent your client effectively and still learn from your bird's-eye view of a worthy adversary's performance on a familiar matter. This applies not only to those core performances before the court—trials, hearings, oral arguments—but also to discovery conferrals, mediations, even an exchange of correspondence. If you can cultivate a civil and resolution-oriented relationship with your opposing counsel, you will gain key insight into how others might view the facts. When you can talk about discovery matters calmly and without posturing, you get free discovery of the opposing theories and themes your client will be facing. You can save your client time and money by fighting only the necessary fights, and fighting those in a fair and efficient way.

I again admit to how fortunate I have been, as many of my litigation adversaries have been excellent advocates, men and women alike. I have learned the hard way and the easy way from opposing counsel. The important thing is to be open to what you can learn from your adversaries.

4. Clients and witnesses

In litigation, your clients may be your most important teachers. The law dictates the analytical framework in which you must develop your case, but the facts give the shape, form, and texture. Juries and judges decide cases based on the facts. Regardless of how familiar you are with the legal framework of your practice area, you start every case ignorant of the facts.

Clients have to teach us the facts. For a corporate client, the employees who have the knowledge we need could be at any level within the organization. Effective learning from our clients requires good listening skills and the ability to relate to diverse individuals. While these individuals may have all levels of education and a wide range of communicative abilities, they always have something we need to learn—expertise in their realm.

5. Formal mentoring programs

My experience is limited to being on the mentor side of formal mentoring programs in law firms and bar associations. The success of these assigned relationships has been mixed, having an inevitably artificial feel. Nevertheless, I cannot come up with any good reason a woman advocate would not take advantage of such programs when they are offered and accept whatever mentoring comes from them. In the rare case, one of those perfect mentoring relationships may develop. If the assigned mentor is not perfect, however, the mentee participants still will have another ally, and no woman advocate can ever have too many allies.

TEACHING—THE JOY OF GIVING BACK

I have found no clean dividing line between learning and teaching when it comes to the collaborative practice of law. While I learn the facts from clients and witnesses, I also am teaching them about the legal system and their role in it, preparing them for testimony or other proceedings and shaping their expectations.

My work with more junior lawyers has produced many learning experiences. The truth is I was not very good at training and developing other lawyers when first I moved into that role. Far too often, I found myself in a crisis situation. Disappointed with the work product that a junior attorney brought back to me, I had to do the work myself, usually late at night or over weekends or holidays. The experience frequently left me feeling angry or resentful, questioning the talent or commitment of the junior lawyer. I confess to using harsh tones and sharp words on occasion. I was setting a standard of excellence on behalf of the client, so I felt justified.

The reality is that successful women advocates must recognize the importance of having others to whom they reliably can delegate work and get back products they can use. The ability to teach others to work with you effectively is crucial to growing your practice. Unless you can develop colleagues you can trust, you never can go on a vacation or take a sick day without worrying about what is happening at the office.

The good news is your delegation and training skills can and do improve with experience. Working with smart, talented junior lawyers who speak their mind and protest when they should is not easy. I was not comfortable hearing the bright young lawyer who challenged why I kept asking him to "think": did I believe he would turn work in to me that he had not thought through as completely as he believed necessary?

My education as a teacher of lawyers in the private practice setting was fraught with too many such conflicts, but I am grateful to the junior lawyers who had the courage to speak up and begin the dialogue with me on how I could best help them be better. The difficulty of teaching litigation strategy and practice, persuasive legal writing and argument, client service and ethical advocacy cannot be overstated. But there is immense pleasure in seeing those you train grow into effective advocates.

I recently was talking with one of my best friends from college. We were discussing the satisfaction we both were finding in our professional lives, despite the troubled economic times and how adversely the current crisis had affected both of our industries. It was a moment of self-revelation when I found myself telling her that what I enjoyed most about my work was the day-to-day interaction with the associates in my office as we worked together on client matters.

It is indeed now my favorite part of lawyering. If I'm lucky enough and keep putting in the effort, perhaps in my remaining years of practice, I'll master the art of teaching as Galapas did. Maybe someday others will look to me with the gratitude I feel for my own perfect mentor, Marvin Barkin.

Taking the Lead in our Firms, Careers, Communities and Cases

12

By Sandra Giannone Ezell

SOME PEOPLE ARE in charge. You can tell they are in charge, because they have a certain title or rank. Other people are leaders. You can tell they are leaders, because people want to follow them. Or people just DO follow them, whether they want to or not. These leaders are of interest. It is especially interesting that the legal profession is seeing the rise not only of women who are in charge by virtue of the grant of a title but also of women who are leaders by virtue of the fact that they have vision, people who follow them, and people who help the leaders to manifest their vision.

I imagine that the practice of law is much like other businesses, although it is the only business I have been in for the past twenty years. We have an organized structure of individuals who all work to provide quality service to clients. Every day I have not only had the good fortune to be called upon to handle and try some of the most interesting cases throughout the country, I am also charged, whether I am in the office or at 30,000 feet, with managing, leading, mentoring, molding, teaching, cajoling, and evaluating other lawyers. So, it is against this background that today I evaluate the particular challenges faced by women who are not only asked to practice their particular version of the legal craft, but who are also asked to lead, or who lead whether they are asked to do so or not. This is a small group of women nationally. But, the fact is that the trajectory of these numbers is upward, and, with that increase, there are new challenges for our profession—both for the women and men within it.

This increase in law firm women leaders presents several challenges. No two people are the same, nor are any two firms. Therefore, to analyze the obstacles women face with leadership, as well as the positive new perspective they bring to the leadership landscape, one can look only at general trends.

As a starting point, consider the training of leaders. Traditionally, there was no formal leadership training at law schools or within firms. This resulted in men disproportionally receiving the informal mentoring and training necessary to become future firm leaders. We must also consider that men still hold the majority of positions of power both in-house and in firms of all sizes. This means that the vision for success, the performance matrices that measure success, as well as the rules for how to communicate your successes, were and still are, by and large, created, endorsed, ratified and measured by men. This creates some challenges for women leaders operating within a pre-existing business vision. This is not, however, an excuse for women to fail at leadership. It just means that, if you create your own business vision, you will have to superimpose your vision onto a system with norms of doing business predating the female visionary. It is important, therefore, to remember that success today rests on your ability to accept *today's* reality even while you aspire to create a different one tomorrow. To accept does not mean endorse, it means acknowledge.

So, it's not easy. And, it is different for men than women. If that strikes you as an insurmountable unfairness, you may be right—for yourself. But, for those of us who want to accept and meet challenges, it is important to remember that just coming through the door differently does not define the success of the venture. In fact, women have been and will continue to be both highly successful firm leaders as well as profound failures at this task. The ways we lead may be affected by our gender, but success or failure is not gender-defined.

Ironically, being perceived as a successful and dynamic leader within the current system is easier for women than for men. This is based on the principle that if you exceed someone's expectations, they will hold you in higher regard than if you simply meet them. Because those who measure success in the legal profession do not expect women to be effective leaders, managers, strategists, and mentors, women enter a managing/leadership role with a presumption of mediocrity or inadequacy. This is a great advantage for true leaders, because, by rebutting the presumption and surpassing expectations, your stock will raise more highly and quickly than any man's. This is, of course, a double-edged sword. You do enter the equation with the expectation of failure and mediocrity, and, if you do not excel, you will be seen as less effective than a man who is similarly mediocre.

So, how do you leverage these realities to your advantage today? How do you lead your people in a way that accomplishes all of the goals that you are attempting to achieve? How do you do this without training and against a background of anticipated failure? You just do. You have the same benchmarks for running a successful law practice that a man does. You must recruit, train, retain, and promote good people. You must be able to manage some of the most difficult people on earth (lawyers, of course). You must promote practices, policies, and procedures that ensure systemic best practices designed to provide the highest level of client service. You must make sure your systems also provide a fulfilling, challenging, fair, and encouraging work environment for your staff. You must maximize your fees and minimize your costs. You must not sell out or change who you are in the process. Then, you must remember that this is your job, not your life, and you must sometimes go home.

To do all these things, I follow a few simple rules. I do not follow them all of the time because it is impossible to do that. But because I aspire to follow them at all times, I have a game plan every day. To illustrate my philosophy, I will focus on how I approach leadership regarding a single one of our office core objectives: the goal of delivering the highest quality trial advocacy for corporate clients with the most diverse legal teams.

- Create a vision. I have a vision for what I want my office to be. I developed that vision with the input, buy-in, and consensus of all my partners. There are many things for which a law office can be known. I believe ours should be known for delivering the highest quality trial work from the most diverse group of lawyers. I often boast that I have the pleasure of running the most diverse law office in the City of Richmond, Virginia. I always follow that with the caveat that if I am challenged by someone who feels they have a more diverse office, I will seize upon that challenge as an opportunity to increase our diversity. This is my vision, shared, professed, and critically important.

- Believe in the vision. I know we have the potential to compete and win on both essential prongs of this vision when compared with any other firm in the city. I act in accordance with this belief both as it regards core business and my non-billable activity. I write about the vision. I speak about the vision. I push my clients to promote this vision. I feed the pipeline. No one who knows me doesn't know that this is my vision. I walk the talk.

- Communicate the vision. I make sure that this vision is known 360°. My clients, to whom I report, know this about my office vision. My partners in other offices, including all of the members of my executive committee, know that this is my vision. The lawyers, paralegals, and staff of my office know this. This message is communicated early and often. This message is communicated up, out, and down, and it is the same message irrespective of the audience. I am often rewarded to hear people to whom I have communicated the vision communicate the vision without me.

- Communicate confidence in your leadership. Communication is the key to success of any vision and any visionary. This is true not just about what you communicate but how you communicate it. Leaders communicate both verbally and non-verbally. They have control of their body language. They communicate through their carriage that they are in charge and that having them in charge is a good thing. People want to follow someone who makes them feel like they will be reliable when things are going well and, more importantly, when they are going wrong. This is an area where women are often challenged. Who really wants a woman with her finger on "the button?"

Grace under pressure, the ability to make a move rather than stand and think, and a pronounced and well-established track record of sharing glory and taking all the blame are all things that make people confident in you—no matter your gender. The ability to give public praise and private criticism is an essential leadership quality. Leaders have this as a philosophy of managing people. When it is time to take responsibility for a project or result that is not what was anticipated or hoped for, or simply to tell the client or firm that a mistake occurred on your team, a leader owns that. It happened on your watch and represents a failure of your system and an opportunity for system and personal improvement. This is not something women are trained or socialized to do necessarily. But, whether you have this as an inate quality or a learned one, a leader has this quality and followers look for it and rely on it.

Your track record of confidence, carriage, longevity, and resolve are essential to building a following and becoming a leader. Communicating confidence, therefore, is a key to being a leader. People have seen me pursue this vision when it has been easy and when it has been difficult—I am still here and still have the same message. I communicate that if we follow this vision, it will not only be the right thing to do but the smart thing to do, and we will be rewarded. I will communicate that again tomorrow.

- <u>Communicate the method of obtaining the vision in the past, present, and future</u>. In any organization, there will be people of many ages and stages of life and experience. Your method of accomplishing your vision must withstand scrutiny of the life lessons of those who have been around the longest as well as convince the newest and fastest on your team that it is cutting edge and current enough to get their buy in. This is a reality. It is a challenge. However, as with any challenge, you cannot accomplish it if you do not factor this spectrum of scrutiny into your planning process. There are always lessons from the past, which, like statistics, can teach us anything or nothing. There is always a better, faster, newer, more technologically advanced way to do things. But as with any technology, there are always risks. So, consider the input you receive, and, then, be a leader. Establish that you have considered what must be considered, factored in all of the viewpoints of merit along the spectrum, and come up with a method of accomplishing the vision that you support and which others should support. This, of course, requires consideration of, but not imitation of, the competition. You will be followed as much because of belief in your vision as trust in the process by which you arrive at it.

- <u>Have passion for the vision</u>. Women resist passion because it feeds stereotypes of bringing emotions to work. I approach business without emotion but with great passion. It is often described by others as enthusiasm. I express the need with a heartfelt business desire and a well-fashioned plan. I believe that passion, when it is true, is contagious. I also believe that without it you can only be a functionary and never a true leader. There's no doubt that when I speak about the diversification of outstanding trial lawyers in our shop, I mean it passionately, and you can see it. I mean it every day.
- <u>Have a reputation for ethics, fairness, and professionalism</u>. Ethics and professionalism serve as a cornerstone for some leaders. While we can all call to mind leaders who did not embrace ethics, fairness, and professionalism, there is no place for that in our profession. The practice of law is a self-policing profession, and these must remain cornerstones of our profession. I believe the importance of this is profound to being a woman leader in the legal profession. Not only do we have to demand it of ourselves but of our profession. Establishing this reputation and factoring these issues into all your decisions and reactions will set you up to lead people both today and in the future. The issue of "trust" in leadership is timeless. Professionalism is always a good business model that makes people want to help you attain your goal.

Like any good lawyer, I would like to end with a disclaimer. There is no magic bullet. There is no tried and true "leader formula." What has worked for some will not work for others. I know it when I see it and so do you. Some women are leaders who need no teaching and others will never be leaders no matter how much you teach them. It is both interesting and exciting that this is a subject that now warrants discussion. That we have moved away from the notion that women should lead the same way men have always led is a milestone worth celebrating. So, too, is the fact we have thrown away the notion that there is only one way to be a successful woman leader.

Take from this what feels like it will help, discard the rest. But in so doing, take a step that so many others before us did not have an opportunity to take—start developing your own formula for how you will one day lead. Maybe that day is today. If it is, remember, you may be in charge, and, for that, you can generally check your website, your nameplate, or your paycheck. But, if you want to see if you are a leader, look around you, is anyone following?

The Elements of Style | 13

By Janet S. Kole

Every lawyer has his or her own style when it comes to appearing in court, in depositions, and in meetings. Like all successful trial lawyers, I have honed my personal style over a period of years—in my case, let's just say more than twenty-five. I am comfortable with my own courtroom persona, and I have found it to be effective. All successful trial lawyers have their own inimitable styles that work for them. Often, this style is the same one that defines how we present ourselves in our professional lives beyond the courtroom.

Finding the right style is particularly difficult for women lawyers. Men and women are different, and people perceive each gender differently. Style is about more than just how you dress, which is constantly in flux as you age and society changes. Style is how you present yourself, and how you can convey competence. The question for the newer lawyer is how to find a style that works for her. The answer depends on basic personality, age, and geography.

We are all, of course, creatures of our times and experiences. When I began practicing, the discussion of the "appropriate" courtroom persona for a woman lawyer was centered on the culture shock of having a woman in the courtroom in the first place; big issues included the proper attire for the woman litigator, and hairdos and makeup. With chagrin I remember that women lawyers pretty much without exception wore man-tailored navy blue suits (with skirts) and little "ties" to court for years. I was no different, at least for a while.

Then the big issue became whether women could wear pants in court. Some judges, in the Eastern District of Pennsylvania where I practiced, forbade women from wearing pants. The concept seems quaint, now, but it brings up an important consideration—how you present yourself isn't about you, it's about doing what is most effective for your client. You may love to wear flip flops when you're out with friends, but it's a no-no when meeting clients.

I have managed to escape both the uniform look and the pants ban to come into my own as a litigator and a "persona." And who might that be, you ask? Well, you've heard of the "reasonable man," as all of us have who went to law school. I am—the reasonable woman. And the great thing about this lawyer character of mine is that it's really me, not some role I'm acting. Those who know me know that I'm relatively calm, reasoned, and forthright in "real" life.

But getting the "real" me into my courtroom appearances took some hard work. And, while portraying the "real" you may be the way to win your cases, maybe not all of your characteristics should be included in your court persona. Your own style will be made up of the "real" you, your vocal inflections, your clothing, your pacing; but it may not be the same "you" you present to your family, partner, or child. (For example, when my son aggravates me, as he'll tell you, the reasoned and calm Mom disappears during the time it takes for me to shout at him.)

It is worth noting that your persona at work is as important as your persona in court, particularly if you are an associate looking to get ahead in your firm. You should try to match your style at work with that of those around you. Are your colleagues laid back and relaxed? Are they over reactors? Don't put on an act, but if you work with more frantic types, your best style is more fevered. When I worked at Schnader as an associate, Buddy Siegel, one of the senior partners, unwittingly gave a clue to what worked best there for associates. He pointed to one of our young male associates, and said to several of us in the hall: "You see how fast he's walking? You can tell he's a good lawyer." You can bet we all put something of a spring in our steps after that. It may sound petty, unimportant, or even ridiculous, but the truth is that small things like conveying a sense of urgency can make the difference in how your colleagues perceive you. With a little modification, therefore, the rules below can also apply to audiences other than the judge and jury.

How do you figure out what works for you? What should you leave in, and what should you leave out? I have a few "rules" for creating a personal style.

1. Be Comfortable With The Lawyer "You" You're Presenting In Court.

Don't try to be someone you're not.

I suppose my role model in the courtroom as well as in my every day life has been my father. First as a lawyer, then a judge for many years, both in the trial and the appellate divisions, my father was unfailingly described as courteous, bright, warm, and intellectual. His manner was courtly and quiet. He was exactly the same at home. I found his courtroom demeanor one that I could emulate comfortably. It suits my personality, too.

You won't find me pounding a table. I don't throw books or papers. If a witness for the other side lies on the stand, I don't sigh and roll my eyes. When a judge of the Court of Common Pleas in Philadelphia stepped down off the bench to take my hand and kiss it, in front of the jury and my client and opponent and a courtroom full of witnesses, I didn't flinch, grab my hand away, or make a cutting remark. I didn't do anything except discreetly wipe my hand off on my skirt, wait until the judge was back on the bench, and begin my opening statement.

But how did I get there? When I first started practicing trial law, my calmness was more feigned than real. I remember my first motion argument, at which I attempted to show how relaxed I was by leaning on the jury railing. I felt like an idiot, and I never did that again. Trial and error, and getting comfortable being in a courtroom, helped me figure out what moves to make to both appear to be, and actually be, in control.

I am comfortable being a low key advocate. My demeanor and my clothes both contribute to my "reasonable woman" persona. I wear low heels, comfortable pants suits, small earrings, little to no jewelry. It works for me. But it might not work for you—you may be excitable, you may want to play on that as your style. I have seen several women advocates in court whose personae seemed counterproductive, but, in fact, worked for them.

My favorite is the woman who argued in front of the Pennsylvania Supreme Court wearing the full "Annie Oakley"—a buckskin skirt, cowboy shirt, and cowboy boots. She wore her hair in a long braid that reached to the small of her back. She was a sight, but she was competent and presented her argument cogently and simply. (I should note that the Pennsylvania Supreme Court, until fairly recently, had a justice who wore his black robes lined with red silk, which he showed as he walked up and down the dais behind his colleagues during arguments. This may have given this advocate the idea that nothing she wore could top that.) She pulled off her look as a simple country girl who could bring down a moose with one shot by speaking the way she looked, simply and to the point. Her persona was well thought out and coherent.

I also admired the style of a former colleague of mine who was six feet tall, blonde and gorgeous. She looked a lot like Dolly Parton, and she emphasized the similarity by allowing her Georgia accent to remain undimmed by her stint at Harvard Law School and at a large northeastern megafirm. She wore her hair long and lush, wore extremely high heels and short skirts, and allowed her blouses to show just a little more cleavage than we are used to seeing in court. She was also brilliant, but the men in court—opposing counsel, judges, members of the jury—didn't notice until she had lulled them with her voice and her looks into a false sense of security. The whole package she presented was the iron fist in the velvet glove. If any of you have seen the TV show "The Closer," you'll understand how effective she was as an advocate. Her style was great for her, but not something I'd be comfortable with (apart from the fact that I'm a shrimp).

Here is what you don't want to do. Don't try to be what you're not. Unless one of your characteristics is off-putting to decision makers, don't change it. Sometimes, you are the best judge of that, sometimes not. You may think your chest tattoo, for example, is lovely, but your colleagues may think it offends the sensibilities of judges, who tend to be conservative in things like personal style. Other personal characteristics can be a net neutral if they are so much a part of you that changing them would feel unnatural. For example, a female colleague of mine was told that her voice was too high, and that she should learn to lower it. She was, and is, a brilliant lawyer. Her response was to leave the firm where she received that advice and to keep her normal speaking voice.

Some lawyers go so far as to change personas, at least somewhat, to suit the circumstances. And that brings up point number two.

2. Be Attuned To How The Judge And The Jury Are Reacting To You And Be Flexible.

Fine-tune your presentation.

One of the most effective adversaries I've faced is an environmental litigator who chairs the Litigation Department of a major firm. I'll call him "Jim." He is bright, and unyielding in the defense of his many corporate clients. He stands about 6 feet 4, and he can be intimidating when he wants to, by drawing himself up to his full height and using his booming voice.

But he doesn't always use that grizzly bear persona. I discovered this when, much to my surprise, the "other Jim" appeared at a sanctions hearing on a Rule 11 motion I filed against him and his client. Jim's client, a chemical company, was in the process of remediating a number of Superfund sites in New Jersey. I had asserted in a complaint I filed on behalf of my client, a developer, that the chemical company had polluted the developer's property. Jim filed a motion for summary judgment, asserting in his affidavit (let this be a lesson, lawyers, about the pitfalls of verifying pleadings and motions instead of having your client do it) that not only did the chemical company not pollute my client's property, he was completely unaware of any Superfund sites being remediated by the chemical company anywhere near my client's property. I resisted the motion with an affidavit of my own from the New Jersey Department of Environmental Protection showing that the chemical company had applied for and received permits to remediate a Superfund site that included my client's metes and bounds description. I also filed the Rule 11 motion.

When I saw Jim in the lobby of the courthouse before the hearing on our two motions, he tried some of his bluster on me. "That Rule 11 thing was a little over the top, don't you think?" he growled at me. "Not when my opponent lies to the court," I said.

When he entered the courtroom, it was clear that the woman judge was extremely peeved at Jim and his client. Her demeanor at the hearing made that patent. The look she gave Jim was like a deep freeze. But from that moment on, the Jim we all saw at the hearing was a cuddly teddy bear, not a grizzly. While not obvious, his stentorian tones had taken on a trace, a mere hint, of a southern twang. Instead of squaring his shoulders, he let them get round. He drooped his head a tad, and his hair was slightly unruly, with his forelock hanging down over his forehead. He actually sold to the judge the "I'm-just-a-country-boy" act. His version went something like this:

"Your honor, my client is a huge corporation with offices all over the country. The activities that the government complains about in the Superfund suits happened so long ago that there's no longer anyone at the company who knows anything about them. Here I am in New Jersey, trying to figure out what went on twenty years ago when no one who works for my client can help me. That's why I signed the affidavit—I did as much investigation as I could with very little help. I had no idea Ms. Kole's client's property was part of the Superfund site. I'm not very good at reading metes and bounds descriptions. I'm a trial lawyer, not a real estate lawyer. There was no bad faith here, your honor." And he opened his blue eyes very wide at her.

I don't know who was the most surprised that day by Jim's performance, the judge or me; but it was nothing compared to the surprise I felt when I saw the judge palpably thaw toward him. He kept those big baby blues focused on her, and she actually blushed. All these years of hearing men complain that women lawyers try to use their sex appeal to win cases, and my first actual view of sex in the courtroom was from a guy!

What Jim gained that day was a respite. Although the judge's clerk told me, and I presume told Jim, that the judge's habit was to read her ruling from the bench after oral argument, the judge told us that she would take my Rule 11 motion under advisement. She denied Jim's motion for summary judgment from the bench. And the respite gave Jim the time to put together an attractive offer for my client to settle the case (which included attorneys' fees in lieu of the Rule 11 sanctions).

This story warrants a brief digression on "sex appeal": I prefer to call it animal magnetism, and it isn't either a bad thing or a good thing. It just is. All human beings are attracted to or repelled by others based on many factors. To the extent you can maximize your animal magnetism, you should do so. I was helped tremendously by a trial advocacy program where the mock jury told me my eyes were my most compelling feature, and I should use them more. Again, like my father, I have a "warm" look, and if I look directly at a judge or juror, it imparts my sincerity. It isn't "sex appeal"; it is more like a motherly or teacherly look. But it is a kind of attraction, and I use it for the benefit of my clients.

Whether or not you decide to play up various attractive features you have, even after you have created your courtroom "you" and you feel comfortable inhabiting that skin, there may be some slight changes you want to make to your persona if you are finding that the judge or the jury are responding indifferently or badly to you.

3. Be Prepared For Anything, And Know How Your Persona Should React.

As we all learn in a trial advocacy program, litigation boot camp, or the courtroom of hard knocks, the best way to be sure you're not blindsided in the courtroom is to try to anticipate everything that could possibly go wrong. How do you handle a witness who goes off the deep end or changes her story? What do you do about the expert who is suddenly tongue-tied? While we all can learn the various techniques to deal with these surprises, what will work best for each of us depends on our personal style. One person might use humor to defuse an ugly situation, another steely anger. But unless you've got a razor-sharp wit and can think of funny lines on your feet, don't try humor. Similarly, if anger is your reaction of choice, be sure you have the emotion completely under control if you're going to use it in open court. You don't want to go overboard.

One well-known defense attorney has perfected the art of eye-rolling when a witness lies on the stand—he doesn't overdo it, but he gets his point across. Another pit-bull litigator I know turns bright red and conducts the rest of his cross-examination through gritted teeth. I tend to look mildly incredulous, and either patiently point out earlier statements by the witness that are inconsistent or ask him if he remembers telling me the exact opposite during an interview.

Above all, however, be prepared. I remember proferring as a piece of rebuttal evidence during a federal bench trial a document, which was not in the pretrial order but which had been produced by one of the parties in the case. (Of course, the pretrial order reflected my statement that I reserved the right to use any other evidence made necessary by way of rebuttal). My opponent objected. "Your honor, I've never seen this document before!" she said. " And it's not in the pretrial order!"

I pointed out that the pretrial order permitted me to use anything in rebuttal, that it had been produced in discovery, and, more importantly, that I had hand-delivered a marked copy to her office the evening before, with a cover letter saying I was going to use it in court for rebuttal. Far from being speechless, my opponent claimed never to have seen it. The judge was not impressed, gave opposing counsel a minute to look at it, and admitted it into evidence.

I had prepared for my opponent's possible ploy by providing a catch-all in the pretrial order and by writing to her the night before and also faxing her the document I intended to use (belt and suspenders). Because of my preparation, I was able to be completely unflappable when she objected. I could present my calm, reasonable woman exterior.

She, however, was completely unprepared to deal with the appearance of the document. "I never saw it before" is a lame excuse. And, had she been prepared, she could have chosen to cross-examine on the document, purposely ignore it and pretend it was not meaningful to the case, or claim it was unfairly prejudicial. In fact, if it were true, she could have presented herself as outraged that she had never seen the document until that moment. As it was, she presented herself as merely an incompetent advocate. Looking foolish doesn't help your case or your client, and after all, that's why we're all here.

4. It's About The Case And The Client, Stupid! Leave Your Ego At The Door.

I am amazed when lawyers get so wrapped up in warring with their adversaries that they forget about the actual case they're trying. Often, it will happen at a deposition—one lawyer will make a long-winded speaking objection to a question, only to have the questioning lawyer retort with ad hominem remarks, resulting in a colloquy back and forth for pages of deposition transcript. This does not, as one of my law partners who loves football says, advance the ball. It has sent to college, however, many children of many court reporters.

To war over minutiae in a deposition is stupid, but to war in court is, I believe, completely toxic to your client's interest. I tried a jury case several years ago in which I represented one of two defendants. The plaintiff's claims against each defendant were identical, and the evidence applied equally to both defendants. My co-counsel (male) and my opposing counsel (female) hated each other. At every opportunity, they referred to each other as "my esteemed opponent," or words to similar effect, in a tone of voice that dripped sarcasm. Toward the end of the week-long trial, my co-counsel actually screamed at opposing counsel, who yelled right back at him. The judge admonished both lawyers to cut it out. (He actually pointed to me, the good girl, and told my co-counsel that he should try his case "more like Ms. Kole does.") I frankly didn't like either of the other lawyers, but I contented myself with defaming them to my paralegal back at the office. At the end of the case, the jury rendered a verdict against the other defendant, my co-counsel's client. In keeping with my co-counsel's temper, he blew a gasket and left the courtroom. His second chair remained, however, and the judge let us interview the jurors to determine their reasoning. And what do you think they said? They hated my co-counsel. They thought he was so mean to that "girl attorney" on the other side, that he must be evil, and if he was evil, his client was obviously in the wrong. One juror leaned over and stage whispered to me, "But we liked you!"

My co-counsel's bad-tempered behavior was devastating to his case. Even though our opponent behaved just as badly, the jury thought that because she was a woman, she was less at fault.

Don't let your ego, bad temper, histrionic personality, or stupidity get in the way of your client's case. Remember, when you're in court, you're not the "real" you but a simulacrum of the real you. You are playing a role, a character, and that character only has the client's best interests at heart.

5. Don't Forget Your Client's Feelings; Be a Caring Person as well as a Vigorous Advocate.

Even a corporate representative has feelings. And particularly if that corporate representative has been a witness in your case, he or she has a vested interest in seeing the corporation vindicated. Louis XIV said "L'état, c'est moi!" ("The State, it is I"), and similarly for many corporate officers, the corporation is inseparable from their own self worth.

So while you never want to lose sight of the legal issues in your case, and while your judgment tells you that your adversary's annoying remarks about your client (or the witness himself) don't impress the jury, sometimes, for client relations purposes, you need to soothe his ruffled feathers. Don't make the mistake of thinking that just because the client is a sophisticated business person, he knows nasty remarks are just part of the advocate's job.

For example, many years ago I represented a close corporation that was the plaintiff in a business dispute. The corporation had been started by one man, who had turned the reins over to his kids. Damages in the case revolved around the credit-worthiness of the company: could it have raised the capital it needed to expand its business had the defendant not committed a fraud on the company? Dad was a dream witness: white-haired, kindly, and with a manner that sang of integrity. His son, by contrast, was blunt and uncooperative, even on direct examination by me. He was so angry about the entire subject matter of the case that he let his anger leak out in the courtroom. My opposing counsel took advantage of the situation by baiting him on cross-examination, and then arguing in closing that although Dad could be believed, Dad's testimony was not relevant to the case, because he wasn't in daily control of the company. And the son? "You can see how he stonewalled," said my opponent to the jury. "You can tell from his demeanor he's a liar."

Now, this was at the conclusion of a four week trial, and I could tell my case had gone in well. Opposing counsel was reaching for everything he could think of to throw a monkey wrench into my case, but both of us knew he was blowing smoke. When he trashed the son during his closing argument, the son turned beet red, and I knew he was good and angry. I leaned over to him at the table and whispered that the guy was going for broke, and he shouldn't take it personally. "I know that," he said. But I was not convinced that my client wasn't still smarting.

So during my closing, I gave my story of the case to the jury, and, at the very end, I took off my glasses and moved closer to the jury box. "The last thing I want to say is this," I said. "I am personally offended at the remarks my opponent made about my client. There is no evidence that he lied to you. You can tell he's angry at the defendant for putting him through this. And it takes some nerve for my opponent to suggest that he's lying because he's angry."

I know that statement added nothing to the argument on behalf of my client's lawsuit. But I could see it instantly mollified my client. After the judge's charge, and after the jury filed out of the box to begin deliberations, he stood up and offered me his hand to shake. "Thanks for saying what you said in the closing," he said.

Don't forget you're a human being as well as a courtroom actor.

In short, the rules I've outlined above are designed to help you focus on those aspects of your personality that forge a bond with your audience, and urge you to lose those things that detract from your effectiveness. To help you shape up, it's a good idea to get some formal training, through an advocacy workshop, such as those offered by the National Institute for Trial Advocacy. I've taken courses through NITA, and I've taught some, and both taking and teaching have been valuable learning experiences.

Above all, practice. Take every opportunity to get to court—argue motions, do arbitrations. When you stop worrying in court about who you are, congratulations—you've got style!

Having Fun 14

By Nan Joesten

Lｉｔｉｇａｔｉｏｎ ｃａｎ ｂｅ demanding, draining work, which is why finding a way to have fun is a key to longevity in this profession. For lawyers in big firms with increased billable hour requirements, this has become ever more challenging, but, at the same time, even more necessary. Even if taking (or making) the time to have fun were not a priority because of workaholic tendencies, there are innumerable benefits to doing so that have nothing to do with creating a satisfactory life while making a living, and everything to do with using your free time to become an even better litigator. How so, you ask?

By definition, litigators are called upon to solve complex, intractable problems between people. This is true whether you handle high stakes commercial disputes or a neighborhood tree trimming complaint. The easy problems get resolved without our help, and we are most needed when parties are too far apart to resolve their disagreements readily. Fair enough, but how does having fun fit into that framework? In addition to the need to maintain sufficient good health and stamina to keep up with a demanding job, it's a lawyer's ability to bring a broader view to a problem that makes her so effective. Her ability to connect her client's story to the everyday world is critically important, because that allows her to find and mold the persuasive arguments she needs to advocate her client's position best. Of course, none of this would be possible without the requisite law to support her point of view, but great lawyers are more than just great researchers—they are also able to combine the facts with the law to tell a compelling story.

Being out in the world, "having fun," helps us all to engage in the world, making it easier to weave together the storylines that will bring the case alive to the judge, the mediator, the arbitrator, the jury, or even the other side. Staying connected to the world beyond surfing the internet or commuting to the office is what fuels the suppressed storyteller within or provides the spark of creativity or genius to bring the story together.

There is also the proven link between rest and relaxation and productivity and creativity. Whether it's the joy of learning a new technique in cooking school, the satisfaction of conquering a portion (or all!) of the Pacific Crest Trail on a backpacking trip, or the decadence of a nap on a sunny window seat, it's widely accepted that taking the time to do the things that we enjoy brings innumerable dividends. While trial lawyers can all tell war stories from trials that demonstrate our ability to live on adrenaline when necessary, we all know that there are times when we hit a wall and need a period of rejuvenation to be back at our best. Finding ways regularly to have fun and relax can help provide the creative spark that inspires both your work and your life and keeps you fresh.

Making a regular point to enjoy life also has a benefit in developing a rapport with the jury. While fewer and fewer cases go to trial these days, it is important for a versatile litigator to be facile in working in front of a jury, and a big part of success in that forum requires the ability to come across sincerely, pulling from a variety of life experiences to communicate your point effectively. It's not just about connecting with the jury either. Lawyers who are healthy, happy, and fun-loving people often have a superior ability to connect with the people around them, which is an important part of rainmaking, that always-needed skill so critical to long-term success in private practice. And even though in-house or government litigators may not have a need to grow a law practice by cultivating new paying clients, they still need to build relationships effectively with internal clients and seek out new and better ways of running their practices, which is often facilitated through networking and engagement with others who enjoy similar pursuits. Indeed, those in the business of providing professional services can tell plenty of anecdotes about finding commonalities with clients that help ease the relationship along, particularly when dealing with otherwise difficult problems that we are hired to solve.

The experience of successful veteran women litigators confirms both the importance of finding ways to have fun throughout the demanding practice of law and the many and varied ways that can be done. Senior partner Deborah Ballati, at the San Francisco firm of Farella Braun & Martel, describes herself as being "enormously happy" over the course of her more than thirty years as a litigator. Why? She thrives in the field of construction and insurance law. Fortunate to have exposure early in her career to the ABA's Construction Forum, Ballati quickly found herself meeting interesting people, learning more about that practice area, and becoming ever more involved in putting on the highly regarded Forum programs. This engagement led her eventually to become the first woman chair of the Forum in 2002, a personal and professional achievement of which she is rightly proud, and which paid big dividends for her in developing her practice. But she did not view her interaction with the Forum as drudgery, instead, finding it fun. As Deborah says, "find something you like to do and where you're likely to shine because you enjoy it."

And that is the key to Deborah's happiness factor—choosing to do things that enriched her and the lives of those around her. She also finds fun outside of her professional interests. Deborah's been married to Judge David Ballati of the San Francisco Superior Court for 30 years. A two-career couple from the beginning, the Ballatis have made spending time together having fun a cornerstone of their successful partnership and a platform for their professional success. They decided early on that they would commit to make time to be together on a regular basis, doing things that they enjoyed, like traveling the world. But their time together also includes the simple pleasures of getting up each morning to walk the dog together through their neighborhood before parting ways for another busy day.

At the other end of the spectrum, women who are just entering the profession also seek a satisfying role for their law practice within their lives. There are fewer and fewer new attorneys with a single-minded focus on their careers, particularly if it comes at the cost of not being able to do other important things, including enjoying life outside of work. For these women (and many others) the phrase "work-life balance" doesn't even make sense. Work is a part of life, not something that is on the opposite side on a "life" balance scale. The challenge is to find a meaningful place for work within the twenty-four hours we have each day.

Mary Cranston, the former chair of what is now Pillsbury Winthrop Shaw Pittman LLP, and a fellow of the American College of Trial Lawyers, is a winner of the ABA's prestigious Margaret Brent Award. The award is bestowed by the ABA's Commission on Women in the Profession in recognition of women lawyers who have excelled in their field and paved the way for other women lawyers, as Mary certainly has done. The first woman litigation partner at Pillsbury, the first woman to chair a Global 100 law firm, and also the mother of two children, Mary has been a pioneer in the legal profession. Her contributions as a trial lawyer, law firm leader, and community volunteer are legendary. Her advice for women attorneys seeking to master the demands of the practice of law while building a rewarding life is simple: figure out what energizes you, in every aspect of your life, professionally and personally—and maximize the time spent on those energizing activities. Conversely, find ways to minimize the time spent on what is de-energizing, either in the office or outside of work. By increasing the ratio of energizing activities to de-energizing tasks, you increase the likelihood of finding the satisfaction that will allow you to have a challenging career over the long haul. And, by definition, doing things that you find fun are energizing and revitalizing. Whether that means baking your daughter's first birthday cake instead of buying it, ordering take-out instead of cooking on a weeknight when you're running late, lobbying to take on sole responsibility for a less high-profile cause of action in a big case so that you can have more of a first-chair role, or planning your first trip to explore wine tasting in Provence, go for it! Make the choices that put you in a position to be energized by what you're doing, both inside and outside of work, and you'll be richly rewarded many times over.

PART III

What Our Environment Is Like

Life in a Big Firm

15

By Kourtney L. James
Gillian A. Hobson
Paula W. Hinton

PART ONE

By Kourtney L. James

Life in a Big Firm: An Associate's Perspective

BOSS LADY

A few weeks after I started as an associate at a large firm in Texas, the head of my section gave me my first major project. After locking myself in my office for several days, in hopes of impressing the partner with my best work, I completed the project and went down to his office to turn it in. As I waited for him to arrive back from lunch, I began talking with his administrative assistant. We chatted casually about the firm—how I was adjusting, where my office was located—the usual pleasantries. Then she asked a question that took me completely by surprise—"So who works for you?" I paused for a few seconds as I tried to process the question—*What does she mean, "Who works for me?" I just started here—no one works for me, I work for other people*. Before I could reel off the names of various partners and senior associates for whom I had completed tasks during the few short weeks I had been employed at the firm, she interrupted my thought process by answering her own question—"Julie* works for you, right? Oh, you'll love her. She's great to work with." At that moment I realized someone *did* work for me— my professional assistant. The day I started my position at the firm, I went from being a broke law school graduate who had never held a full-time job, to a highly compensated attorney who could direct the actions of her professional assistant as well as dozens of law firm staff (paralegals, project assistants, etc.).

Yep—I was officially a "boss." Interestingly enough, with all the preparation I received learning the legal skills, and with all the advice I received from current and former law firm attorneys about the importance of excelling on every project and turning in each assignment on time, no one ever mentioned the instantaneous transition I would be expected to make—to manager of more than a dozen people—once I entered the firm. While there are plenty of resources that advise new associates on how to hone their legal skills and how to make themselves "visible" within the firm, few resources discuss non-legal components of a large law firm and how management of these non-legal components can ultimately translate into a better practice. Management

---

*All names have been changed to protect identities.

skills, along with other relational proficiencies not taught in law schools, are skills that new associates are required to master quickly in large law firms—no matter how inadequately prepared they may be for the task. Thus, while I could provide a "to-do" list on how to improve your writing skills, how to make the most out of client contact or how to network within the firm, after more than three years of practice, I thought it best to share with you my experiences with management and relationship building that will prove invaluable to new associates entering a large law firm.

MANAGEMENT 101

Becoming a good manager of the assistants and staff that support you in your daily tasks is critical to excelling as an associate in a large law firm. This can be a challenge for someone who, like me, was never employed full-time until entering the firm. Going from a 25-year-old fresh-faced law school graduate to a full-time attorney giving orders to people old enough to be your mother or father can be intimidating. However, learning how to manage your team of "helpers" can prove invaluable to your developing practice. Recently, I drafted a document on behalf of one of my firm's most valued clients regarding termination of a guarantee that the client had given to various third parties. The letter had to be sent to third parties for the termination to be effective. I spent a great deal of time making sure the letter complied with the requirements of the agreement. I meticulously checked each letter for the correct wording. I handed the letters to my professional assistant and asked her to mail them out that day. Around three o'clock that afternoon, when I noticed that she was still making labels for the letters, I asked if she thought she would be finished by the end of the day. She responded that she would, but that the mailroom closed at five o'clock, and she was not sure if the letters would make it to the post office. My heart skipped three beats! For the termination to be effective, the letters *had* to be mailed out that day. Usually, when I give my assistant a mail-out, it is not urgent and there is not a problem if it goes out the next day. On this occasion, I failed to relay to my assistant the urgency of this matter and, as a result, she worked under our normal arrangements. Fortunately, we were able to get the letters out that day, and all was fine.

This recent incident reminded me how important effective management is to my practice. No one would have cared about the meticulously drafted letter if it was not mailed on the appropriate date. The brilliant research memorandum that you write for the senior partner that develops a key legal argument for the case will not be nearly as impressive if your administrative assistant cannot read your mark-up and the final draft has numerous typos. And the hours you spend coordinating a major deposition will go unappreciated if the paralegal that you are working with misunderstands the schedule and the partner gets the witness file an hour before the deposition. Consequently, effective management skills—giving clear, concise instructions, detailing deadlines and ensuring that assigned tasks are being done in a timely manner—can make or break your reputation at the firm.

Effective management also means understanding and recognizing the humanity in everyone you work with. Everyone has good days and bad days, everyone wants to be greeted with a warm, genuine smile and everyone wants to be respected. Thus, managing is not just about effective delegation; it also means taking into consideration the human needs of your assistants. So when you see that your assistant is under pressure to get a project done, be thoughtful about the situation and do not request that he or she handle more tasks if they can be held off for another day. And when the paralegal who normally assists you is dealing with a family emergency, be mindful of that and offer your condolences and concerns. Try not to have your assistant work overtime for you unless it is absolutely imperative, never raise your voice or bark orders to any assistant, and, in general, be kind and considerate of their time and expertise. Believe me, your humanity will not be forgotten and will most likely be returned in times when you need it most.

THAT PARTNER

New associates know they will face many challenges in a large law firm, but many associates fail to consider the challenges presented by becoming a manager. In fact, some associates never master the task of effective management and go through their entire legal career without ever sharpening their managerial skills. They become the partners who bark orders to their assistants and forget to tell the associates working with them about upcoming deadlines—only to have the associates stay up all night finishing work that the partner failed to tell them was due (but that is another article!). They become the partners who *no one* wants to work with or for. As a new associate in a large law firm, you should make it your priority to perfect your management skills—sound managerial and relational skills will not only benefit your legal career, but will serve you well in practically all walks of life.

PART TWO

By Gillian A. Hobson

The Road to Partnership: A Junior Partner's Perspective

THE BEGINNING

Growing up in St. Croix, I was always interested in the somewhat unique legal relationship between the United States and the U.S. Virgin Islands. When I went to Harvard College to pursue my undergraduate degree, the fact that a significant number of students were going to law school seemed to cement the notion in my mind that I too would go to law school. To be clear, I really didn't know what being a lawyer meant. There were no lawyers in my family, and I knew very few lawyers growing up. My mother is a hair stylist who owns her own salon, and my father was an insurance salesman. Neither of my parents attended college. Still, I wanted to go to law school.

It wasn't until my summer experiences at law firms that I really began to understand what lawyers actually do on a daily basis. My current firm is the second firm I have worked at since starting my legal career. I started my career at a law firm of approximately 350 lawyers. The firm was the largest one I worked at during law school summers, and I made that choice, because I believed the firm would be small enough to offer a more nurturing environment but large enough to attract complex work. We had a relaxed, non-hierarchical environment at my old firm. The people were very friendly and entrepreneurial. I recall wandering around the office on my first day of work in search of the library and having a senior partner ask me what I was looking for, then actually walking with me to the library. However, after a year and a half of practicing at the firm, most of the partners in my practice group decided to leave in search of a better "platform" for our practice. For those partners, a better "platform" meant moving to a larger firm with more depth and breadth. After carefully weighing the pros and cons, the similarity of the cultures of the two firms and the prestige of working at what I viewed as the best firm in Texas, I was convinced that bigger was going to be better.

In hindsight, the decision to come to the big firm was absolutely the right one for me. We have an excellent group of lawyers with significant experience in many practice areas and a very open culture. Our lawyers, no matter how senior, are generally accessible and available to assist whenever called on.

This firm has never felt too big to me but that may be due, in part, to my level of involvement at the firm. I know many of the firm's lawyers through work and have been heavily involved in firm activities and in the local community.

SECURING GOOD WORK/THE PLAN

Despite all of the benefits of being at a large firm, the main challenge for an associate is to get good work. When the economy is good, that challenge is less of a concern. However, when the economy slows down as it did in 2001 and 2002, work opportunities tend to decrease. Not long after I arrived as a lateral attorney in August 2000, the work flow slowed. I had not established any significant relationships with the new partners, and my old partners were establishing relationships with new associates. I inadvertently fell through the cracks and struggled to get good work. Although I was initially tempted to leave, I rallied myself in my fourth year and decided to seek out anyone who might be a potential mentor and/or source of work. I began to forge relationships with women partners at the firm and would meet with them for breakfast, lunch and drinks. I also forced myself to go outside my comfort zone and tried to develop more personal relationships with a number of male partners. I had fallen into the trap of focusing only on doing good work and would often eat at my desk. With my new plan, I made sure I went out to eat with different lawyers. I also decided to become a self-appointed "expert" in a few specialized (but less "sexy") areas of law and conveyed my decision to all the lawyers in my practice group, many of whom were happy to direct those issues to me. Finally, I made a concerted effort to meet senior women attorneys who were practicing in-house. Through those combined efforts, I managed to raise my profile, and, over time, my work flow increased.

My intent was always to stay and make partner. As I reflect on the type of person I am, I readily acknowledge that I have always been very goal-oriented. At a law firm, the brass ring is making partner. Even though I considered leaving when I felt I was not getting my fair share of work opportunities, and my career was not progressing, I ultimately decided that the goal of making partner was achievable. Once I made that decision, I came up with a multi-faceted plan to do everything I could to achieve it.

Although I knew that the journey to make partner would be challenging, I have been surprised at how difficult the journey actually has been. In high school, college and then law school, if you studied enough, your efforts would typically translate into good grades. As a lawyer on the partner track at a large law firm, doing excellent work does not guarantee that you will make partner. Similarly, billing the most hours does not guarantee that you will make partner. The actual formula for making partner at a large law firm is an amorphous one that typically involves doing excellent work, working very hard, being well-regarded and a good firm citizen, and, ultimately, being able to make a business case for why a group of partners should share their pie with you. Although I did formulate a plan for making partner and discussed it with various partners within and outside my practice group, there were no guarantees that my plan would work.

THE COSTS/THE GOOD HUSBAND

Spending all that time and effort on making partner greatly reduced the amount of time I could spend with my family, which greatly increased my stress level, especially in the last few years before partnership. I know that my male colleagues also shared similar experiences, but I think the problem is more acute for women. Although my husband has been and remains extremely supportive of my career, even his patience was tested a few times. In the final years leading up to making partner, I tried to be smarter about my time and achieve the illusory "work-life balance." This, however, really did not mean I worked less; rather, it meant that I would, for example, schedule business development events that my husband and son would enjoy attending. I also introduced my husband to some of my male clients, and they now golf together.

Although I see balancing work and life as a long-term endeavor, I have never felt the need to choose one over the other. I grew up with a working mom, as did my husband. Virtually all of the women we knew growing up were working moms, so the idea of having children and working is normal for my family. My husband's children came to live with us when they were each nine years old. They are now 21 and 16. I am fortunate that my husband has always been completely supportive of my career so having children has never affected my decision to try to make partner. We simply found an allocation of responsibilities that works for us. I am the planner—doctor appointments, birthday parties, trips, special events—and my husband executes whatever directions I give him. He works in the software industry and has typically had a more flexible schedule than I have, so our arrangement has tended to work fairly well. I am, however, very sympathetic to women with younger children, especially if their husbands have equally time-demanding jobs, because I think the challenges are more difficult.

LOOKING FORWARD

Having been a partner for just one year, I think it is too early to comment on whether it meets all of my expectations. I do have a tremendous sense of pride in achieving this milestone and have garnered the respect of many in my local community. However, with the accomplishment comes a sense of obligation to help other minority and women associates accomplish the same goal if they want to. I also feel an increased sense of responsibility for my own career. As an associate, partners feed you work. Once you make partner, the paradigm changes. I am fortunate to have clients with whom I have relationships and from whom I get some of my work. As a partner, in addition to generating work for myself, I have to be mindful of generating enough work for associates as well. Given the 2008 downturn in the economy, these concerns have become more acute.

At this point in my career, my primary career goal is to be a successful lawyer—and I am still sorting out precisely what that means. In part it means that although I have been recognized by the Texas legal community for my legal skills, I intend to expand that recognition beyond Texas. I also intend to expand my client base by developing more of my own clients. I have established some fairly sizeable goals for business development and have given myself a five-year timeframe. And, perhaps most importantly, I want to help other minority and women attorneys achieve success in their careers. I've had a number of mentors—women and men, attorneys and non-attorneys—who have been invaluable in guiding and nurturing me along the way and I hope to be able to do the same for others.

When younger associates ask me for career advice, I tell them to work hard to develop a reputation early in their careers for doing excellent work. They should also spend a fair amount of time developing relationships with more senior attorneys in their firm. I misjudged early on how important relationships would be in my career development. I would also encourage them to look for mentors in the not-so-obvious places. Sometimes, we need to go outside our comfort zones to look for guidance in our careers. Associates should also take ownership of their careers by setting short-term goals for themselves and considering sharing those goals with a friend or mentor so as to hold themselves accountable. In my early career, I focused only on the amorphous concept of "making partner." I think I would have been better served if, at the beginning of each year, I had established a few concrete goals for myself and focused on accomplishing those goals.

If I had to tell associates what <u>not</u> to do, I would advise them not to eat at their desks unless they have a conference call. They should spend time getting to know other attorneys at the firm as well as clients. They also should not be afraid to ask for help or advice. A first-year attorney recently asked me to explain some of the concepts in a fairly complicated matter. I was glad she felt comfortable enough to ask me, because understanding the fundamentals will help her do a better job. I think it is perfectly acceptable to ask those questions but often women are reticent to do so. The failure to ask for help can make an already challenging job more challenging. In summary, do exceptional work, set goals, and reach out to others for support and advice. Your future is truly in your hands.

PART THREE

By Paula W. Hinton

Life at the Top? or, "To Keep a Lamp Burning We Have to Keep Putting Oil in It."

THE PASSION IS BORN

There was never any question in my mind as to what I would become. I would be a trial lawyer. In fact, there was no free will for my brother and me until we received our law degrees from the University of Alabama—as our father had three decades earlier. My father practiced law in a mid-sized Alabama city, and I was "Scout" to his "Atticus." Yes, he did know Harper Lee at the University of Alabama in the 40's, and I have watched "To Kill a Mockingbird" more times than you can imagine—in part, because Dad knew Miss Lee, in part, because my godparents' nephew played the role of Jim in the movie, and, in part, because it spoke to me about standing up when injustice surrounds you.

When I was little, I accompanied Dad every Sunday morning to the county jail before we went to Sunday school. Dad visited his clients about their upcoming court dates while I ate biscuits with the guards and trustees in the kitchen of the jail. I followed him to court and watched the trials, and he paid me a nickel for each supplement I put into his books in his law library. He represented many who otherwise would not have had representation, and the judge who gave one of his eulogies said he was legal services before there were pro bono legal service agencies. I grew up in a time where the law made such a difference in people's lives, and many desperately needed representation from "Lawyer Hinton."

My passion for the law and for being a trial lawyer was in my blood. I loved law school and graduate school; particularly since it was a place where it was okay to be a smart Southern girl. I no longer was the overweight, red-headed valedictorian with thick glasses; I was part of the best group of people I had ever met. I was embarking on a profession I loved then, and I love now. Yes, I faced the awkward firm interviews of the 70's, but I never gave up. I kept reaching for more. My Dad had said I could have the best of both worlds, and I was out to get it.

HOW DID WE GET HERE? THE LAMP

As I complete my 30th year in the practice of law, I have had occasion of late to raise two important questions: "Where did all of those years go? Why and how in the face of so much change have too many things remained the same for women over the past three decades?" Both are serious questions for me, but the latter is important for the legal profession and for the future careers of women like Kourtney and Gillian in the large law firm. As Mother Theresa observed "To keep a lamp burning, we have to keep putting oil in it." But why do we have to keep relighting the lamp?

Many of us can still recall the time when we were told we couldn't be a trial lawyer and a mother. I recall when I was pregnant with my son in the late 1980's being told by a young male partner (now in another firm) that being a mother was a choice—like his choosing to play golf. He said, "You can't be a great trial lawyer and a great golfer, and you can't be a great trial lawyer and a mother." I think many of us have shown that isn't so. I still scratch my head over that analogy—motherhood and golf? You can manage your life to have the best of both worlds, and never let anyone tell you that you can't. Nothing is easy, but our profession gives us flexibility we wouldn't have in many other occupations.

Women of my vintage are the first significant group of women lawyers to approach 30 years of practice. We are the group that faced the same challenges, opportunities and obstacles. We climbed the career ladder at the same time, and, sadly, we probably all made the same mistakes at work and at home. But we are not alone. We were and are supported by a sisterhood, and some good men who worked with us in our efforts to obtain and provide equal opportunities for women in our profession. Now, we must protect and enhance those opportunities. We achieved a great deal, but so much more remains to be done. We must be sure that this vast wealth of experience helps those who follow behind and beside us; we must be sure we put more oil in that lamp.

With the passage of the years, many of my friends and classmates are now judges, politicians, general counsels, law firm leaders and bar officials. It is difficult to believe that enough time has passed for us to be part of the so-called "establishment." We have made great progress, but problems remain in that women still aren't a significant part of the power structures of law firms. How do we best recruit, retain and promote women attorneys in today's law firms to be leaders in the future? These issues are at the heart of today's large law firms where the costs of talent are so enormous.

Some of us are the senior partners in major law firms, decision-makers in major institutions, and have achieved a great deal. We are now the role models that we so desperately wanted and needed when we were young lawyers. With all of the changes around us, why is it then that the number of women partners in major law firms has not changed significantly in the past decade? What do we need to do to create real opportunities for young women attorneys? Why does stereotyping still hold so many back? How do we deal with all of the changes that affect those of us who have been practicing for decades, while assisting those who are climbing up the steep and slippery ladder to success?

Young attorneys, male and female, frequently ask for advice and guidance. They want to know how I handled things when I was a young associate, mother and wife, striving to be a partner in a major law firm. The best advice I give them is "Do as I say, not as I have done." We have all made so many mistakes in our careers, and we learned from them and can help those behind us avoid them. How many times have you been silent when you should have raised your hand and made your voice heard or spoken out too much when you should have remained quiet?

SHARP ELBOWS/DID SHE SAY THAT?

We all started in our large law firm with the same excellent grades, the same work ethic and the same burning ambition the men had, but having weathered a few decades, we see that we still face challenges. We <u>must</u> continue to set new expectations for ourselves and others. These challenges change as we advance in a firm and we must adapt to meet them. Women at all levels face the same issues in the workplace—most associated with old notions of stereotyping. And stereotyping is not limited to just the thoughts of men. Women also engage in stereotyping. Stereotyping sees a world where women "take care" and men "take charge." We all know that an aggressive woman litigator is still viewed differently than a male—we know what they call her, while the man's aggressiveness is viewed as an asset. These notions were around decades ago, and they are still here today. We must work to counter these stereotypes and work towards advancement for all.

Catalyst noted in recent studies, including "The Double-Bind Dilemma for Women in Leadership; Damned if You Do, Doomed if You Don't," that women face many obstacles in obtaining and retaining leadership positions. There is so much more to do to close the gap between perception and reality for women lawyers. Women need <u>actual</u> opportunities, as well as the responsibility and power to take advantage of them, in our still male-dominated legal profession. We must continue to help those behind us and adapt ourselves to meet the challenges facing us.

WHO AM I? ADDING OIL

Acting like a man is not the answer. You have to find your place and voice. Recent research indicates that women are perceived to be less likeable as they become more successful, but you already knew that. We are likeable if we don't achieve or strive for achievement, but why can't we succeed on our terms? McKinsey is working on an analysis about women in leadership for release later this year which will help many of us in our efforts to advance. A wonderful article, "Centered Leadership—How Talented Women Thrive" from the McKinsey Quarterly newsletter from the fourth quarter of 2008 points out that studies show that women who vigorously promote their own interests are seen as aggressive, uncooperative and selfish. However, they note that other studies show that the failure of women to promote their own interest results in a lack of female leaders. We are seen as too soft or too hard. Never "just right." Stereotyping is just part of the problem. We need to understand the system and make it work for us—not against us. That will not be easy, but some resources are becoming available to assist us in understanding what is happening and how to work within our firms to change things for us, and others.

Like it or not, women need to be more careful than men of making negative impressions if they wish to advance within their firms. As noted, women lawyers who are aggressive and hard-charging are perceived as difficult to deal with and not team players. It isn't fair, but it is the reality of our profession and others as they exist today. I often ponder how counter-intuitive these criticisms are about women trial lawyers—who hires a non-aggressive and demure trial lawyer? The answer is no one. You have to find your own voice and vision within your firm and be prepared to confront and deal with the demands of your practice, your family, and your life.

I found my place; but now, at the peak of my success, I suddenly find my market getting smaller. The reason is simple. Now that I am a successful "older" attorney, my billing rate is higher, and clients now tell me that there are areas of rate-sensitive litigation where they will no longer be able to hire me. Also, cases for which I was hired only a few years ago are now not large enough to justify the higher billing rates. Instead, clients now look to hire me only in those "bet-the-company" lawsuits or cases of large exposure or large potential returns. I'm now viewed as the senior partner who can try the big case or the client service partner who ensures that the right lawyers from my firm are staffing particular matters. Lawyers my age and with my experience are learning how to re-position our practices and marketing efforts. The changes never cease.

NOW WHAT?

I recently met with the younger women lawyers in our Austin office. The big topic was the issue of "balancing" work with motherhood and life at home. I told them that this emphasis on "balance" is nonsense. Law firms, consultants, and bar associations push this notion of "balance," and I believe balance is not achievable, and to tell young attorneys there is "balance" is unfair and sets unrealistic expectations. We never have "balance." It's just about managing your time, managing your life, and using the resources available to you. It's about doing the best you can on a day-to-day basis and ceasing the constant guilt when you are not "balanced."

I closed that meeting with the Austin lawyers by telling them a story about my son who was born my first year as a partner. He was discussing his future job prospects and the hours required for a particular position. When I noted that his Dad and I had worked long hours, he said, "Oh Mom, you and Dad didn't work that hard when I was growing up." It was at that moment I knew I had been successful—we had done it! He was clueless how hard we had worked and how much time we spent working when he was small. He just knew we always had time for him and were there for him.

A few days later, I received a note from a young associate and mother who was in that Austin meeting: "Paula: Thank you for sharing your many words of wisdom to us Austin gals this afternoon. The story of how your son has no clue that you worked so hard literally brought tears to my eyes. I can only hope that I survive this working mom gig so well—and with such fun pizazz!"

Life in a big law firm is tough, and each stage is full of new experiences and challenges. This is not a profession for the faint of heart or thin of skin. It will batter your ego, but you must know that you will bounce back, that you are exceptional and will succeed. You got here, you stayed here, and you will excel on your terms. Never take your eye off the prize, but be aware that the prize will change in the different stages of your career. You will face new difficulties as a result of your successes and your advancement up the ladder. Women fought to be where we are, but we face even more difficult hurdles that surface with each level of our success. I know I have, but it is part of the challenge for now. Embrace it. The large firm is right for me, but you will have made it when you find happiness and self-satisfaction in your career and your life.

Becoming a Successful Women-Owned Law Firm: My Life in Law Before, During and After*

16

By Beth L. Kaufman

THE FIRM THAT I walked into on April 3, 1978, my first day at my first job as a soon-to-be admitted lawyer, looked very different than it does today. Then, it was composed of five male partners, most emanating from large New York law firms, in office space in one of New York's original skyscrapers that, while it was all on one floor, was separated by a building corridor. I was the first woman associate, fresh out of law school. Today, the firm still is in the same building, occupies the entire original floor (no longer divided by a building corridor) plus one additional floor, has opened an office in Chicago, and is a certified women-owned law firm of 11 partners, nine counsel and seven associates. How did we get here?

That story begins with some personal history. Although I had worked at a law firm as a summer associate and then part-time during law school and had helped out my brother-in-law as a quasi-paralegal during college, I was naïve about the practice and business of law, when, all of 23 years old, I began my career. I knew from my summer experience that I wanted hands-on work and to learn to be a lawyer sooner, rather than later, and so I jumped at the chance offered me by a boutique firm composed of well-credentialed lawyers who had the skills I wanted to acquire and who wanted to grow their firm and teach young lawyers, a firm that was looking for a young lawyer to handle what my classmates and I would have characterized as "real work." I also thought I would begin to have children in the next few years and wanted to continue to work full-time as a lawyer, have the ability to continue to develop professionally, and to work independently for good clients, but also be an ever-present mother, who raised her children. In short, I wanted it "all."

The firm I joined in 1978, which has evolved into one of the largest women-owned firms in the U.S. today, not only allowed but encouraged and facilitated my pursuit of these goals. It was clear to me that that would be the case from the very beginning. It is that story that provides the keys to becoming a successful women-owned law firm.

Step 1 to becoming a successful women-owned law firm: As a young lawyer, find the right professional setting in which women lawyers will thrive.

That setting must be a place that allows women to develop professionally, while shouldering other responsibilities—to children, spouses and parents—that inevitably fall on their shoulders. Back in the late 1970s and throughout the 1980s, there was not a lot of technology available to facilitate doing both, but whatever there was, I used. I vividly recall sitting at my home computer on numerous evenings, waiting for software named "Remote" to transmit a document to the office, where a secretary was waiting. It often took an hour or more to transmit particular documents back and forth, leading to curtailed sleep, but the documents were all completed and timely served. On other occasions, I would come home from the office in time for dinner, playtime, bathing and reading bedtime stories to my one baby, then two, then three small children, only to hop on a train to go back to the office at 8 or 9 p.m. to make sure that a midnight deadline was met.

Throughout those years, our firm did more than just tolerate those habits. Once I proved that I was a good lawyer, who wanted to take on responsibility and could produce a first-class work product, the firm *encouraged* me to meet my family responsibilities as well, provided the resources I needed in the evening and on weekends to get my work done and often re-scheduled meetings so that I could attend. Work assignments were made with regard to merit—expertise and experience, prior dealings with a particular client—and not gender. The clients with whom I worked and with whom I maintain friendships to this day, all knew about my children's exploits, and they delighted in the stories; the firm never hid any of that from these clients (as some firms seemed to do), deciding, quite correctly, that it all was a part of who I was and would be a part of the relationships I was building with clients.

For me and others at our firm, professional development meant involvement in national, state, and local bar associations; for me and other women, the national bar association involvement often meant travel—with families—to meetings. When my children were teenagers, I contended with their ever-present question (complaint?) about whether we could ever go on a family vacation that was not associated with a bar association meeting. (Now my adult children want to know where the next meeting of such and such bar association is taking place, and whether they can tag along!)

My own career thrived at our firm: the nature of the work was so stimulating and challenging, and our clients were not only involved in interesting businesses, but were so helpful and supportive, that I wanted to do a first rate job and pushed myself to be my own harshest critic and taskmaster. The result? Great results for very pleased clients, and great experience and exposure for an increasingly more experienced lawyer.

Step 2 to becoming a successful women-owned law firm: Develop your own clients from within and without the firm.

Having no pre-existing client relationships of my own, my first client relationships were with existing clients of the firm. To get good work as an associate, which will help you develop professionally and allow you access to those from whom you will develop your own practice and independence, you must do unequivocally excellent work for those you are working for—the partners and the clients of the firm. In my case, that eventually led to partners letting me run litigations substantially on my own, to trying cases on my own and to clients feeling comfortable turning to me for advice and assistance without going through a partner. Without such confidence being expressed in me and my judgment, I never would have been able to nurture the entrepreneurial spirit that has proven so necessary to being an owner of a women-owned law firm. Without clients feeling that level of comfort with me as their lawyer, they never would have continued as our firm's clients and never would have referred other clients to us.

Step 3 to becoming a successful women-owned law firm: Understanding the responsibility of becoming a partner.

Everything already expressed in this chapter is pretty much self-evident for any lawyer, male or female, whose ambition is to become a partner in any size firm. Having achieved this level of success as a lawyer and within my firm, after eight years of hard work and three pregnancies and childbirths, I became an equity partner. Still relatively young (not quite 32 at the time) and unsophisticated, I did not understand that my partnership status was economically feasible only because of the loyalty of clients who were important to the firm and the generous spirit of existing partners, who made sure those clients thought of me as their primary lawyer at the firm.

It took me many years to realize the responsibility that being a partner carries with it, particularly at a small firm. Again, this is true for both men and women, but I believe its ramifications may be somewhat harder for women to grasp. Certainly in the late 1980s and early 1990s, there were few women partners among law firm partner ranks, no matter what size the firm. And there were even fewer women who were equity partners, and fewer still who held leadership roles within their firms. Men, it seemed to be thought back then, were groomed more directly for the responsibilities of partnership and understood how to assume them.

I set out to assume the responsibilities that came with partnership in the same way that women usually take on new responsibilities—whether at work, in the home, or in community organizations: I painstakingly learned all aspects of the business, the economics, the business development dynamics, the human resources concerns and demands, and the competitive environment in which our small business operated. I worked to maintain good relationships with our excellent staff—indeed, to a large extent, I had matured as a lawyer with their support, and many had watched as I raised my children. One even remembers pulling out my first gray hair! But I had to figure out and navigate the new relationship of employer-employee with each of them without losing the personal connections.

I was encouraged and supported in that effort by the male partners in the firm. And I do not mean to say that I alone was so encouraged—indeed, the wise forefathers of our firm knew that, to be successful, all younger partners needed to be engaged at the entrepreneurial level, and everyone was, with varying degrees of success. Those who became fully engaged remain at the firm and are owners of it; those who did not left, usually for larger firms where firm management and, in some instances, business development—some of the most important responsibilities of being a partner—were the responsibilities of others.

Step 4 to becoming a successful women-owned law firm: Business Development.

I quickly learned that excellent legal work for existing clients for which I may receive some management, but not origination, credit under our firm's compensation formula, was not, by itself, going to lead to the success I wanted to achieve—for myself and, more important than I then knew, for the firm. I knew that I had to develop business in different areas from existing clients, so that I could share in the origination credit, or I had to develop new clients for the firm, for which I would receive full origination credit.

Although I usually was not aware of it, I was being mentored as a business developer during my associate years and my years as a young partner. Doing excellent legal work, networking to establish relationships within existing corporate clients and with potential new corporate clients as in-house lawyers left to go to other companies, networking with other lawyers in professional organizations—all keys to successful business development—were all supported and encouraged by our firm. But I had to learn something that does not come intuitively to women: I had to learn how to ask for work from those clients. Whether it was fear of rejection, or a sense that if I was a good lawyer, the work should just come to me (as opposed to anyone else), or an inherent shyness, I am not sure, but no matter how many times I heard from consultants at programs and on panels that women just have to ask for work, I could not bring myself to do so directly. This was the case even though I thought I had mastered the economics of how we did business, and I knew and understood completely how important new business and new sources of business were to a law firm. I plugged away, indirectly soliciting new business from existing and new clients, in my own (discreet) way. Slowly but surely, I am learning to be more direct. I also am learning that a few gray hairs (not too many) and ascension to a leadership role within a law firm facilitates being able to do this successfully.

I was successful to a point. In the early 1990s, my efforts produced a significant milestone: I became the highest revenue producer in our firm, and in 1999 our firm name was changed so that my name was in it (a key piece of recognition that definitely helped the generation of business, again attributable to my (mostly) male mentors/partners and to the hard work I had put in).

Up to now, the story set forth here has been largely personal. But I was by no means the only woman at the firm or the only one to become a partner. In the early summer of 2005, when the firm's financial statements for 2004 arrived, we learned that women owned more than 50% of the firm's equity, which qualified the firm for women-ownership status. This had been achieved due to hard work of the women partners and the encouragement and promotion, by the original male partners of the firm, of the best lawyers in the firm without regard to gender.

We promptly applied for certification by the Women's Business Enterprise National Council (WBENC) as a women-owned business, a prerequisite to being recognized by corporations as a diverse business that allows the firm to be added to the list of counsel the corporate in-house attorneys can select from and also permitted us to join the National Association of Minority and Women-Owned Law Firms (NAMWOLF).

This development has allowed us to begin to ask for business—from existing clients and from new clients—in a manner that exudes a confidence that we now know is hard for a client to resist. Whatever success we had in developing business before our certification has grown significantly since women became the *principal* owners of the firm and its leaders.

Step 5 to becoming a successful women-owned law firm: Having fun in and navigating the waters of women ownership.

One of the most delightful by-products of our new ownership status was the wonderful messages of support and encouragement we received from colleagues, judges and clients. One, in particular, led to another significant development for our firm, our expansion to Chicago.

A long-time friend of mine was a litigation partner at a large Chicago firm and we had similar practices. We had talked for years about the various roles that women litigators were most effective in, both in the courtroom and outside, and shared a similar view of the legal world. She had heard many stories from me about the fun we were having with our new women-owned status and how well-received it was, when she decided that she wanted to exchange her partnership in the large firm for a partnership in ours. Knowing that did not mean she would move to New York, we opened our Chicago office in March 2007. At first, that office had one partner, one woman attorney who was of counsel, and a secretary. In short order, and as a direct result of the publicity the firm received when that office opened, it was composed of seven women attorneys and one male attorney, all of whom are highly skilled and well credentialed attorneys and many of whom take advantage of the flex-time, project-based working arrangements we offer.

As you might surmise, the women of the firm were thrilled with our new status and many of our male partners were as well. I have to admit, however, that, at first, certain male partners were not comfortable with having our women-owned status a focus of our website and marketing efforts. Being sensitive to those concerns was an important component of leading a firm made up of both women and men. We recognized that there would be those who would emphasize the women-owned status of the firm, and those who would not. Our website did and does let those interested know that the firm is women-owned, but not in a heavy-handed way. When profiles of the firm have been published, principally in publications highlighting diversity in the legal profession, all partners are included. Over time, even those most resistant have softened their stance and have begun to emphasize the firm's women-owned status themselves.

The women of the firm do manage it as well. Our managing partner is a woman, our management staff is composed of all women, and our key policy decisions are made by the equity partners, the majority of whom—in both pure numbers as well as percentage of ownership—are women. The head of our litigation practice is a woman; the head of our real estate practice is a woman; the head of our trusts and estates practice is a woman.

We often are asked why our ownership status matters. On the most fundamental level, it does not—our lawyering skills, good judgment and successes are what matter. But I like to believe that most lawyers have good skills, good judgment and are successful in their areas of practice. Our women-ownership status distinguishes us because it reflects a culture that is the polar opposite of the culture at the large law firms surveyed in the National Association of Women Lawyers Survey that shows such low statistics for women equity partners. This culture was instilled in our firm by some enlightened male lawyers beginning in the late 1970s. It rewards and encourages excellence in a gender-neutral way, promotes and encourages the advancement of women lawyers, and lets them ascend to be leaders of their firm and the profession.

Life as a Corporate In-House Counsel

17

By Barbara A. Moore

I NEVER DREAMED OF being a lawyer. In fact, when I started at Penn Law, I didn't know one single member of the profession. It never occurred to me what I would do with my degree; I simply wanted to extend my education, and a college professor suggested law school. As I consider it now, it was quite a casual way of starting such a bold journey. But then, starting out on a straight path to anywhere has never been normal for me. And so now, as I contemplate my career as an in-house lawyer working for a French chemical company, I can truly say this was not the journey I mapped for myself 30 years ago when I graduated from Iowa State University with a degree in English.

If you knew me, you'd realize how bizarre it is that I claim ISU as my undergraduate alma mater. I hale from a small town in New Jersey. My mother and father were originally from North and South Carolina, respectively. I am African-American, and both my parents were born to sharecroppers. Neither parent attended college; neither had ventured farther west than Pennsylvania in their lifetimes. I had never even been on a farm. So what was an afro-wearing 22-year-old black woman from the Northeast doing in Ames, Iowa in 1974? I asked myself that question almost daily for the first six months of my residency. Finally, the answer became obvious—I was trying to make the best out of an emotionally charged and hastily made choice to get married to a man I'd known for about two years. He had decided to go to ISU to study agricultural business after growing up in Harlem. It made absolutely no sense at all.

So, instead of finding a job in Ames as a computer programmer (the trade I had acquired after graduating from high school in 1970), I started college in May 1975. And I excelled. I graduated in 3 years with a 3.8 GPA, a degree in English and started looking around for something else to do while my husband made plans to get his MBA. I will forever be indebted to the college professor who suggested that I apply to law school. Clearly, it was never a choice I would have made on my own. I didn't know one person who had either practiced law or even attended law school. I knew some people who had been in courtrooms, but they were not wearing blue pin-stripe suits. Thank goodness I had seen "The Paper Chase" at least once. Years later, I would be introduced to the courtroom in a real way, when I appeared *pro se* at my own divorce proceeding, because my lawyer failed to appear. Even though it was an uncontested proceeding, and I was still in law school, I considered that to be my first legal victory. It could only get better.

As much as I loved college and the opportunity to learn, I really disliked law school. I wanted to be independent, to be able to earn a living. Without having anyone to talk to about the experience or the expectations of law school, I simply muddled through. It probably wasn't until the last semester of my second year that I began to figure out that there was never a single right answer and that any point—including black letter law—could be argued. For a post-sixties black woman who had learned that you needed to play by the rules to get ahead, the Socratic method seemed a difficult if not an impossible lesson. I just wanted to get to the point, draw the *right* conclusion and move forward.

I have often said that, if asked, I would never go back to law school. But I take that back. If I went again, I think I might get more out of it and, perhaps, even enjoy it. I was an older student in law school the first time around; I think it made me skeptical of the idealists and visionaries. But now I'm even older—old enough to speak my mind and argue with conviction. I always thought that there was something wrong with me because I just didn't think like those people. Now I know that it's our experiences that give us shape and value, and our diversity is what law school should be about. The best answer is, "It depends!"

I probably disappointed a few people when I decided to practice in my hometown of Morristown, New Jersey. After all, I had a Penn education. But since my desire was to settle down and get to work, home had a nice feel. After living in Philadelphia, I had no desire to live in another city. Iowa had left its mark in more ways than one. My transition to a corporate law firm in New Jersey was fairly smooth. I had enjoyed a summer internship and been invited back. Although I was assigned to the Litigation Department, I thought I really wanted to be a corporate lawyer. Once again, my perceptions were colored by my limited knowledge. Much later, I would realize that what I really wanted was to work for a corporation. It turned out that I was well suited for litigation. I liked the variety of the assignments, and the people in the department were the most social. I was a good writer (thanks to my days at ISU), and I worked long hours. I found out later that I didn't bill enough, and that ultimately would be a problem. But it was a good experience. I had interesting cases, the firm had an excellent reputation, and I learned quite a bit. After about three years, I began working almost exclusively on products liability litigation, which served as the means by which I would ultimately acquire my corporate position.

As a litigator in a corporate law firm, my clients were mainly in-house counsel. In the mid-1980s, I became friendly with an African-American woman who worked for a diversified manufacturing company that included batteries and chemicals. One day, she got a call from a headhunter who was hoping to fill a position with a new company that was about to purchase one of the subsidiaries she counseled. He wanted to know if she could recommend anyone. They were looking for someone with about 5 years' experience. The timing was perfect. She gave him my name, and—as they say—the rest is history. I started with the new company about 2 months later.

When I walked in the door for my first interview and then when I returned on my first day, I understood that my own personal experiences would be invaluable in learning to adapt to the new work and lifestyle that in-house counseling would require. Our corporate offices would be undergoing a make-over in a couple of months. But, for now, we'd have to settle for the photography of the old regime—pictures of sheep grazing near a manufacturing site somewhere in the Midwest. The somber shades of grey depicting endless miles of steel amidst an equally grey sky led into the corporate executive wing, where I'd be stationed temporarily until our new president arrived. My next office would be a small closet-like file room that was immediately available and would suffice until my permanent office was prepared. The sheep reminded me of Iowa and the closet—well I'd had bigger. It took about 18 months, but we got new pictures, new wallpaper, new furniture and many new employees. And, as we look back on those early days, my boss of 21 years and I share some very special memories and some hearty laughs. All of these changes early on helped my ultimate adaptation to what continues to be a fundamental truth of corporate life—change is constant.

Corporate change is done without apology, with the goal being continuous improvement. This concept was true even before it became a "Total Quality"[1] mantra. Change is usually preceded by the entry of new management, under-achieving financial results, competitive pressures, or all of the above. Corporations are also known for their unending initiatives (an earmark of change) and the legal department is not immune. We've studied and been studied; we've been centralized and de-centralized. We've cut costs, reduced budgets, consolidated outside counsel, developed preferred counsel, written business plans, policies and guidelines, developed training tools, been trained, conducted video conferences, web conferences, and set up e-Rooms and databases. We know how to make spreadsheets, presentations, use graphics, and pie charts. We belong to associations, go to seminars, get CLE, and have represented the Company in various capacities within its industry.

---

1. Total Quality Management is a set of management practices incorporated throughout an organization to ensure the organization consistently meets or exceeds customer expectations. Although it originated in Japan in the 1950s, it is widely associated with the principled teachings of Dr. W. Edwards Deming. *See* Free Management Library, A Complete Integrated Library for Nonprofits and For-Profits. Authenticity Consulting, LLC (1197-2008) at http://managementhelp.org/quality/tqm/tqm.htm

Given the potential for new initiatives, it is most important for corporate counsel to be ever mindful of the client's best interests. The client is not the chief executive officer, the shareholders or the business executives of the most profitable divisions. Rather, the client is the corporation—the intangible entity that exists to be profitable but must act in accordance with its by-laws and articles of incorporation. As in-house counsel, our legal and ethical duty is to keep the corporation's interests paramount. Practicing in a corporation means sometimes being in conflict with management, sometimes advising against the latest and most popular management program, and sometimes being the lone voice for reasoned and measured steps. It doesn't make you the most popular among the functions, but, hopefully, when it counts, you will be recognized as one of the most valuable members of the team. It is that learning—to be both a team player and a singular drummer—that is hardest to grasp.

I can remember during the interview process when the general counsel asked me if I had any concerns about working for a French corporation. Before becoming a lawyer, I had worked for a corporation, and the experience I had there had been great. So it never occurred to me that the emphasis of his question was on the word "French." I had never met a French person, I didn't speak French, and I had never been to Europe. A corporation was a corporation. To me, the fact that it was French made it all the more interesting and diverse, and that was a good thing.

Now, 21 years later, I think I understand the emphasis. There is a cultural difference for sure. But what made (and continues to make) it easier for me to prosper within the French corporate setting is that I have always had to deal with an uncertain environment—whether as an East Coast transplant in Iowa, a member of a distinct minority at Penn Law (about 10% of the incoming class in 1981 was African-American), or one of two women left in the class of 1981 at the law firm six years later (neither one of whom would be named partner). Indeed, I spent the first three years of elementary school as the only black kid in my grade. Like so many of my peers whom I would meet at later stages in life, I held many firsts as a fairly intelligent black kid growing up in the 1960s in a majority white population. So when it came to being American in a French corporation, I felt up to the task. What I wondered under my breath as I thought about his question was what it would be like to be one of five attorneys in a corporation that was about to grow exponentially. For the first time in my short career, I would be in the minority because I was a lawyer.

Once hired, I soon found out that rather than having to prove myself as a worthy employee, people counted me as an expert. I was the in-house litigation lawyer. People came to me for advice and assumed I knew what I was talking about. My boss was busy establishing a department, hiring other experts with whom I would eventually work hand-in-hand. There was no partners' committee; the legal department was headed by the general counsel and he had named an associate general counsel to run the department on a day-to-day basis. Meanwhile, the general counsel worked at the direction of our French parent to grow the company in the US. The associate general counsel—my immediate boss—was my contact and provided the guidance and oversight I needed. Amazingly, although we were in a corporation, there was little bureaucracy the first few years. We were establishing ourselves and assembling the acquisition assets amassed from the frenetic growth spurt lasting just about three years.

Those first few years went by in record speed. I traveled about 25% of the time. Literally, I was on the road at least one week out of each month. Sometimes those 5 travel days were split over two or even 3 weeks. I became a frequent flyer and went through at least three garment bags and a multitude of leather brief cases. I learned the ins and outs of air travel; learned how to use calling cards before there were cell phones; experimented with driving myself to the airport; tried long-term parking, off-site parking, valet parking, and, ultimately, selected a reliable car service.

I've traveled to places as varied as Paris, France and Butte, Montana. Frankly, between the two, I was probably more out of place in my own country. It's amazing that there are still many places, court rooms and judges' chambers that have not had the "pleasure" of hosting ethnically diverse counsel. Although it was admittedly almost two decades ago, I still remember in 1989 walking into one of two major restaurants in Butte and having everyone in the place stop talking and look directly at our party. I thought the stares were for us all as obvious visitors, but then one of my hosts told us that there weren't any black people in Butte or its surrounding towns. The stares were for me—the only woman and the only African-American in the group. Several years later in the same state, I had a federal judge tell me to my face that he once saw a black guy at a football game. I think he was trying to make me feel comfortable. Still, I saw the Big Sky and marveled at how beautiful our country is—warts and all.

My work has been just as varied. Over the years, my specialty became tort liability defense. We had products liability claims, class action litigation following plant upsets, environmental releases resulting in mass shelters and evacuations, and severe personal injury claims arising from these incidents. We had an affiliate involved in the blood products field, and, early on, we learned about a terrible disease that was being passed to hemophiliacs through blood transfusions—it was the beginning of AIDS litigation. Another affiliate was the major defendant in litigation arising from an incident involving watermelon allegedly poisoned by pesticide-contaminated irrigation waters. A recall of watermelon was instituted throughout California over the weekend celebrating July 4th, which I soon learned was the highest watermelon sales period of the year. The commercial claims and personal injury claims were in the millions. I've managed numerous wrongful death cases and won two class action cases involving thousands of plaintiffs. I have counseled a group of engineers in France who were defending claims of defective technology arising from an asset sale to a company in India. I've served as a liaison in litigation where we have had layers of lawyers—Paris counsel, New York counsel, state counsel, and local county counsel. Some of my most interesting and challenging cases are still pending. And, like most litigators, I can say that my portfolio is never boring. There's always some new product, some new claim, or some new twist on an old law that keeps the practice fresh.

In the last several years, my work has focused more on commercial litigation. Interestingly, I find that the business people are more passionate about these cases than they are about multiple-plaintiff personal injury litigation. It's not that they are dispassionate about human injury; it's that they are closest to what they do day in and day out. And, when the issues between competitors become heated or when the company is at odds with an asset seller or purchaser in a multi-million dollar deal, it reflects directly on management's style, choices and decisions.

It is in these situations that in-house counsel must excel. We need to understand the sensitive business issues, identify the legal ramifications and select and educate outside counsel once litigation is either contemplated or instituted. Litigators are not business counsel; and good litigators realize that their business counsel colleagues are necessary partners. The same conclusion will be made by good business counsel. I have managed to develop solid relationships with my colleagues in the Legal Services group, and I must say that my experience over the years has resulted in a high level of respect among the business leaders themselves.

It was not always so. I do, however, remember when the tides began to turn. It was in my third or fourth year. The company had completed a worldwide acquisition of a chemical company that was international in scope. One of its subsidiaries owned a manufacturing facility that had a history of plant upsets and environmental releases. It had been involved in significant litigation, including the unsuccessful appeal of a punitive damages award. Less than a year after our acquisition, the same plant had an unexpected release of chemicals in the middle of the night. The next day, six separate putative class action lawsuits were filed. We knew we were going to have to resolve the consolidated cases short of trial. The president of our company at the time was adamant that we had to "win."[2] He called me into his office to tell me that he had done his own research and found that there were only six reported cases in the country where punitive damages actually had been awarded. I looked him straight in the eye and told him that I didn't know where he'd done his research or gotten the numbers but that, assuming the numbers were correct, it was still the case that one of the six was the verdict involving our newly acquired subsidiary. He had no response.

We ultimately resolved that lawsuit and, after another such incident less than a year later, the plant was closed. Some accused the legal department of trying to run the plant, and I found out how the game of company politics was played. That was probably the most stressful time in my career. Still, I grew tremendously. The next president of the company, who had successfully run one of our more profitable enterprises, suggested that I become a plant manager. I found out later that his suggestion was a serious compliment inasmuch as plant managers in chemical companies are basically the equivalent of business directors. They are the point persons on every front—operations, maintenance, finance, human resources, engineering and health and safety. Their desk is where the buck literally stops on a daily basis, well before it reaches corporate headquarters. Of course, I was not really qualified to be a plant manager, but this President believed I had the basic talent to make the transition. I've always remembered that suggestion; it was the one thing that made me realize that I really wanted to be a lawyer—even though it had never been my original dream.

When I accepted my position as litigation attorney, I imagined that I would be at that company for 3–5 years and move on to a corporate setting a little closer to home. Based on my own assessments of corporate life, I

---

2. Since this encounter, I have begun my discussions with business representatives facing new litigation with the definition of success. What does winning the dispute mean? Together, we determine the best outcome for the Company and map our strategy to that goal. This way, when we talk about winning, we're speaking the same language. I believe that this one practice is a key factor in my successful performance over the years.

thought that working for a pharmaceutical company might be as challenging and offer better job security at the same time. At the time, I lived within ten minutes of three major pharmaceutical companies. Twenty-one years later and still commuting an hour both to and from work, the company has changed, but our legal team has remained fairly intact. Some of the original company's assets were spun off at the end of 1997, and most of the Legal Department went with a newly created smaller and more focused specialty chemicals manufacturer. We've had our challenges, but we've managed to retain our core. The pharmaceutical industry is still more profitable, but it's had its ups and downs as well. Mergers, acquisitions, and divestitures have changed all of the companies whose affiliations I once secretly coveted.

Working for a corporation allows you the opportunity to work with lawyers all over the country and—when it comes to global companies such as mine—all over the world. This is probably one of the biggest differences on a day-to-day basis about my practice in-house when compared to practicing at a law firm. I have cases across the country, and I also assist in litigation involving our foreign affiliates. As a result, I get to work with all kinds of lawyers, with all kinds of talent. Over the years, I've made many acquaintances and I've also made some life-long friends. My focus is not on New Jersey when I'm at work; in fact, I've had very few litigation matters in this state. The differences among the states and even the distinctions in the federal courts were, at first, surprising. But, in the end, those distinctions brought back the sage lesson of law school that had taken so long to sink in—it really does depend.

Similarly, the people within the company with whom I interact outside the Legal Services group have equally diverse responsibilities. Plant managers, toxicologists, marketing managers, human resource professionals, business directors, accountants, tax professionals—the list of in-house contacts and client representatives goes on and on. My job is to explain the legal system, make sense out of seemingly baseless claims, bring reason to disputes among business partners, and teach lessons learned once the fires are extinguished.

In addition to pure legal work, I am also responsible for a good deal of administrative tasks. I am the initial contact with the outside auditors and I coordinate reporting tools for our material litigation and that of our affiliates and parent. I also supervise another lawyer and two non-exempt employees—a paralegal and a legal assistant. Making time to understand their individual challenges and ensure their development and performance are key to good management. It is also just easy to be interested in those people with whom you spend such a large amount of your time on a daily basis.

Probably one of the most valuable consequences of my career as a corporate lawyer is the time it has allowed me for family and other social commitments. I work hard every day, and now that we are more prone to telecommuting, my computer is online at night and all weekend. I respond to email from Paris, Beijing, Sao Paolo, Lyons, New York, Texas and wherever else things are moving on fast track. But even before the advent of telecommuting, I didn't go into the physical office on the weekend. Nor do I log hours for the sake of billing. It's not expected; we are encouraged to spend time with family and make contributions to society outside the workplace.

My only child was born after several traumatic miscarriages. Her birth became a celebration for all who worked with me. Now, 15 years later, I can honestly say that my daughter has an extended family among my colleagues. We've all shared in each other's joys, heartbreaks, trials and celebrations. Some of our team has left for other opportunities, others have been downsized (an unfortunate term from "corporate speak"), and two of our team members have passed away. We've watched children grow up, marry, and have their own children; we've said good-bye to parents; we've lived through 9/11; we've gone on retreats both stateside and abroad; we've climbed rocky cliffs, been on scavenger hunts, and maneuvered canoes in the Mediterranean all in the name of team building.

I've become a volunteer in my spare time, working for my church, for social organizations, and for charities. I've been honored by my company and placed in various leadership roles throughout my career. I've advanced in position and salary, been given long term-incentives, and included among the top managers in the company. My husband of 24 years is a great support; as is my faith. My hope is that I can inspire my daughter to choose a career that is as challenging and rewarding as mine has been. I want her to dream and think big, but I also want her to be courageous enough to make choices that she never envisioned.

View from the Bench

18

By Hon. Gene E. K. Pratter

A JUDGE OUGHT NOT have trouble writing about "the view from the bench." After all, expressing "views" is an integral part of our job. Much of a judge's "view" is, literally, from the bench. We see and hear lawyers, litigants, jurors, witnesses, victims, probation officers, case agents, security officers, supporters, reporters, observers, and countless others. Writing figures prominently in a judge's efforts to communicate results and reasoning. Generally, our goal is to impart honest judgments and useful guidance as clearly and concisely as circumstances warrant and permit.

Therefore, it is a pleasure to contribute to the new edition of The Woman Advocate. I will resist listing platitudes or, even worse, admonishing the reader to do as I say, not as I did. The challenge is to choose from among a judge's many vantage points that which best serves as the bully pulpit. Should I recount prior judicial trailblazers' travels and travails or describe my decidedly less rutted path? Should I look into the well of the courtroom to describe the poignant, perfect, or painful performances of the professionals I see? Or is the best view the one ahead to predict how women lawyers and jurists will fare in the future? These are all ripe opinion topics.

One part of my job is to issue opinions. Of course, "opinion" is something of a misnomer for a judge's work product. Strictly speaking, a judge is not free to impose her or his personal opinion on the cases awaiting resolution. A judge who has never issued a ruling she or he personally wished could have been different may not be performing the job correctly or taking it seriously. Because this publication deserves the same respect for objectivity, accuracy, and potential usefulness as does opinion writing, I will make the earnest effort to discharge my duty here by offering a few thoughts and actual observations from the bench I am honored to occupy.

GETTING TO THE BENCH

There is no sure-fire formula or recipe for becoming a judge; no GPS can be programmed to arrive at this professional destination. As I briefly critique my own journey, please forgive my presumptuousness in paraphrasing George Washington's assessment that geography and "an epoch when the rights of mankind were better understood and more clearly defined" were largely responsible for the success of the American Revolution. G. Washington, Circular to the States, June 8, 1783. While I embrace Ralph Waldo Emerson's observation that "[t]he world makes way for the [wo]man who knows where [s]he is going," I credit my attaining a federal judgeship to being in the right place, with the right-enough credentials, at the right time, and encouraged by the right people. In addition, I had the strong and strategic support of my family, and the good fortune, after 30 years of private practice, to withstand the pay cut if a federal judgeship came my way. Thus prepared, I was able to remain alert to opportunity if it arose.

It is a harder and more frustrating journey for some than it is for others. Many capable candidates are derailed. If I had had to mount a campaign to win a judicial election, I never would have donned a robe, but others might relish that thrill. The launch pad to a judgeship may be academia. Some judges come from the ranks of prosecutors or the criminal defense bar; others, as did I, came from private civil litigation practice. Many federal judges already enjoyed successful tenures in state court.

People often ask whether it is harder for a woman to become a judge than for a man to do so. My personal response sometimes causes raised eyebrows, jaw clenching, or polite grumbling. Frankly, it is something of a roll of the dice for both sexes. In the last few years, and perhaps for some years into the future, it may prove easier for any given woman to become a judge than for any given man to achieve that goal. However, in my estimation it is hardest of all for a woman to become a judge (or a leader of a law firm, for that matter) if she allows even a justified chip on her shoulder to become a heavy boulder that slows her down and holds her back. At least the chip never, ever helps her reach her goal. Does that mean women have to work harder? In my view, that's a "definite maybe."

I am a late-phase baby-boomer. About a third of my law school class were women. In our district, I now work with five other women judges, as well as five women magistrate judges and two women bankruptcy judges; our Court of Appeals has four women members. Most of these judges were here before me. I do not claim trailblazer status. Rather, I see myself and my female contemporaries as part of a bridge generation. Women who began their professional trek before 1970 carved remarkable and inspiring trails, but we who followed them are by no means out of the woods.

One amusing personal experience might put the trail's true distance in some perspective. Students of the history of women lawyers recognize Belva Lockwood as the woman first responsible for opening up the federal courts to women lawyers and as the first woman to argue before the United States Supreme Court. In 1874, when she tried to plead a case before the U.S. Court of Claims, Judge Charles Drake silenced the courtroom (and Belva), looked her over, then refused to allow her to proceed, declaring as if it was a key precedential ruling: "Mistress Lockwood, you are a woman." Some 133 years later, I discovered I shared an experience, albeit far less dramatic, with "Mistress Lockwood." Mine was thanks to no less an oracle than *The New York Times*, reporting on an opinion I had issued in a case that garnered some national attention. In the article, the reporter used a masculine pronoun to refer to me and my ruling. When a correction was published, the paper excused the mistaken reference to the presiding judge's gender as "an editing error" and proclaimed authoritatively: "Gene E. K. Pratter is a woman." Good to know, thank you very much. Though I can chuckle at the declarative on my account, I am certain that, in her case, Belva Lockwood could only silently fume and search for a male co-counsel to present the winning argument she had crafted.

Mail routinely comes to me addressed to "Hon. Eugene Pratter," even from lawyers who have appeared already before me. I also receive law clerk applications inquiring when "he" will be conducting interviews; and, inevitably, I get invitations to have my wife sign up for the garden tour while I attend judicial conferences on the latest sentencing statistics. Perhaps more blame belongs to my parents than to a presumed, inevitably "sexist," social order. However, there is a chance that how I spell my name merely gives easy vent to latent, hopefully benign, expectations that jurists are more likely to be men. Thus, however notable the gains made by women aspiring to the bench are, the parity that would negate those expectations has not been attained.

For fans of demonstrative exhibits, plotting data about women judges makes the results look dramatic. Some will say the statistics are disappointing; others will say they are impressive—or at least encouraging; still others may say they are alarming, and leave it enigmatically at that. As with so many matters, our perspective tends to dictate the adjectives and adverbs we use. In any case, the documented facts merit mention.

The first woman federal judge, Florence Ellinwood Allen, joined the Sixth Circuit Court of Appeals in 1934. She remained the sole female federal judge for 15 years. Forty-one years later, in 1975, when I graduated from the University of Pennsylvania Law School, there were six female federal judges nationwide. By 2004, when I was sworn in as a federal judge, the national number had increased to 226, due in large measure to the expanded opportunities for women when Congress authorized 152 new judgeships during Jimmy Carter's presidency. It also helped that, during that time-frame, the ABA amended its judicial candidacy evaluation criteria to take into account certain differences in women's career patterns, with the result that the ABA's prior ratings disparity between women and men shrank. In 2005, women made up 17.4% of all Article III judges. As this essay is being written at the start of 2009, the federal courts' Administrative Office counts 243 women federal judges.

Nonetheless, as Chief Judge Judith Kaye retires after 25 highly regarded years on the New York Court of Appeals on which she was the first woman to serve, to her chagrin (at least as reported by *The New York Times* on Dec. 28, 2008), no women are among the seven replacement candidates. This may be especially surprising given that, while women have gained in numbers on the federal bench, female representation on state courts has increased even more notably. Although no one keeps national statistics on the number of women state judges, the best estimates suggest that there are approximately 25,000 law-trained judges nationwide, and roughly 20% are women. By 2005, there were 17 women serving as state chief justices. Data from some states and big cities shows that many judicial opportunities exist for women. For example, about 30% of the judges in Massachusetts are women; approximately 27% of the Florida state court judges are women; about a third of the judges in Chicago's circuit court are women; and, as of 2009, women will be president judges of all three of Philadelphia's divisional courts. The largest numbers emanate from urban areas, where many women serve in lower courts of limited jurisdiction, such as family and juvenile courts. In the words of Judge Leslie Alden of Virginia, women judges are visible at the top and concentrated at the bottom. They are rare in rural communities. Reportedly, women have harder times when they must raise war-chests to pay for runs for judicial office, but they make great strides in jurisdictions that use merit selection or other appointment processes. The National Association of Women Judges was established in 1979 to address the isolation felt by the mere handful of women judges, and, now, the NAWJ serves as a resource for the growing ranks of women judges and enhances the opportunities for more women to join them.

My experiences with the confirmation process and arrival at the courthouse bear little resemblance to Judge Allen's experiences seven decades earlier. Allen's nomination predated the advent of the ABA evaluative role, but the FBI gathered opinions from members of the bar and bench who considered "her appointment as lamentable, laughable, disastrous and would make the [Sixth] Circuit Court appear ridiculous and would lower the high traditions of that bench. Many members admit[ted] a natural prejudice against women in the judiciary, particularly Federal, as being naturally unqualified." Memorandum for the Director of the Federal Bureau of Investigation by F. A. Tamm (2/15/39). Following her investiture, Judge Allen was subjected to overt sex discrimination by some of her judicial colleagues:

To say that she received a very cool reception from her new colleagues is a gross understatement. In addition to one judge who, it is reported, was so upset at the idea of a female colleague that he literally took to his bed for several days, three of the remaining five judges refused to offer her congratulations. Id.

Judge Allen was even excluded from joining her colleagues at lunch because they dined at an all-male club in Cincinnati.

My experience was certainly different. As far as I know, practitioners questioned about my possible selection expressed no shock or dismay about a woman with litigation and professional responsibility background filling an opening on a district court bench that already had five women. All of my new colleagues—female and male alike—were immediately, and continue to be, welcoming and ready to be helpful without presuming to tell me how to do my job. Our court's mix of independence and collegiality is authentic, lively, mutually respectful, refreshing, and without guile. Our Eastern District of Pennsylvania judges genuinely appreciate the arrival and participation of new judges. (In 1978, when our district's first woman judge, Norma L. Shapiro, arrived, apparently things were different. Eventually, Judge Shapiro won over even the hard-core doubters at the bar and on the bench with her intelligence, diligence, generosity, and courteous tenacity to be held in high regard by all, smoothing the way for the rest of us in the process.) I'm told that the conversation in our judges' lunchroom (co-ed, of course) changed somewhat with the arrival of women judges—especially now that we number a half dozen women. Of course, it helps that most of the judges (without regard to gender) tend to be versatile and accommodating conversationalists. While the exciting particulars of informal judicial discourse must remain confidential, I do not think it would be a violation of black-robe trust to say that even if Monday noon-time conversation starts with an animated recap of the weekend's sports events, it soon ventures into a host of other topics, often led by the women to include the day's headlines, worthwhile movies and books, kids, pets, trips, cars, bargains, statutory gaps, and, of course, new opinions coming from the Court of Appeals. Regretfully, we have been singularly unsuccessful with the luncheon menu, but that has more to do with the mysteries of bureaucracy than the mysteries of gender. In this lunchroom ritual, our court is much the same as my former law firm where the kick-offs for the weekly partners' lunches were lively expressions of the lawyers' self-proclaimed expertise with Monday-morning sports strategy, second-guessing, and statistics. It seems it never matters what the season is or what the athletic experts' day jobs are.

I do know I was exceedingly fortunate as an associate and partner in a remarkable law firm, and I am grateful that I was able to take advantage of the opportunities the firm and the Bar provided. I owe thanks to a great many talented people who encouraged me without regard to their gender or mine. But even if I was enjoying my work and my colleagues too much to notice some slight caused by gender bias, the lesson I take—and, hence, the lesson I offer—from my own law firm experience, and those of successful women whose careers seem to soar, is this: A work environment that is a meritocracy where hard work is both expected and rewarded, and where there is an honorable pursuit of excellence without bias, prejudice or discrimination is a priceless platform on which to build a worthwhile career. It is the level playing field we all seek. As crucial as personal drive and goal-setting is to the achievement of success, a fundamentally fair and discrimination-free professional environment can make an enormous difference.

WORKING FROM THE BENCH

My good fortune continues in terms of my work environment on the district court. Of course, while we speak metaphorically about "taking the bench" or being "on the bench," most of a trial court judge's work is in a considerably less public setting. A federal district court judge spends far more time in chambers reviewing the steady stream of incoming motions and briefs, researching diverse issues hidden in esoteric statutes or created from whole cloth by a creative lawyer's mind, and often discussing those issues with law clerks in anticipation of oral arguments and trials. We work on drafting and editing opinions and orders, attempt to decipher novel and sometimes mysterious submissions from *pro se* litigants (and from some lawyers), and re-routing correspondence from criminal defendants who are awaiting trial, anticipating sentencing, looking for new counsel, crafting their appeal from prison brief banks, requesting re-designation to a preferred prison, or some other problem a prisoner presents to the court. We have law clerks and interns to mentor, and court and bar committees to convene. We also perform community outreach functions by presiding over naturalization ceremonies for new citizens, teaching civics classes to middle and high school students, coaching mock trial teams, participating in Inns of Court, presenting CLE courses, and hosting visiting jurists from around the globe, to name just a few extra-curricular activities. These do not line up along gender lines. Each judge has his or her strengths and preferences, as well as those tasks that inevitably hide at the bottom of the pile. Some of the male judges are the most nurturing of their clerks and the quickest to sign up to teach teenagers; some women judges shine when the subject is technology.

Women judges are frequently asked if women judges "see" things—or decide cases—differently from their male counterparts. Retired Supreme Court Justice Sandra Day O'Connor puts it this way:

> I am often asked whether women judges speak with a different voice. This is a question that generates widely differing responses. Undaunted by the troubling history of their view, many writers have suggested that women practice law differently than men.

Sandra Day O'Connor, The Majesty of the Law, 190 (2009).

Justice O'Connor expresses surprise at any suggestion that gender differences lead to judicial differences, and she appears to bristle at the notion that her opinions "differ in a peculiarly feminine way from those of [her] colleagues." Id. at 191. Rather, Justice O'Connor concludes: "There is simply no empirical evidence that gender differences lead to discernable differences in rendering judgments." Id.

Justice O'Connor quotes Justice Ruth Bader Ginsburg to the same effect about gender-based "voices" from a 1994 address:

> When asked about such things I usually abstain. Generalizations about the way women and men are . . . cannot guide me reliably in making decisions . . . At least in the law, I have found no natural superiority or deficiency in either sex. I was a law teacher until I became a judge. In class or in grading papers . . . and now in reading briefs and listening to arguments in court . . . I have detected no reliable indicator of distinctly male or surely female thinking—or even penmanship.

Id. at 192.

Recently, I served on a panel with Justice Ginsburg at the National Constitution Center, and the moderator, a female broadcast journalist, put the same question to us. After acknowledging that any jurist from the ranks of some minority group may well exhibit greater sensitivity to injustices visited upon others, and observing that she and Justice O'Connor may have had a greater tendency to "stick to the arguments" than their male colleagues, Justice Ginsburg answered the question by quoting Justice Jeanne Coyne, formerly of the Minnesota Supreme Court, who has said what most judges seem to believe: "a wise old man and a wise old woman [will] reach the same conclusion." Remarks of Ruth Bader Ginsburg, The Peter Jennings Project For Journalists and The Constitution: Women and the Law, March 8, 2008, quoting from D. Margolick, "Women's Milestone: Majority on Minnesota Court," New York Times, Feb. 22, 1991.

I certainly do not disagree with the Justices. Rulings by women judges shake out the same way as those by male judges, although there is some empirical data that men judges may be slightly more lenient in sentencing women defendants than women judges are. It may be that women judges, simply by virtue of their life experiences or their relatively shorter tenure in practice or on the bench, initially or stylistically may approach litigants or lawyers differently than do male judges. Maybe it is something else. I have said more than once—and only partially in jest—that parenthood and running a household are useful experiences for any busy trial judge to call upon. (What better way is there to develop those "eyes in the back of your head," or to learn to tell at a glance who threw the first verbal punch, or to know when there is simply no choice but to "multi-task"?) But to deny that both men and women have the innate potential to develop those skills would be to fall prey to the very stereotypes we profess to abhor. In any case, on the ultimate question—do men and women judges ultimately judge differently—I would bet confidently that the gender of the judge could not be ascertained from the gender-blind reading of an opinion or from the outcome of a case.

I know there are anecdotal challenges to this thesis. Periodically, professional publications ask lawyers to rate judges' relative courtesy to lawyers and litigants. Law blogs are bloated by such efforts. I am unaware of any such survey in or around our region, but one from the far west reported that practicing lawyers ranked female judges as significantly less courteous than their male counterparts. Apparently, two-thirds of the respondents were men. We all know that reading surveys is a practiced art, and we probably all learned enough in Psych 101 to figure that attorneys and litigants likely will favor a judge similar to themselves, whether in age, ethnic make up or gender. Then again, this reported disparity may arise simply from the fact that, when a male judge acts sternly or impatiently, he is regarded as firm or strict, whereas a woman who conducts herself the same way is labeled as strident, obnoxious—even, sad to say, in our region—to learn of courtroom conduct where male attorneys try to push around relatively new female judges by talking over them, arguing back with contemptuous "with all due respect, Your Honor" lines thrown in to offset their rudeness, and basically just refusing to accept the judge's rulings as final. To be fair, I cannot determine with confidence whether the behavioral difference is in the gender of the judge or in the gender of the advocate. However, I surely doubt the same would ever occur if the genders were reversed all around.

In spite of periodic anomalous behavior, however, there is reason to be optimistic. New generations of male attorneys whose mothers may have practiced law, who went to law schools with equal numbers of men and women and had female professors, and whose wives are lawyers or whose daughters aspire to be lawyers, will be less affected by the gender of the judge and more open to criticism and authority coming from a female on the bench. Women judges, too, will continue to develop their own judicial personae which presumably will lead to beneficial behavior modification for all concerned.

When I ask my colleagues if they see themselves as "male" judges or "female" judges, the responses are uniformly no, they do not, at least not in any fundamental way. One colleague mentioned, however, that he recently was told by a woman lawyer who had previously clerked for him about an experience she had had in my courtroom that might highlight judicial gender differences. I had arranged to have coffee service for all brought in to the courtroom where I was holding a case status conference one morning for about 40 lawyers, most from out of town. The former clerk told her former boss that she doubted that a male judge would have ordered the coffee for the conference. In truth, I cannot say whether my chromosomes made me do it, but I do know I really like my morning coffee, and there was no reason not to share.

Perhaps we develop habits (quirks, some would say) that have their roots in our gender. For example, my being a woman may explain why I routinely include a reference to the influence of the "Founding Mothers" during my basic welcoming remarks to incoming jury panels as I explain the constitutional origins of the jury system. Perhaps, too, my gender prompts me to admonish criminal defendants to turn to face their mothers or grandmothers who come to court to ask for leniency at sentencing and apologize to them for the heartache caused by the defendants' conduct. One of my male colleagues leaves the bench and stands at a lectern in the well of the court to present lengthy jury instructions at the end of each case. That could be agony in high heels. None of this, of course, goes to the heart of judging.

So, what do I see when I look at my fellow judges and our predecessors? Though they rarely speak in these terms, judges know they may be called upon to show great courage to decide cases based upon the law without regard to the social or political consequences that might result, and certainly without regard to their own gender. Sadly, sometimes unexpectedly harrowing risks follow the every day fare of cases, such as occurred with the death of the Fulton County judge killed by an escaping defendant or the slaying of a Chicago federal judge's husband and mother by an unbalanced and disgruntled civil litigant. Such risks notwithstanding, judges remain committed to the tasks of administering justice in small matters as well as matters of grave constitutional and international significance. Gender has nothing to do with it.

Judges are servants to the public, sometimes traveling to remote regions of the world to teach legal principles, assist in drafting constitutions, implementing court systems, piloting and staffing education programs for teens, and assisting *pro bono* projects. Thanks mainly to bar associations, judges' service is often recognized. Women judges are more and more frequently receiving the profession's highest accolades alongside their male counterparts. The John Marshall Award recently was earned by Judge Deanell Tacha for her lifetime of service. New York's Judith Kaye was honored as a tireless reformer for juries and children. Col. Linda Strite Murname received the 2008 Margaret Brent Women Lawyers Achievement Award for her service as an Air Force attorney and judge assigned variously during her career to Japan, Germany, Latvia, Iraq, Rwanda, as well as being a former prosecutor and Executive Director of the Kentucky Commission on Human Rights, and, now, Senior Legal Officer at the International Criminal Tribunal for the former Yugoslavia.

Throughout the country, local bar associations and community organizations are generous with public recognition and praise of judges, all of which the jurists themselves certainly appreciate. In particular, I would be remiss if I did not applaud the efforts of the ABA and other professional groups to urge Congress to rectify the overdue and merited restoration of judges' salary levels. These efforts are appreciated by all judges, and we look forward to their eventual success. Most often, however, judges' service, by both men and women, goes unrecognized, and, by and large, that is fine with the judges. In the main, they are not in it for the plaques or platitudes.

IMPROVING THE VIEW

Even an active "big city" litigator is likely to get an unexpected eye-full and ear-full upon becoming a judge. Most—but not all—of the professional performances I have seen have been gratifying.

As a career civil litigator, I had had no meaningful experience with the criminal side of the docket that makes up so much of a federal judge's work. The prosecutors and criminal defense bar routinely perform at impressively high levels. Women make up a large portion of both. They, like their male counterparts, rarely fail to demonstrate their respect for the Court, their clients, their opponents, firm leaders who ponder the proper professional development—more so than their civil-side colleagues—recognize that their

cause is far better served by keeping their powder dry for the truly determi-
native issues and presenting to the Court only those matters, those witnesses
and those exhibits that really count. Due no doubt to the frequency with
which they appear in court, these lawyers have an infinitely better grasp of
the art of questioning witnesses and using the Federal Rules of Evidence.
They also have a more thorough understanding of, and respect for, the individual judge's preferences and practices. At least in my experience, they are
far less inclined to try informally to contact the Court in order to seek accommodations for their own personal non-dire scheduling issues or to ask the
Court or Chambers' staff how to frame an issue or argument without first
checking the rules themselves.

I frequently suggest to private law of young litigators that an invaluable
and economical training tool for young civil litigators that is often overlooked would be to have them sit in the back of a federal courtroom and simply watch a few, short criminal trials. One of the many "visuals" to experience on such a field trip is something I am seeing more and more frequently,
namely, proceedings where the prosecutor, the primary law enforcement case
agent, the defense counsel, the probation officer, and, yes, the defendant are
all women. It happens frequently enough these days as to go unnoticed as
often as not.

The criminal cases also serve to bring to mind the many other professionals who make the judicial and justice system work: The United States
Probation Office and the Pre-Trial Services Office, the U.S. Marshals Office,
the court security officers, the FBI, the DEA and other law enforcement
agencies, and, of course, our Clerk's Office. Our Circuit Executive is a
woman. Women perform at all levels with impressive results. I mention this
not only to express some much-deserved credit to these professionals, but
also to suggest some additional vocational opportunities available for women
with law and other professional degrees.

I will skip the familiar admonitions about comporting and presenting
oneself at all times "like a professional," of never compromising on matters
of ethics and honor, of treating everyone with courtesy and civility, and of
being prepared and punctual. I eschew a fuller discussion of these characteristics not because they are unimportant, or because I doubt their high value,
but rather because they are so fundamental that anyone who has picked up
this publication already knows of their importance and does not need to be
told again. Instead, I offer a few other comments that may be a bit out of the
mainstream of advice from judges.

First, do not assume that in court—or, for that matter, in life—being a woman is always a disadvantage to be overcome. I am not the first woman judge to say this. Sometimes being a female will create the opportunity to seize the dynamic favoring the perceived underdog. Other times, it can offer an element of surprise or sympathy. Seeing, as I do, so many juries made up of a majority of women, I often hear them say after a trial has concluded how they took personal pleasure in the abilities demonstrated by a women advocate or, on the other hand, felt more personal discomfort in one who performed poorly. But this can be a double-edged sword, and the delicate balance is to recognize what we are without over-using what we are. Women lawyers—like women judges—often do need to be tough, but that toughness must have a purpose. Being a woman lawyer certainly will not necessarily cause a verdict to be one way or the other, but it can affect how the professional's performance is perceived, and it can help deliver the client's message.

Speaking of "the message," permit me a comment or two about marketing. My remarks on this subject may sound like outright apostasy. Nonetheless, I long have been puzzled by the efforts and resources devoted to create and dispatch a law firm marketing machine to tout someone as a "great lawyer." Frankly, if you want to be known as a great lawyer, be one. Put a slightly different way, I have yet to hear any judge or jury refer to a winning argument or a withering cross-examination presented by a marketing department; I have not read a single stellar brief written by a press person; and no marketing personnel have yet stepped up to the lectern to answer my questions during oral argument. (As for non-litigators, as far as I know, no one from marketing ever negotiates or documents an iron-clad contract or structures a deal to meet a new tax regulation, either.) None of this is to say that, in the highly competitive world lawyers now inhabit, there is not some appropriate supporting role for marketing. However, no amount of marketing will mask or make up for a failure to do the hard work of crafting the tailored—not "commoditized"—professional products clients deserve. For what it may be worth, someone recently reminded me that the difference between "try" and "triumph" is a little "umph."

The reference to hard work leads me to my final point. Few professional publications hit our desks without some article about "life-work balance." Most women litigators (and, to be fair, many of their male counterparts) are probably too busy to read the articles; besides, we surely know what the articles say. But do make time to skim them, if only to glean even a single idea or trick that might make your personal situation even temporarily better or more manageable. I have read, with some considerable distress, of recent studies that report documented higher levels of stress for women lawyers, leading to greater frustrations and more permanent departures from the profession. Discuss these issues without rancor with other women professionals. A recent study at UCLA documents that women professionals who "tend and befriend" other women have less stress.

It behooves us all to figure out ways to find personal and professional satisfaction. For women litigators, there surely is no single answer; everyone has to undertake her own search. The search for satisfaction starts with oneself. A person who is realistically self-confident will demonstrate that to her clients, her opponents and the court. The comfortably confident women litigators are the ones who realize that it is not who you are that holds you back; it is who you think you are.

Of course, the best brand of self-confidence comes from mastering the matter at hand. It also comes from being essentially happy with your own lot in life. I have yet to see a high-octane lawyer who can perform at reliably high levels for a sustained period if her or his personal life is in long-term disarray. If this means having to periodically set different priorities, so be it, as long as you do not too quickly completely abandon or sacrifice one part of your life for another—most often accommodations can and should be made. I also strongly encourage women lawyers who have families to share some of their work experiences with their families. You will find they are interested to hear about your work. You will make them proud of you. Knowing something about what you do and why you do it may lead them to cut you a little slack when you need it in the middle of trial.

Professional satisfaction for women litigators often means including extra-curricular activities in their lives—usually some combination of personal hobbies or interests with sustained professional volunteer activities. The smart litigator soon realizes that being active in the community produces important by-products, by making her better attuned to judges, juries, and witnesses, not to mention opening up avenues to new clients and new friends. Obviously, it matters less what the extra-curricular activities are than sticking with them and following through.

My concluding comment is more of an invitation to women litigators to take appropriate opportunities to share with judges the view of the bench that you have. How can we perform our jobs up to the highest traditions and expectations of the public and our shared profession? Let us hear from you.

Life in a Public Interest Organization

19

By Margaret Lambe Jurow

Dᴜʀɪɴɢ ᴍʏ ᴄʜɪʟᴅʜᴏᴏᴅ, I attended Catholic school, and public service was a constant theme at school and at home. Not as in, "you should work for the ACLU," but rather as, "take care of widows and orphans, clothe the naked, house the homeless, feed the hungry."

At Catholic school, in those days, we were encouraged to think not only of what we wanted to do for a living, but about what was our vocation. While some of that encouragement was surely in the hope that some of us would join a religious community, there was also a genuine attempt to focus each of us on our purpose in life beyond our own selves. Although they didn't attend college themselves, my parents and grandparents valued education highly but also expected that our education would be used to serve both our personal needs and those of the community. Both my brothers and my sister are col-lege-educated and work in government or public service.

Now, an adult with two grown sons, I consider the concept of being a member of the legal profession in much the same way I consider my vocation as wife, mother, sister, daughter, and community member. My profession is not just my job or career, but a fully integrated aspect of how I spend my time and talents with the community at large.

When I attended college, I did not have a firm idea of what I would do for a living, and my family was not able to provide much guidance. I strug-gled with meshing my educational interests with the need to support myself. I held a variety of jobs during college, including one at LeBoeuf Lamb Leiby & McCrae, which, at that time, had a well respected partner named Kimba Lovejoy. I worked at the petty cash window and Ms. Lovejoy wouldn't have known me from Eve but, seeing her function at that prestigious law firm, in-spired this young college student. Like many first generation college stu-dents, the legal profession, like the medical profession and the engineering profession, seemed accessible and held some concrete appeal to me.

In 1981, I was accepted to Hunter College's Inaugural Class of Revson Public Service Scholars. The program was a Godsend to me. It included a generous stipend and an internship with a "high level" person in government. My internship was with Ross Sandler, Mayor Koch's Transportation Director. Through this internship, I developed a deep appreciation for government and public service and the people who serve those institutions.

I continued working in government after I completed my internship. I married Steve Jurow, who was a deputy director of the Mayor's Transporta-tion Office—at the time office romances were not so politically incorrect as they seem to be today. Steve and I started a family soon after.

In 1985, part-time professional work was virtually unheard of, and it certainly was not available in the agency in which I was working. So, I decided it would be a good time to go back to school and, given my continued interest in serving the less-fortunate and drawing on my childhood ideas about vocation and profession, law school beckoned. I started at Brooklyn Law School when my oldest child was an infant. I chose Brooklyn Law School, because it had a part-time day program, which suited my needs at the time.

I was an unusual law student for the time. Although I was as young as the majority of students, I was closer in experience to the women who were embarking on second careers or who had already raised families. I'd had my first child the March before I started law school and had my second child the summer between my first and second years, so I didn't have much time for pondering the larger issues. I was just getting my work done. I did not have a concrete plan of where I was trying to go, although I presumed I would try for work in some form of public service at some point. Although I was expecting my second baby in July following my first year, I hoped to participate in Law Review. But my circumstances didn't square with the policies in force at the time. I clearly recall the young woman student editor of the Law Review telling me that I really shouldn't apply for Law Review if I couldn't spend July and August cite-checking articles. My second baby was due on July 13th, so, in May, when we had this conversation, it was pretty obvious what I would be doing during my summer vacation. This very bright student editor informed me that many of the students seeking to serve on Law Review would be foregoing their summer vacations to do cite-checking for their articles and that everyone had to set his or her own priorities. I informed her that giving birth, nursing an infant, and caring for a fifteen month-old was not a vacation and decided that Law Review—or at least that one—wasn't for me.

That summer, we moved from Brooklyn to New Jersey and my second child was born. I arranged to transfer from Brooklyn Law School to Rutgers Newark; however, I needed to complete some core courses before I could do so. So, just five weeks after my second son was born, I was back in school at Brooklyn Law School. I had the opportunity that term to study with Professor Elizabeth Schneider, who had been a women's rights litigator for many years, having been an innovator in the defense and representation of domestic violence survivors. Professor Schneider had been affiliated with the Women's Rights Litigation Clinic at Rutgers University in New Jersey, and she assisted in arranging for me to have a summer internship with Professor Nadine Taub of the Clinic the following summer, which ultimately proved a better preparation for my future career than Law Review. The Women's Rights Litigation Clinic, at an earlier time, had included now Supreme Court Justice Ruth Bader Ginsberg and had, for me, the right leaning and values and was affiliated with the Women's Rights Law Reporter—a different kind of law review—where I later served as a Notes and Comment Editor.

In between my third and fourth years, I felt I needed to work in a law office. Public interest law firms like Legal Services and the ACLU were extremely competitive, far more so than private practice, and I simply did not feel up to it at the time. I checked the career office and carefully looked for a private firm that might be a good fit. In the course of my research, I learned that the managing partner of then Podvey, Sachs, Meanor & Catenacci had, in 1969, represented a Roman Catholic nun in connection with her refusal to cooperate with a criminal investigation, claiming the priest-penitent privilege. I thought a firm like this might be a good fit for me value-wise, and I was right. One of the other partners there had been a public defender and the firm was generally populated with all-around good guys. I accepted a clerkship at Podvey for that summer and, upon my graduation the following year, became their first part-time commercial litigator, breaking some new ground on behalf of the women associates and, later, men and women partners, all of whom chose part-time work for a variety of reasons at different times of their lives. I stayed there for several years, made partner and served on the management committee.

Podvey was in 1989, and is now, a medium-size law firm by New Jersey standards, with an active litigation practice. I was thrown right into the mix, with the safety net of Bob Podvey as my mentor and supervisor, a firm-wide open-door policy, and a "we're all in this together" attitude toward each and every case the firm handled that has been unrivaled anywhere I have worked since (and they've all been great places). The training and experience I received as a young associate at the Podvey firm has served me well in each and every subsequent career move. My best friend is a physician, and I think of my early Podvey experience as the equivalent of a legal residency. I don't think I would be nearly as effective as a litigator today were it not for the training and experience I received from my partners and friends at the Podvey firm.

While I believe that direct moves from law school to public interest law are as competitive today as they were when I was in law school and that many very bright and talented attorneys go directly into public interest law from law school, I do not regret my path and recommend private practice to law students, especially those who want to try cases and directly represent individual clients.

During my time at Podvey, I did some pro-bono work with the approval of the firm. My mentor also continued to represent a women's religious community, a municipality, and some other non-profit organizations as part of his regular clientele, and I was privileged to be able to participate in some of that work. I also performed some charitable work in my personal life through my church and synagogue memberships (that's another chapter).

I also progressed in my career and began to carry a heavy trial schedule, which was difficult to reconcile with my family obligations. An opportunity arose for me to go work at the United States Department of Justice ("DOJ") Office of the United States Trustee as a trial attorney representing the public interest in bankruptcy cases, and I took that opportunity, leaving private practice, at least temporarily. My friends at Podvey were supportive of my decision, and we have stayed in regular communication through today.

I was happy to return to government and enjoyed the ability to have discretion over the cases I prosecuted. I continued to do community work in my personal life, especially with the Interfaith Hospitality Network of Essex County New Jersey, a homeless shelter alternative for families. Through Interfaith Hospitality Network and my membership in both a Roman Catholic parish and a Reconstructionist synagogue, I coordinated transforming the worship buildings into a shelter for families a couple of weeks a year. The experience of hosting families in distress, eating, chatting, and sleeping overnight with them is truly transformative. I continue to think it is so much more transformative for the volunteers than for the clients. Housing and wealth inequality became an increasingly compelling cause for me in this period. Participating in Interfaith Hospitality Network had the added benefit of being something that I could do together with my husband and children. It was a public service that we did together, which was also a high priority for me at the time. Thus, I continued to integrate my personal values in both my professional activities and my home life.

Professionally, as a trial attorney at the Office of the United States Trustee, I oversaw all of the bankruptcy cases that were filed before one or more particular judges. I worked with terrific attorneys and non-lawyer colleagues in an ombudsman and public interest capacity. I became acquainted with many members of the bankruptcy bar and the bankruptcy judges. While there was no shortage of work, I enjoyed having input into which cases our office would become actively involved in and especially enjoyed being able to spend the time and effort a legal issue needed as a matter of right and justice and not simply economics. But, with passage of bankruptcy reform legislation in 2005 that, in my opinion, favored the financial industry to the disadvantage of consumers, was not very lawyer friendly, and was certainly not consumer lawyer friendly, the dichotomy between my legal work and my personal views became untenable. I decided I needed to leave the Trustee's Office when, while giving the DOJ's answer to a question at a seminar, the audience hissed out loud, and I realized I agreed with them. It's always been my conviction that every client should have a lawyer who is completely committed to his or her case, and I could no longer be that lawyer after bankruptcy reform legislation passed, at least as it related to consumer bankruptcy work. So, I decided to leave, and my first inclination was to call my old friends at Podvey.

I was warmly welcomed back at the Podvey firm. Although Podvey agreed to accommodate my desire to do pro-bono work and develop my own practice, I soon began to miss certain things that had been available in government, such as the ability to pick and choose cases and to devote as much time to an issue as it requires, irrespective of the monetary value of the claim. Also, at $350 an hour, even the smallest brief or the simplest court appearance seemed costly, especially for the more modest of my clients, and this nagged at me.

My children were now nearly grown, and I desired to integrate my professional and personal life more completely. I didn't want my work for poor people to be only after-hours and on weekends; I wanted to devote myself entirely to this cause. I saw an advertisement for an experienced litigator at Legal Services of New Jersey ("LSNJ") for someone to take on cases on behalf of defrauded homeowners and to work on a project called the anti-predatory lending project. Although I didn't then understand how legal service organizations operated, I interviewed in June and, soon after, was offered the position, which was for much less salary and a longer commute. (When I sat down to tell my dear friend Bob that I was leaving Podvey again, he asked me, "Peggy, if we cut your pay more, will you stay?") The sum of all my experience, not the least of which was my volunteer work with Interfaith Hospitality Network, contributed to my being selected for this single statewide legal services position.

I started working at LSNJ in July 2007. The next month, the mortgage market collapsed, and I've been working at a feverish pace ever since. At LSNJ, I work with a small group of extremely dedicated poverty lawyers. We represent very low-income clients trying to help them keep their homes. In the course of my work, I often interview families in their homes, and I have had the privilege of meeting scores of people throughout New Jersey of all races and creeds, all with the common problem of limited resources and vulnerability to sharp home mortgage lending practices. This has broadened my appreciation of my own circumstances, and reaffirmed my initial instinct that this is the right work for me.

Being a public interest lawyer is different from being in private practice or government. Public interest law offers the freedom—almost the obligation—to litigate only the most meritorious cases and to consider what the effect of the case will be on those other people who were not able to attract representation. In short, it's all impact litigation. Public interest lawyers are universally hard working—I work longer hours for less money than at any other time in my career, yet I am more professionally and personally satisfied.

Legal Services work is also very different from commercial litigation or government service in the emotional impact it has on me. I listen to a lot of heartbreaking stories, and I now know why therapists limit their sessions to fifty minutes. Actively listening to some of the stories poor people tell is very depleting. Oddly, it is not always the people who have the strongest legal case who are most appreciative of having had the opportunity to consult with an attorney. For many poor people, simply being listened to with dignity, knowing that somebody is on their side and has listened to their problem, and given them advice is enough. I find this to be true in my work with Interfaith Hospitality Network as well. Listening to someone with respect is often the most affirming thing that you can do for someone. It's not that a low income client can't accept more bad news—they can, and they do all the time—but, often, they just want to be heard.

In New Jersey, LSNJ is the coordinator of legal aid for some 1.8 million low-income residents. Of course, we don't have nearly enough staff to serve this client population. In many cases, I had meritorious lawsuits not brought for lack of an attorney. But from my work in both government and the private sector, I knew that there were a lot of private attorneys who would be willing to help if asked. So, together with my colleague, Rebecca Shore, and with the enthusiastic support of our Executive Director De Miller, we embarked on a campaign to recruit and train private attorneys to represent low-income homeowners in defending against foreclosures and prosecuting predatory lenders.

The internet and e-mail also have transformed legal practice in the public interest community. Rebecca and I—only two lawyers in our offices in Edison, New Jersey—are able to confer on a daily basis with hundreds of other advocates throughout the country through an internet service list. We are able to exchange data and information with advocates in other states and with private counsel within our own state. Just yesterday, a late Friday afternoon, we were alerted about a client with an emergent problem that may re-sult in the sale of her home next Wednesday. With the power of the internet, late on a Friday afternoon, we were able to contact the pro bono attorneys we have assembled over the past month and attract counsel to represent her, ex-change model pleadings, and coordinate her representation. That would not have been possible without e-mail and the internet; it provides the potential for each and every direct representation case to be impact litigation.

My work at Legal Services also includes testifying before the New Jer-sey State Legislature, conferring with state and federal regulatory agency staff on issues involving consumer lending and home ownership, and partic-ipating in coalitions and task-forces with other advocacy groups and service agencies.

For me, practicing law is more than a job and more than a career. It's not something that starts at 9 a.m. and ends at 5 p.m., whether you're in private practice, in government, or serving clients in public interest litigation. I be-lieve that every lawyer is privileged to participate in the resolution of his or her client's problems. Regardless of whether my client is a big company or a poor elderly woman, I have always taken that responsibility with the utmost seriousness, and I believe that is true of most of us. It's a privilege to serve in the legal profession. Because of that, it's important to shape your career in a way that works best for you and your family. It also requires thoughtful in-trospection and the need to be honest with yourself about your needs and goals. You need to understand your relationship with money, to be honest about your families' needs, your earning capacity, and your attention, and to realize that these priorities will change over your life. My experience has been that the contacts, connections, and relationships I've made at each stage of my career have served me well in subsequent phases, even though each job has been so different from the others. For example, my contacts and friends in private practice and the many people I regulated while at the United States Trustee's Office have served me well at LSNJ in helping me attract private practitioners to carry some of the load of representing low-income residents during this mortgage foreclosure crisis.

I think a perspective for a young lawyer to bear in mind is that nothing is permanent, so you need not be afraid to try new things if you believe that is how you are called at any given time, whether by your profession, your family, your community, or your own beliefs.

Signed, Sealed, Delivered: My Life As A Government Lawyer

By Tiffany M. Williams

PERSONAL EXPERIENCES

Despite having practiced in various sectors of the legal profession over the course of my career, my life as a female government lawyer has been among the most fulfilling and rewarding. My government experiences have ranged from clerking in the judiciary branch of government to serving as an Assistant United States Attorney in the executive branch, and from serving as Chief Counsel to the Speaker of the New Jersey General Assembly in the legislative branch to currently serving as Deputy Chief Counsel to the Governor of the State of New Jersey. On balance, I would characterize my overall experience in government as fulfilling, dynamic and empowering.

In my various government roles, I had the opportunity to fulfill my passion and commitment to public service in leadership positions at the highest levels of my agencies. My desire and heart has always leaned towards giving back to the community and making a difference in people's lives. The impact of my daily decisions and the opportunity to sit at the decision-making table often dominated by men has been transformational to my career development as an attorney. In reflecting on the best way to illustrate the overall experience of my career as a government lawyer, I thought I would present a profile snapshot in an interview with—myself!

Q. What were the most fulfilling aspects of government service?

A. I found the opportunity to bring about global and broad-based change to be most fulfilling. While serving as Chief Counsel in the New Jersey Legislature, I assisted with the passage of the bill that repealed the death penalty in New Jersey. I did not have to write letters and make an appeal to legislators as the advocates did. I sat down with the legislative leadership as the institution's attorney and gave my professional advice on the right course of action—speaking from my seat at the table—despite being one of only two women in senior management. Currently, in my role as Deputy Chief Counsel, I am making recommendations to the Governor on the selection of judicial candidates, personally having a hand in the future of our judiciary and jurisprudence. It is an awesome responsibility, and I am incredibly fulfilled to follow the career of judges that I have interviewed for the job. Additionally, benefits of working in government include:

- Greater autonomy and flexibility of hours/scheduling
- Strict adherence to ethical standards
- Hands-on experience

- Insider's perspective
- Exposure to key government decision-makers
- Incredible relationship-building abilities
- Opportunity to affect larger policy decisions
- Increased client contact
- Fast-paced and challenging work environment
- Development of ability to think quickly on one's feet to make an informed decision
- Low employee contribution costs for benefits
- Pension benefits

Q. What are the most challenging aspects?

A. The most challenging aspects of government service can be the strained resources that are available to accomplish the enormous tasks and responsibility that come with governance. Particular challenges to working in the public sector include:

- Lower salaries
- Restrictions on outside activities (i.e., political activity, outside employment)
- Post-employment restrictions
- Limited resources for formal training and professional development
- Less formal and structured work environment
- Less formal feedback and evaluation on work performance
- Informal mentoring or lack of mentoring

Q. What factors do you attribute to your success?

A. My success in government has come through, one, my ability to define success as personal growth and fulfillment; two, my ability to withstand the ebbs and flows of my own proficiency; and three, my determination to continue to press forward and grow despite the professional challenges I have faced. In government service, given the changes that often occur with changes in an administration, it is necessary to be flexible, competent and self-assured, to adjust quickly, and to build relationships that will give you longevity. All of these factors are magnified for women in government, because, at times, we are in the minority and bring a different perspective and set of skills than existed before we came on the scene. Remaining true to your natural skill-set, yet adapting to the environment, is crucial to success as a woman in government.

Q. What advice would you give a lawyer who is just transitioning into a legal position in government?

A. First, determine the type of skills you want to gain. Government offers opportunities for enhancing your ability to think quickly on your feet and quickly process and evaluate a solution to a problem. In a more autonomous public sector position, ownership over tasks and development of written and oral communication skills are keys to success and by-products of a successful government career. The often fast-paced environment in many government settings requires the skills of multi-tasking and priority setting with no one to monitor your workload or give you strict deadlines for completion. Many government positions require constant communication and coordination with other moving pieces, which may require lots of meetings, letters and e-mails. Second, consider the difference in monetary compensation levels between the government and private sector, but remember that there is no price tag for the feeling of knowing the impact that you made as a government lawyer on the lives of many. Finally, evaluate where you can leverage a government position in your next career move. Lawyers transitioning from the private sector should be acutely aware of their next potential career move so that they can ensure they select a position that will develop a skill-set or experience that can propel their career to the next level.

WORK-LIFE BALANCE

Leadership positions in government tend to demand constant availability and flexibility, which can make it difficult to maintain a healthy work-life balance. In sum, government services at the highest levels can forge an attack on work-life balance against which one must actively guard. Women in government have an extra burden to guard their time zealously and set boundaries. This dynamic can be in direct contradiction to the desire and efforts necessary to excel and advance, which depend on being ever available for the next crisis. I have found it difficult to maintain time for consistently nurturing outside relationships given the cycles and overall pace in government. Whether it is legislative cycles, election cycles, budget cycles or crisis management, government is fraught with the need for tough leadership decisions daily. Communication among and between stakeholders and decision-makers on a daily and frequent basis is the way to survive. Unfortunately, this lifestyle is completely contrary to a scheduled life of priorities, which affect other responsibilities and people in your life. Accordingly, to achieve work-life balance, government leaders have to make tough choices and set boundaries early on. Further, they must have outstanding competency and energy, yet maintain respect and reputation as a team player and hard worker.

WOMEN OF COLOR IN GOVERNMENT

Women of color in government have an entirely unique experience. In light of the dismal numbers of women of color at the highest ranks in government, typically, the experience can be both an opportunity to stand out and distinguish oneself, yet a challenge not to carry the entire burden of your race on your shoulders. Inevitably, as a woman of color, you typically become the go-to person for dealing with similar constituency groups, which can be an opportunity to bring voices to the table that may not have been there previously. These opportunities can translate into experiences that non-minority colleagues may not experience and can lead to interactions with decision-makers and agency heads that non-minority colleagues typically do not encounter.

On the other hand, women of color in government can experience unique challenges that can lead to isolation and lagging professional development, since there are generally so few women of color in government leadership positions. Personal experiences shared among women of color repeatedly reveal that they are often overlooked for mentoring and development opportunities. Women of color often relate to watching majority colleagues get informal social opportunities or invites to lunch or choice assignments with greater frequency. Moreover, despite often having opportunities to become the go-to person for representing one's own constituency group, women of color can mistakenly become the sole spokesperson, which essentially can reduce women of color to a generalization. Women of color are confronted with the reality of defying generalizations, yet the advantage of opportunities to bring underrepresented communities to a position of power and influence in decision-making that they otherwise may not have had.

The most challenging professional aspects for women of color involve confronting negative stereotypes. As an African-American woman, I have had to fight continually against the negative stereotypes characterizing me as confrontational, bossy and overbearing. Anytime I demonstrate any aggression, passion or ability to stand up for myself, I do so at risk of being characterized as a stereotype. I have witnessed repeated instances professionally where white women may have had the same reaction as I did to a situation. My reaction, however, was characterized as angry or as having an attitude, but the white woman was characterized as a real go-getter and tough. At times, women of color also have to confront more overt aspects of racism where their authority is undermined and deference given to their white male subordinates.

ISSUES UNIQUE TO WOMEN OF FAITH IN GOVERNMENT

As an ordained minister, I thought it was important also to address issues unique to women of faith in government workplaces. Women of faith, whether they are the clergy or just those with professed belief, are a positive force and can bring a perspective of a higher consciousness to the workplace. These are women who are typically held in high esteem by colleagues, tend to field questions, and are sought after for advice and mediation in resolving disputes. In my own experience as a minister in government, I have provided confidential counseling to co-workers dealing with sensitive and vulnerable personal issues outside of work and possibly affecting work. I have also been called upon to provide a moral compass for the environment overall. However, these responsibilities do not come without their own set of challenges. There can be significant social challenges with after-work socializing focusing on the consumption of alcohol or a disproportionate number of activities conducted at bars. Most common is the challenge of dealing and managing offensive language and inappropriate jokes without appearing overly sensitive. I have encountered environments in government where I have been ostracized or not included in outside social activities because of fear of offending me. I have also experienced environments where my views were ridiculed and characterized as dogmatic. Women of faith are typically held to higher ethical standards and any human mistake can also be magnified because of the pedestal effect. A final significant challenge is dealing with the accusations of inappropriately bringing religion into the workplace because of the strength of one's beliefs. I have had colleagues challenge me on having my Bible on my desk, praying in my office and speaking about the fact that my values are based on the Bible. Nonetheless, because I cannot separate my faith from who I am, I press on along with women of faith throughout government. Despite the challenges, there is room for us at the table in government, and our faith and belief in higher purpose will keep us strong!

TOP TEN LESSONS LEARNED

My career in government has been a laboratory of experience and life lessons that have developed and strengthened my character and career in ways that are unique. Here I share ten of those lessons:

1. Treat every person with respect and kindness.

A common maxim in government and politics is that you never know who your next boss will be. That intern that you were too busy to mentor or the colleague who uses speakerphone with their office door open could potentially be your supervisor or your agency's director one day. Leadership positions for lawyers in government are often a result of a combination of skills, ability and the right relationships. It is difficult to predict which relationships your colleagues possess that may propel them into your path in the future. I am often reminded of a former colleague in one office who treated me poorly, only to have to contend with me as a supervisor a few years later in a different environment. Moreover, you may never know which co-workers and colleagues that you may need as a resource for future opportunities later in your career. My positions in government have convinced me that there is no better advice than to treat everyone that you encounter with dignity and basic human respect—after all, they deserve it.

2. Manage office politics.

Knowledge and awareness of the lay of the land is a vital assessment from the beginning of an employment relationship. If there is one thing about a work environment that can make or break an employment experience, it would have to be the ever present office politics, which includes office cliques and difficult personalities. Cliques and overly politicized office environments are polarizing and can lead to demoralized staff, perceived inequities, and reduced productivity. Most of all, handle difficult colleagues with kid gloves. These types of personalities can come in varying shapes and forms but typically hide behind insecurity, manipulation and competitiveness. The deadliest aspect is that they can show one face to management and another face in interacting with you. Nonetheless, failing to manage these relationships can jeopardize your individual reputation and credibility. To borrow from an age-old football analogy, the best defense is a good offense. Be proactive about building relationships with difficult personalities to demonstrate that you are not trying to be a threat to their value. However, it is vital that boundaries are established to avoid violation of trust. Regular and consistent communication and relationship building with managers and supervisors about your work and value will go a long way in demonstrating your character and integrity in the event it ever gets challenged by difficult colleagues.

3. Develop strong interpersonal skills.

Developing, honing and demonstrating good people skills are a must in succeeding as a government lawyer. The ability to relate to others and treat them well enables government lawyers particularly to procure results, resources and information needed for effective decision-making. Conversely, the inability to demonstrate strong interpersonal skills effectively can serve as a barrier to results. Strong oral and written presentation in daily communications, phone conferences, meetings and e-mail can establish a government lawyer's reputation as a result-oriented leader rather than a mere bureaucrat. It is crucial to take an active role in getting to know colleagues and staff within your organization and other agencies with whom you will be interacting. Going the extra mile to visit their offices and gain insight and perspective on their role and responsibilities will only enhance your ability to leverage them as a resource to achieving your own results. Ultimately, people help and promote people whom they like.

4. *Admit mistakes or lapses in judgment and seek to rectify them immediately.*

Mistakes, mistakes, mistakes. They are bound to happen so prepare to deal with them in advance. Often, there is a bit more pressure in government to cover mistakes because of the detrimental impact they can have on the principal or agency head for which one works. Concealment or denial of mistakes or playing the blame game will erode your credibility and reputation for integrity. I can recall vividly a situation where I made a mistake that I had to rectify and correct immediately. Although the mistake ended up having significant consequences, it was a learning experience, and I can look back and say that I was proud of how I handled it. My reputation is not forever entangled in the mistake, but, rather, I was able to transform it by allowing my integrity to show forth. Similarly, as a manager or supervisor in government, one should prepare to support subordinates as they go through the learning process of making mistakes. Isolating and ostracizing staff for mistakes will only lead to reduced productivity for future projects. Confronting the mistake head on, debriefing the employees and empowering them to build a strategy to avoid the mistake ever happening again is the alternative that will result in the most fruitful team-building relationships.

5. *Stay in your lane and win over your enemies through conciliation and dedication to the end goal.*

Staying in your lane is a huge reality of government practice. Inevitably a bright, ambitious attorney will wander out of her lane with the greatest intentions. What can likely result is a harsh reality that you have now offended the person whose lane you wandered into. The colleague now thinks you are trying to take over his or her responsibility, trying to make your colleague look less than competent or are gunning for his or her spot. Notwithstanding any intention on your part, you have now created an enemy. Perhaps you did nothing but accept a job offer. However, unknowingly, you took the desired position of someone internally who did not get selected. Unwittingly, you have now put a target on your chest. While this now creates an additional challenge, it is not insurmountable. The right approach is to be conciliatory in dealing with difficult relationships. Allow the other person to feel empowered and slowly begin to discover ways to encourage her to let her guard down. Highlight her accomplishments to others without being disingenuous or patronizing. Refer information and opportunities to her that will enhance her decision-making and role. To borrow from a Biblical analogy, the "Promised Land" or end goal can usually not be attained without encountering enemies. Identify them quickly, confront the issues head on using weapons of conciliation and empowerment, and stay focused on the end goal. You will be victorious.

6. Develop a reputation as a dedicated, hard worker— be known for your work ethic.

Government is not a unique environment when it comes to the basic organizational need for productivity and high-quality work product. There is no denying a great work ethic. Inevitably, in every organization, government lawyers will encounter individuals who talk a good game but really do not produce much. Often times, these types of individuals ascend to leadership positions because of strong interpersonal skills or great relationships. However, at some point in their career, these types will hit the wall if they have not developed a strong work ethic. Time will reveal their deficiency. It is best to develop a strong work ethic for being focused on the task at hand, and to be goal-oriented and willing to dedicate the time to hone the skills needed to deliver a quality result. Government practice can sometimes be fast-paced with expectations that extend beyond the resources afforded to the task. Hunkering down and doing whatever it takes to gain the expertise, knowledge or relationships needed will build a solid foundation. Constantly remaining proactive and anticipating the needs of your organization or agency as demonstrated by your constant flow of output and going above and beyond the ordinary expectations of the task will be rewarded in your character development, integrity and the desire for others to promote you. Government attorneys have the challenge of resisting the temptation to "get by," because there are no billable hours or market-driven pressures. Nonetheless, nothing can outshine good old-fashioned hard work.

7. Seek a solid understanding of ethical obligations and demonstrate the highest levels of professionalism.

Government positions are fraught with technical ethical requirements and codes that dictate prohibited and permitted activities with the purpose of avoiding corruption of decision-making by government employees. Typically, there are ethics officers within each agency and, in some states, there are separate agencies charged with ethics compliance for an entire branch of government. Knowledge of ethics rules and requirements that govern your agency is crucial to successful job performance in government. One media report of an ethical lapse can undermine your career as well as tarnish the reputation of the agency, organization or leadership. Adherence to ethical obligations also enhances a government attorney's integrity, professionalism and sensitivity to outside corrupt influences. The power and influence that government entities often have over profit-making private entities sometimes leads to a temptation by regulated entities to receive a favorable outcome at any cost. Government attorneys must be equipped to make good decisions that are consistent with their mission, authority and charge, despite the impact that it may have on the profitability of a private entity. Developing a reputation of an ethical attorney only enhances your credibility and ability to add value to any employment setting.

8. Go the extra yard to meet the needs of others and tackle tough issues.

The ability to be proactive and take the initiative to anticipate the needs of others is a landmark of successful government service. Government portfolios are often amorphous and change based on the strengths of the individual serving in the role. But, what is needed most is a proactive team player that can anticipate the needs of others and is not afraid to take on tough issues. Character and courage become companions that every woman in government should possess, particularly to stamp out stereotypes and generalizations about women being reticent to "step up" or be aggressive in problem solving.

9. Develop an expertise in communication, responsiveness and making hard decisions.

Similarly, hone in on the skills required to make tough decisions and do the hard work that makes an impact. Do not shy away from the difficult and complicated challenges but, rather, seek to identify the root of the complication and bring the stakeholders together to resolve their differences. Assessment of issues, analysis of alternatives and a strong ability to communicate with stakeholders and decision makers will make you stand out when others procrastinate or avoid conflict and challenge. Additionally, being available and willing to take the time out to schedule the necessary meeting, conference calls or e-mail dialogues will also sharpen your ability to become an expert in calming crisis.

10. Be responsive—return calls within 24 hours and strive to close the loop on issues.

A common complaint in government centers on a perception of government attorneys as bureaucrats moving at a snail's pace, waiting for the 5:00 p.m. hour to punch a time clock and go home. I have been fortunate to work in government environments that would utterly shatter this perception. Nonetheless, I am aware that basic norms of communication and responsiveness seem to be deteriorating in our society, despite technological advances in communication, i.e., the Blackberry and cell phone. There is really no excuse not to respond within 24–48 hours to communications. A simple acknowledgement of an incoming communication will often suffice to demonstrate courtesy and interest to the sender. Even the fast-paced government lawyer whose schedule is much like mine has the ability to use resources such as subordinate attorneys or administrative assistants to assist in returning responses within 24–48 hours. Similarly, bringing closure to open issues rather than allowing them to languish is important in developing a professional reputation and seeking to advance in your career. In sum, government service is a wonderful, rewarding career choice for women in the legal profession. Women are increasing in the ranks of leadership at all levels of government and are shattering the glass ceiling. Diverse populations of women, of varying faiths, creeds and color, are making historic strides that are affecting the world and populations of society that have previously been disenfranchised. Dedicating my career to public service was the best decision I could have ever made personally and professionally. I look forward to leaving a legacy of government leadership for all women.

Small Firm Practice: You Eat What You Kill

21

By Amy Messigian

As RECRUITING SEASON ROLLS around each year at my firm of forty attorneys, we use an oft-repeated phrase used to explain the workings of our office to potential candidates. "You eat what you kill." The phrase describes the reality of small firm life that success is possible only if one generates business. The words sound like hyperbole and reek of carnage, but they ring true in more ways than one.

First and foremost, in the world of small firms, you are only as valuable as your list of contacts. It is hard to grasp this concept when you are straight out of law school. I certainly had no high roller contacts then. Strike that—I didn't even have a contact list; meaning that, without resourcefulness or tenacity, I would be doomed out of the gate.

Second, it isn't just the business you generate, though that is the sales pitch to overachievers from law schools across this great land, it is the identity you forge for yourself *within* the firm. Impressions form rapidly in small offices. A class of two or three associates will quickly generate a standout performer, an associate lucky enough to get the choice assignments and, at least for a little while, maintain a bit of a security. While one might suppose that life in a small firm is less cutthroat, less demanding, less emotionally taxing than at a large, marquis law firm, nothing could be further from the truth. In fact, one of the earliest lessons I learned at my small firm was that if I wanted to succeed, I needed to be a lion and not a gazelle.

A LAWYER IS BORN

If this were a movie and not a book, now would be the appropriate moment for a flashback sequence, all the way back to the tender age of sixteen. Sixteen-year-old Amy should be out chasing boys. Someone should be telling her that she can't go out of the house dressed "like that." But that is some other Amy, from some other time and place. This Amy—Amy the Overachiever—has way too much on her plate to worry about boys. She is student body president. She is a cheerleader. She is on the mock trial team, and the debate team, and an elected officer of a political activism group for high school students. She is a founding member of a feminist club and has rallied for teachers' rights. And let's not forget about her grades. She is on her way to becoming a valedictorian.

Sixteen-year-old Amy already knew a few things about a few things. She knew that she wanted to be a lawyer—the first in her family. She knew about glass ceilings. Her mother often reminded her that when she was Amy's age, her guidance counselor dismissed her thoughts of applying to the likes of

UCLA or Stanford. Mom's guidance counselor would say: "Why go? You are going to get married, and there will be no point to it." Mom acquiesced to this advice and had scrapped her plans to apply to a big name university in favor of the local state college.

Not so for Amy. It was never questioned that she would go to a first-tier university. A college fund established at birth was ripe with donations from family and friends, meaning that despite her parent's modest means, higher education was attainable. Amy was predestined to go to UCLA. Everyone in her family rooted for the Bruins, though all had received their education elsewhere. It was merely a bonus when she, of her own volition, added a law degree to the equation. "A lawyer," my father would tell his friends with pride. "She wants to be a lawyer."

There were no lawyer jokes in the family, only lawyerly puns. For her sixteenth birthday, Amy received her first briefcase with a note inside on which was written, "May all of your cases be brief." It was first used for mock trials and moot courts, but someday it would become a repository for genuine legal papers, business cards and about a thousand highlighters. It is still the only briefcase she owns.

Yes, sixteen-year-old Amy was certainly an unstoppable force, full of dreams and ambition and hand-me-down suits. One might even say that somewhere in that overachieving, headstrong sixteen-year-old was a gazelle set on a collision course with a lion.

THE SMALL FISH IN THE BIG POND

After soaring through four years at UCLA, I landed at Georgetown University Law Center. I met the challenge with newfound intellectual insecurity. Intelligence, in my eyes, had always equated to worth. At Georgetown, there were dozens upon dozens of individuals who eclipsed me in their profound intellectual ability. I was smart, but they were brilliant. It was inspiring and deflating at the same time. These were justices in the making. The Scalias and the Ginsbergs. They would clerk with circuit courts. They would end up at global firms with six named partners and annual retreats in fancy locations. They would represent the Phillip Morrises, Exxons and Wachovias of the world.

But who was I? The glitter and pizzazz of the legal world, to me, was found standing at a podium and addressing a jury of my peers. It was painting a masterpiece into a summary judgment motion or delivering a captivating closing statement. Indeed, I could think of nothing more mind-numbing and awful than spending the first three years of my legal career reviewing documents. I wanted to be in the trenches right away.

This is not to say that I did not want to leave my mark on the legal community. To the contrary, it is because I wanted to leave a mark that I preferred a smaller firm. I distinctly remember a conversation during my 2L year with a large group of my female friends in which we discussed our career ambitions. Out of the entire pack, I was the only one—THE ONLY ONE—whose ambition was to make partner at a firm. Most of the group felt that they would leave their firms before the partnership level, either because they saw it as conflicting with the ability to raise a family or because it instinctively was not somewhere they wanted to be long-term. I thought to myself, if I knew that I would not want to stay at the firm, why endure the hassle? Why endure the billable hour requirements or tax on your personal life? Many associates end up making more per hour at a smaller firm working a reasonable work day than they would at a large firm where their $165,000 base salary comes with a hefty price tag in billable hours. And, small-firm lawyers have the opportunity to make partner much sooner than they would at Big, Bigger & Behemoth.

Between my ideals and the flair to my wardrobe, I was absolutely not big firm material. And so it was that I ended up spending my summer at a small Los Angeles firm—a summer associate in a class of one—while my colleagues summered in classes more numerous than my entire firm.

LET'S NOT GET CARRIED AWAY WITH OUR FALSE SENSE OF FREEDOM

Over the course of the summer, there were several group events, but most of the recruiting process was far less formal. Occasionally someone would take me to lunch or suggest I join him or her for drinks after work. There was little fanfare over me. The highlight of the arrangement was that I had my own office—a first—and my name adorned the door. As Mom always said, it takes little to please a simpleton.

I was told that the program was kept simple to convey a true projection of law firm life. My work assignments were relatively discreet and I was never expected to stay late or arrive early. The ability to come and go as I pleased spared me from the fate of my friends at large firms who were coaxed to events almost nightly, a bunch of Pinocchios drawn to the lure of Pleasure Island.

While my experience certainly gave me a *sense* of life to come, I wouldn't call it an entirely accurate portrayal of small firm life. For one, as a summer associate, I was told to take my time with assignments—to prioritize quality over speed. As someone who was never good at timed tests, I appreciated being judged on completed assignments as opposed to my ability to sprint through them. This preference for quality over speed was lost once I became an associate. As I soon learned, the ability to meet or exceed deadlines was crucial no matter how arbitrary the deadline or how full the plate.

In changing these priorities, it was not that the firm did not seek to turn out quality work product; rather, the exigencies of the practice required sacrificing perfection. Having cast a critical eye at my own work product for many years now, it is hard to let go, but I am trying to find a balance. I try not to sweat the smaller stuff and focus on knocking the big ones out of the park. While I would love to catch every typo, replace every colloquialism, and correct every grammatical whoopsie, I understand that, at some point, it is time to hit send and stop worrying.

For another thing, I learned that, even though you do not punch a time card, people are keeping tabs on when you come and go. I, for one, am not a morning person, have never been a morning person, and have often found that I am more productive at night, sort of like Dracula. Part of the draw to working as a lawyer was that I would finally be able to set my own hours, at least for the most part. I could come in at 9:30 a.m. and leave at 7:30 p.m. Heck, I could come in at 11 a.m. and leave at 9 p.m. I did not factor in that I had joined a cult of early birds. Who knew that a firm could have a "morning culture"? Seriously, that sort of information should be in bold lettering on the NALP form. "Diversity committee, part-time option available, **MORNING CULTURE.**" If they could find a way to add blinking lights around it, that would be even better. For what it is worth, I did not learn until it was almost too late that getting in at any time after 9 a.m. was like setting a moving target on my back. It somehow equated to a lack of motivation, even if I was the very last person to leave at the end of the day. Now reformed, I realize that it is in my best interest to crow with the rooster, set the alarm extra early, and anger the neighbors with the aggressiveness of its blaring siren.

I also learned that small firms can lack solidarity, perhaps even more so than their larger brothers. Cliques form. There are haves and have nots; jocks and rebels. While the firm seemed to be a cohesive unit over my summer, it became clear after I began my first year that it was not. There were divides on many important issues: how to effectively market the firm, whether to continue a summer associate program, whether to provide mentorship to the associates or continue with a "sink or swim" mentality.

At the very center of the divide was the role of women in the firm. I am told that in the not so distant past a small army of women led an exodus from the firm and that the partnership was slowly rebuilding its female ranks. It may explain why two out of the three associates in the preceding class had been female, and why I represented the only new edition in the class that followed. While I hate to think of myself as a place holder, it was undoubtedly to the firm's benefit that I was both female and had an ethnic quality to my last name. And yet, while these features may have gotten me in the door, they are part of what make it a struggle for me to become part of the fold and, ultimately, to succeed.

Until I started practicing as a lawyer, I had always thought of myself as one of the boys. My friends are primarily male. I play fantasy football, baseball, and NASCAR. I enjoy hockey and can hurl obscenities at a kicker for missing a game winning field goal. I like beer. I burp, though never in court. I hold my own at poker. Never would I have imagined that I would not fit in with my colleagues just because I use a different bathroom. But it is so. There is a tangible difference in treatment, however subtle its forms may be. It can be frustrating and, at times, overwhelming. Gender lines are drawn both in interoffice relations and in associate assignments. Being part of a 15% gender minority, I often feel I am on the outside looking in and admire the ease with which the male associates are integrated. They go to baseball games with the partners, play golf together, and have drinks together. It is no surprise that, at the end of the day, it translates into some choice assignments and client contact.

THE CIRCLE OF LIFE

Over the past three years, I have thought a lot about my initial lessons at the firm. "You eat what you kill," ever etched in my brain, forewarns all who come there that the amount of disbursable work is limited. Whether you get that work depends on a variety of conditions, not all of which you can control. Therefore the best chance of success is bringing in your own "food." This is certainly true if one endeavors to make partner.

"You eat what you kill" has another salient meaning: to survive in a small firm, you have to forget everything you think you know about small firms. Small firms are not where Big, Bigger & Behemoth ex-pats go to die. They are where people like me who have ambitions far beyond a three-year career in a law firm go to thrive. It forewarns those who would be sluggish that there is no dead weight in a small firm. If you are not fed and cannot feed yourself, there are only two outcomes: a slow death or swift discarding.

My own career started out in a somewhat "rough and tumble" fashion. I didn't really know what I was signing up for when I accepted my job. I was idealistic, and I was a bit snobbish about my education, though both feelings quickly dissipated. I was the eloquent gazelle in big cat territory. I sauntered in at 9:30 a.m. I grazed over my assignments.

To survive, I had to change my perceptions. I had to modify my behavior and project a tougher image, a "hungry for food" sort of image. I had to arrive early. I had to abide by deadlines, even if it meant turning in something that didn't get Amy the Overachiever's seal of approval.

I had to devour the gazelle to become the lion.

Life in a University

22

By Deborah L. Rhode

"CLARIFY A FEW CONCEPTS. Draw a few distinctions. It's a living."

This is the purported response of Columbia University philosopher Sidney Morgenbesser to a cab driver's question about his job. When responding to similar questions about their jobs, law professors are likely to provoke mild incredulity, and sometimes ill-disguised envy among non-academics. "Six or seven hours in the classroom a week—that's all? And lifetime tenure even if you never publish another word?" To many practicing lawyers working sweatshop hours with little prospect of permanent job security, life in the legal academy seems like a "virtual spa experience."[1] To many professors, who find themselves working just as hard as they did in practice under more intellectually demanding standards, the job description looks somewhat different.

This essay offers a more comprehensive picture of life in legal education. What are its advantages and disadvantages? How should lawyers assess their prospects and find the right job fit in academia? What does it take to build a successful academic career?

THE VIEW FROM THE INSIDE

Rewards

There are many rewards about being a law professor. Career satisfaction surveys find that academics are among the happiest groups in America and among the legal profession.[2] This is scarcely surprising; faculty life offers many of the characteristics that professionals find most important, including control, intellectual challenge, self-esteem, job security, collegial relationships, and socially useful work.[3] Law professors have an exceptional amount

---

1. Peter Keane, *Interloper in the Fields of Academe*, 35 TOLEDO LAW REVIEW 119, 123 (2003).

2. Satisfaction rates for academics range between 75 and 90 percent, a substantially higher percentage than other professionals. *See* DEBORAH L. RHODE, IN PURSUIT OF KNOWLEDGE 4 (Stanford University Press 2006); TOM W. SMITH, JOB SATISFACTION IN THE UNITED STATES 3 (National Opinion Research Center, April 17, 2007). The satisfaction rate for the entire legal profession in general is approximately 55%. *See* Stephanie Ward, *The Pulse of the Profession*, ABA Journal, at 32 (Oct. 2007), http://abajournal.com/magazine/pulse_of_the_legal_profession. One of the only studies that has compared legal academics to legal practitioners surveyed Yale graduates and found that 75 percent of the legal academics were very satisfied, while only 44 percent of the legal practitioners were very satisfied. Further, only 24 percent of the legal practitioners in law firms were very satisfied. *What Yale Law School Graduates Do: A Summary of the Career Development Offices' 5th Year Career Development Survey*, Classes 1996–2000.

3. *See* Deborah L. Rhode, *Perspectives on Lawyer Happiness Foreword: Personal Satisfaction in Professional Practice*, 58 SYRACUSE L. REV. 217, 222 (2008).

of freedom to shape their agendas and schedules. A good part of their work involves teaching and writing on subjects they find interesting and important. Legal academics can exercise at least some influence over the direction of law and public policy and help shape the next generation of lawyers. For many individuals drawn to oral advocacy, the classroom can be a rewarding experience. Large courses offer performance opportunities with captive audiences; clinics and small courses allow personal contact and the chance for significant impact on students' professional development. Long vacations and flexible schedules allow faculty to accommodate other commitments; family obligations, public service and outside interests can coexist with a full-time academic career.

Disadvantages

So what is not to like? More than most non-academics think. The most obvious downside is monetary compensation. Average law school salaries in 2009–10 were $64,292 for instructors; $83,491 for assistant professors; $101,045 for associate professors; and $134,146 for full professors.[4] Although law school faculty are at the top of the academic hierarchy, topped only by business school professors, most legal academics could earn many times that amount working for a law firm, and some find it galling that their students will start as lawyers at higher income levels than their own.

There are, to be sure, many ways to supplement an academic salary, such as consulting, writing casebooks, earning honoraria, or even engaging in part-time legal practice (which universities generally cap at one day a week). Faculty perks are also generous; academic communities often offer outstanding cultural, recreational and information services. But for lawyers transitioning from practice, the downward financial mobility can be painful. The tradeoffs are only worthwhile if teaching and scholarship provide sufficient psychic income.

Unfotunately, the academic lifestyle does not provide such intangible benefits for everyone. Not everyone has fond memories of his or her own classroom experience, and being on the other side of the podium does not necessarily solve these problems. John Maynard Keynes once described education as "the inculcation of the incomprehensible to the indifferent by the incompetent." W. H. Auden defined a professor as "someone who talks in other

---

4. Chronicle of Higher Education, *Salary Data* (2008), http://chronicle.com/stats/salary/salary.htm. *See also* Society of Alternative Law Teachers, *SALT Equalizer* (March 2008) (regional breakdowns).

people's sleep."[5] This was even before laptops and BlackBerrys offered infinite other ways for students to while away class hours without the trouble of listening to faculty, let alone reading the assigned materials.

The quasi-Socratic style of teaching that prevails in large courses is part of the problem. In this world, as legendary Yale law professor Grant Gilmore portrayed it: "Never is heard an encouraging word, and the skies remain cloudy all day."[6] And that was at Yale. At institutions where many students are interested primarily in getting a marketable credential and a head-start on preparation for the bar exam, faculty may find the classroom interchange less satisfying than they had envisioned. Even those who enjoy the challenge of teaching early in their careers sometimes find that the novelty wears off and that the inexorable onslaught of exams and recommendations becomes increasingly oppressive.

Scholarship, too, has its downside. To begin with, it involves isolation and sometimes a fair amount of intellectual drudgery. In 1936, law professor Fred Rodell famously observed: "There are two things wrong with almost all legal [academic] writing. One is its style. The other is its content."[7] Not much has improved on either front. The frequently jargon-laden pretentiousness of academic prose constitutes what one of my colleagues describes as "crimes against our mother tongue."[8] Footnote fetishes have compounded the problem. Who wants to wade through 490 pages, festooned with 4800 notes, exploring a single section of a single securities statute?[9] As Rodell put it, the overall impression is that of "an elephant trying to swat a fly."[10] Unsurprisingly, much of this effort goes unread by anyone but the author's immediate family and tenure committee. My own survey for a Harvard *symposium* on legal scholarship found that more than half of some 70,000 articles had never been cited.[11]

Of course, not all published work ends up being unreadable and unread. Many legal academics write for multiple audiences and some have substan-

---

5. JOSEPH EPSTEIN, IN A CARDBOARD BELT 43 (Houghton Mifflin 2007).

6. Grant Gilmore, *What Is a Law School*, 15 CONN. L. REV. 1 (1982).

7. Fred Rodell, *Goodbye to Law Reviews*, 23 VA. L. REV. 38 (1936).

8. Lawrence Friedman, *Law Reviews and Legal Scholarship: Some Comments*, 75 DENV. U.L. REV. 661, 664 (1998).

9. For the intrepid reader, see Arnold S. Jacobs, *An Analysis of Section 16 of the Securities Exchange Act of 1934*, 32 N.Y.L. SCH. L. REV. 209 (1987).

10. Rodell, *supra*, note 7 at 38.

11. Deborah L. Rhode, *Law, Knowledge, and The Academy: Legal Scholarship*, 115 HARV. L. REV. 1327, 1331 (2002).

tial influence. But non-scholarly publications for practitioners or a general audience will seldom help a tenure file: "mere popularizer" likely will be the epithet of choice. For those who want immediate social or policy impact, academic life is not the most plausible route. And for those who want significant scholarly influence, finding an interesting topic on which one has something truly interesting and original to say is not a simple project. With conventional doctrinal or historical work, there is always the risk that someone else has beaten you to the point and that you will discover it only after investing substantial effort. With empirical work, "computers crash, data are incomplete, irrelevant or miscoded; informants refuse to be candid or fail to return [questionnaires] and telephone calls. . . ."[12] Worse still, after considerable time, effort and expense in conducting empirical research, the results may be disappointing. Specifically, the response rate may be too low to permit generalizations, or the results may appear too obvious; they merely confirm what (in retrospect) everyone already knew.

So too, a discomfiting amount of academic life is consumed in what university officials dignify as "shared governance," and most faculty regard as "administrivia." In the words of then Stanford President Donald Kennedy, "the inmates are running the institution," and they are not always suited for the task.[13] Higher education's reflexive response to almost any issue is to throw a committee at it, and, at some law schools, the frequency of mindless meetings and petty politics is a major irritant. Professors can become enmeshed in disputes over inconsequential matters that they can control as a stand-in for all the things they cannot. Whatever their stated agenda, many faculty meetings have an unstated function similar to the animal kingdom's plumage display, in which participants vie to remind each other just how smart they really are. Those who land in academic careers tend to consider themselves especially intelligent and, like one of the characters in Edith Wharton's *Hudson River Bracketed*, "can't rest until the milkman knows it."[14] All too often, faculty gatherings fit the description that writer Mignon McLaughlin offered for meetings generally: "No one really listens to anyone else, and if you try it for awhile, you see why."[15]

---

12. Peter Schuck, *Why Don't Law Professors Do More Empirical Research*, 39 JOURNAL OF LEGAL EDUCATION 323, 331 (1989).

13. DONALD KENNEDY, ACADEMIC DUTY 139 (Harvard University Press 1997).

14. EDITH WHARTON, HUDSON RIVER BRACKETED 216 (Appleton 1929).

15. McHale, Wit, 257 (quoting McLauglin).

What makes these occasions particularly annoying is that they waste faculty members' most valued commodity: time. Time is an invaluable resource, particularly in the early years of an academic career, when professors are preparing new courses and launching new research. For all their fabled flexibility, academic schedules are also unbounded. Many professors feel that they never truly have "time off." They could always do something better if they invested more effort. Further, part-time schedules are difficult to accommodate. It is possible to reduce a course load, but not to meet with half a student, attend half a faculty meeting, or write an only half-decent law review article.

Finally, the obvious benefits of a tenure system carry some less obvious costs. Because the stakes are high for both individuals and institutions, the standards can be demanding and the risks of failure considerable. The expectation that most academics will pass muster intensifies the humiliation of those who do not. Although few law faculty are turned down by a final vote, a substantial percentage are pushed out before a vote becomes necessary. Not all of them live happily ever after.

None of these disadvantages should be overstated. As noted earlier, the vast majority of faculty are exceptionally satisfied with their careers. But not everyone has the talents and temperament for a life in legal education. Prospective academics should not choose this path by default.

TRANSITIONS FROM PRACTICE

Assessing Your Prospects

Deciding that an academic life may be right for you is, of course, only the first step toward that career shift. The second is determining whether you have a realistic prospect of landing the kind of position you want. Competiveness varies across institutions, but the overall statistics are sobering. The most recent hiring data from the Association of American Law Schools (AALS) found that only approximately 14 percent of some 950 applicants at the annual hiring conference landed positions; the rates were slightly higher for women (15 percent) and candidates of color (18 percent).[16]

What distinguishes the successful applicant? Although law schools vary somewhat in the importance that they ascribe to particular credentials, the most common credentials considered are law school attended, grades, prac-

---

16. Association of American Law Schools, *2006–07 Statistical Report on Law Faculty, Faculty Appointment Register Data* (2008).

tice and teaching experience, publications, law review position, judicial clerkship, and other advanced degrees.[17] The vast majority of law school faculty have spent some time in practice.[18] Working in a field closely aligned with your scholarly and teaching interests is an obvious asset, particularly if it guides your research agenda. However, spending more than a few years in practice can raise concerns about your academic commitment and ability to start over at the bottom of the career ladder. To an increasing extent, schools are seeking evidence of scholarly capabilities. If your resume is weak on conventional markers of academic promise, such as an advanced degree, prestigious clerkship, or high grades from an elite institution, it may benefit you to seek an additional credential or to publish a substantial article before entering the teaching market.

You could also consider positions other than a tenure-track appointment, such as directing an academic program or research center, running a public interest program, or teaching clinical or legal research and writing courses. These jobs offer many of the rewards of academic life without the publication pressures but often also without the potential for future.

Testing the Waters

For individuals seeking to buff up their credentials or to test the waters before making a permanent commitment to academia, a fellowship or visiting lecturer position makes obvious sense. These opportunities are helpful at least one or two years before entry into the market and provide some time to produce a substantial academic publication. A growing number of law schools have fellowships specifically designed to launch individuals into scholarly careers.[19] Legal research and writing or adjunct teaching positions can also provide a taste of academic life, along with contacts that can help in subsequent job searches. But you should approach these positions with caution if your objective is a fulltime tenure-track appointment; many provide neither the prestige nor sufficient time to write that can secure your ultimate goal.[20]

---

17. Elyce H. Zenoff and Jerome A. Barron, *So You Want to Be a Law Professor*, 69 A.B.A.J. 1712, 1714 (Nov. 1983).

18. Robert J. Borthwick and Jordan R. Schau, *Note: Gatekeepers of the Profession: An Empirical Profile of the Nation's Law Professors*, 25 U. MICH. J.L. REFORM 191, 218 (1991).

19. A list of schools with formal programs is available at http://taxprof.typpad.com/taxprof_blog2008/03/teaching-fellow.html.

20. Kevin H. Smith, *How to Become a Law Professor Without Really Trying: A Critical, Heuristic, Deconstructionist and Hermeneutical Exploration of Avoiding the Drudgery Associated with Actually Working as an Attorney*, 47 U. KAN. L. REV. 139, 141 (1998).

Finding a Fit

As with any job search, there are obvious tradeoffs between the likelihood of getting any position and the likelihood of getting one you really want. Casting a broad net will enhance the chance of being hired somewhere but at the cost of ending up with a location or teaching package that fails to accommodate key concerns and desires. Being brutally honest with yourself and diplomatically honest with any potential employer is essential. Can you really be happy as a single Latina in a small town with few professionals of color? How interested are you really in teaching bankruptcy?

As a strategic matter, it helps to identify a reasonably broad range of first-year and upper-level courses that you are willing to offer, but it is a mistake to stray too far from your comfort zone. If you did not like contracts much as a student, you may not feel different as a professor, and switching to a more congenial alternative is not always easy. You incur considerable costs in preparing a new course and often encounter turf issues in trying to "trade-up" the curricular hierarchy. If a school you like is already well stocked in faculty with your substantive interests, do not assume that they will welcome a competitor. If your main focus is in a field with limited student demand, you may want a commitment to let you offer at least one course in the area.

Getting a sense of a particular institution's culture and priorities is always important. What are the backgrounds and expectations of faculty and students? How significant is teaching, compared with research, and how much tangible assistance is available for scholarship? Will colleagues value your research interests? Are you likely to find a critical mass of faculty for support and friendship?

When I came to Stanford Law School three decades ago as the second woman on a faculty of 36 men, I was clueless about the importance of such questions. I was particularly unprepared for the dean's ill-disguised horror when I proposed teaching a course on gender discrimination. "It would," he explained, "type you as a woman." I responded with what I hoped was faint irony: "That probably won't come as a shock to most colleagues. And what, after all, are my alternatives?" But, of course, his point was academic credibility, and I could never establish that with a "fringe" course on women. He suggested teaching negotiable instruments instead. Fortunately, times changed, as did deans, but it was five years before I managed to sneak gender into the curriculum.

Whether or not a school's prestige is particularly important to you, it will be important to others, so it is helpful to know how the institution's ranking affects institutional priorities. If a school is under pressure to improve its scholarly reputation or bar exam passage rates, you should be prepared to respond accordingly.

Entering the Market

The nicest comment I have ever heard about the academic hiring process is that it is "not quite as horrible as I expected." More typical descriptions do not bear repetition in polite company. The lynchpin of the process is the AALS' annual faculty recruitment conference (aka the "meat market"). In essence, the event is a form of academic speed dating. Appointments committees grill selected applicants during half-hour interviews and then invite promising candidates back to their school for one-to-two-day look-over visits. For many applicants, especially those with unfilled dance cards, the conference atmosphere can be truly toxic. The anxiety in elevators is palpable, and if misery loves company, it is not apparent at this event.

Part of the problem is that there are infinite ways to screw up. The most common stem from ignorance, either of a particular school or of courtship etiquette generally. A lack of basic knowledge about the institution signals indifference, indolence, or both. Specific questions about salary and research assistance for an offer that has not yet been extended can seem presumptuous.[21] And overly pointed inquiries about divisive issues are more likely to evoke discomfort than candor. Save those concerns for less formal settings. Also save any extended chit chat for another occasion. You do not have time, and a hiring committee does not generally have interest.

Interviews for academic positions tend to be much more substantive than those for legal practice. You should have some brief, well-prepared summaries of your main publications, work in progress and other research ideas. Prepare several questions of your own that indicate some familiarity with the institution or with those conducting the interview.

During on-campus visits where you will have more extended office meetings with small groups of professors, it is always helpful to know something about their work. Faculty who have little interest in your teaching and research agenda are generally happy to talk about its relevance to their own. But avoid allowing anyone else to hijack the conversation for an extended interval. You want those present to be impressed by *your* intelligence, not by a colleague who already has a job.

---

21. Zenoff and Barron, *supra*, note 17 at 1715.

Good manners and conventional attire are essential. What might be tolerated as harmless idiosyncrasies in an established academic may send up warning signals in an entry-level candidate. If you come across as even slightly rude, arrogant, disingenuous, or fashion–impaired when seeking a position, many interviewers will worry about what might happen once you have it.

The campus job talk is an art form that requires significant preparation, preferably including a trial run with academics. Do not simply assume that the verbal skills that have worked in other contexts will ensure an effective scholarly presentation. In academic contexts, you need to come across, above all, as an intellectual, not as an advocate. Finding the right topic is part of the mission. Choose work that is far enough along to showcase your scholarly talents and likely to interest non-specialists in the field. Avoid appearing pompous, defensive, or evasive. Answer the questions, and try to show a sense of humor. It is generally better to be honest about what you do not know than to duck or wing it.

DEVELOPING YOUR CAREER

Priorities

Many of the strategies that make for a successful academic career are common to other professional contexts as well. One of the most obvious is to set priorities and to be proactive in pursuing them. Know your school's expectations and be reflective about your own. How many and what kinds of publications are necessary for promotion? Does anything besides scholarly publications really count? How is quality assessed and what are the standards for tenure? Schools vary considerably on all of these issues. You need to know whether you will be expected to be one of the nation's leading scholars in the field or just to show promise and productivity.

You also need a clear sense of typical teaching and administrative loads. Do faculty get extra credit for taking on unpopular courses or attracting blockbuster enrollments? Do they lose credit for offering curricular frolics and detours? How is classroom competence assessed? What is the relative importance of student and peer evaluations? How much value is placed on committee work, student counseling and public service?

It is important to ensure that your school's expectations are reasonably consistent with your own aspirations and that you are making reasonable progress toward meeting both. Junior faculty members should be sure to get annual performance evaluations and to respond effectively to any significant concerns. If, for example, your teaching evaluations are weak, you can observe some classes of outstanding colleagues or invite them to your own. You can also take advantage of university resources, such as teaching experts who will videotape and analyze one of your class sessions. If the problem is scholarship, ask for help on developing ideas or reviewing drafts from others in your field.

Once you have tenure or a long-term contract, you should raise concerns if your contributions are not being fairly valued or your basic needs are not being met. Initiating that conversation may not come naturally. As the title of a leading book on gender differences in negotiation put it, *Women Don't Ask.*[22] An unwillingness to seem "pushy" or "difficult," or an undervaluation of their own worth, often keeps female professors from getting the support they require.

Boundaries

Learning when to "just say no" is another critical skill. Women who have been socialized to be helpful and caring often end up with disproportionate shares of academic housekeeping. Faculty of color also end up in similar situations, given their small number in relation to the demand for diversity on decision-making bodies. The problem is compounded by the "learned helplessness" of some professors, whose reputation as undependable, unavailable, unprepared or uncivil exempts them from any heavy lifting on administrative matters. Egregious shirking does, however, arouse resentment among more dutiful colleagues. So the prudent course is to assume a fair share of administrative work but not to become the "go to" person for demanding or divisive assignments.

Setting limits is equally critical for other add-ons to academic life, such as conferences, panels, symposia and non-scholarly writing opportunities. It is nice to be asked, but, often, opportunities that look attractive in principle turn out to be unexpectedly time consuming and inconvenient in practice. If in doubt, never accept on the spot. Take a cooling-off period to assess whether a given invitation will provide significant enough personal or professional benefits to be worth the hassles. Opting for the occasional boondoggle is, of course, a treasured reward of academic life. Subsidized meetings in appealing locations are the "leisure of the theory class." But too much time spent responding to other people's agendas can get in the way of pursuing your own.

---

22. Linda Babcock and Sarah Lashever, Women Don't Ask: Negotiation and the Gender Divide (Princeton University Press 2003).

It is also important to know when enough is enough. Just because there is a hoop, you do not need to jump through it. Banal though this advice sounds, it is surprisingly difficult for many high achievers to internalize. Awards, titles, invitations and prestigious publications are all coveted signals of success. In French sociologist Pierre Bourdieu's phrase, they are the "cultural capital" of campus life. But, for a large portion of the academic profession, the relentless scramble for status is a setup for frustration. There are so many ways of falling short. You can be at lesser institutions, hold lesser positions or publish in lesser journals. There is limited room at the top, and even those who get there can always find someone who does some part of the job better.

Moreover, a single-minded pursuit of prestige comes at a price. Most psychological research on happiness suggests that people often overvalue tangible but ephemeral signals of status. The more you get, the more you need, and their pursuit squeezes out time for family, friends, and leisure activities that, on a daily basis, may be far more fulfilling.[23] What constitutes the right balance often changes over time, and it is important periodically to take stock of whether you are really doing what you want and like.

The point came home to me at one point during my early years of teaching. I was attending a conference for new women faculty at a beach resort in San Diego. One of the first activities for participants involved placing someone in the center of a circle and assigning everyone on the outside a particular role: students, children, partners, colleagues, deans, committee chairs, law review editors and so forth. These individuals then began simultaneously shouting their demands. The point of the exercise was to give people an experiential understanding of competing responsibilities. The effect, at least on me, was to raise my already heightened anxiety level. I skipped the next sessions and social events to hole up in my room, catching up on everything that had been set aside to attend the conference. It was not a conducive work environment, and I felt too guilty and overwhelmed to engage in and absorb the content of the conference or even to enjoy the beach. In T.S. Eliot's classic phrase, I "had the experience but missed its meaning."

Values

After three decades in academic life, what I take from such experiences is the importance of defining success in your own terms. These may not always correspond to conventional markers of status. Many contributions of

---

23. Rhode, *supra*, note 3, 228-229.

academic life do not end up embellishing your resume, but they matter enormously to others and to the institution: helping a student get the job of her dreams or cope with a personal crisis, or improving university policies on important issues. There are also innumerable contexts in which self-promotion is self-defeating, and virtue is its own reward. At conferences, you can avoid entrapment in the debilitating in-group/out-group status hierarchies that are often enforced with all the pettiness of junior high. In public speaking and related social contexts, you can avoid the sins of the sharing-impaired. You can observe time limits and pay attention to needs other than your own.

The greatest privilege of university life is freedom. To a degree unparalleled in most professional contexts, academics have the chance to shape a career that reflects their own fundamental values. If you take advantage of that opportunity, you can do more than just "clarify a few concepts." You can also leave your field, your institution and your students slightly better than you found them.

PART IV

Where We're Going

Bridging the Generational Divide

23

By Beatrice O'Donnell
Anne Marie Seibel

GENERATIONAL DIVIDES ARE OFTEN as challenging in the law firm setting as divides between the genders. In law firms, you may easily find four generations working side by side. In fact, some studies claim that every 5–10 years there is a new generation in the practice of law. Law firms generally do not evolve at that quick a pace, however.

In the larger population, generations currently in the work force break down along the following broad lines:

Traditionalists:	born 1925–1942
Baby Boomers:	born 1943–1961
Generation X:	born 1962–1978
Generation Y/Millennials:	born 1979–1995

With this many different generational viewpoints working together, conflicts are inevitable. While it may not be the same as being from Venus and Mars, understanding how the generations think is critical to building successful litigation teams today.

If you listen to discussions of senior partners regarding new associates, it is not uncommon to hear complaints that the associates are focused on receiving large salaries and perks and are not as interested in working as hard as the partners were when they were associates. The associates, in contrast, cannot understand the partners' lack of appreciation of the associates' interests and pursuits outside of work. The following are perhaps imaginary, but not far-fetched exchanges:

OVERHEARD IN A PARTNERS' MEETING:

"Associates are seeking increasingly high starting salaries but are willing to put in less effort at work."

"I am here later than the associates working for me."

"Associates want constant feedback."

"Associates don't take ownership of cases."

"I can't get associates to invest in marketing activities."

"There is no loyalty among associates to our law firm."

"I can't find associates in the office when I need help."

"The associates spend more time on 'Facebook' than they do in the library."

OVERHEARD IN AN ASSOCIATES' MEETING:

"I don't know why the partner didn't give me comments on the memo I e-mailed."

"I don't want to work as hard as our partners."

"The partners don't appreciate the sacrifices I am making."

"No one is taking interest in my career."

"I'm not informed enough about firm decisions to feel invested in the firm."

A successful litigation team hinges on seamless communication. So, it is important to find a way to understand and bridge the gaps in perception and communication. But, how? First, we must understand where the generations are coming from. Second, we must work to understand the perspective of the other generation and find some common ground.

HOW DID WE GET WHERE WE ARE?

Associates have arrived in the legal profession fresh from the law school environment, which was only their most recent progression in the expected steps to career success. Their accomplishments were marked with great grades and much praise given along the way. These Generation X and Y lawyers are the children of Baby Boomers who lavished attention and praise on their every move. Every sports game was covered like a professional athletic event. Every bit of participation was marked with a certificate.

Moreover, these same Baby Boomer parents frequently micro-managed their children's lives. The same people who were told to "go outside and play" after school by their parents, heavily scheduled their own children's play dates and sports. The Baby Boomers were involved intimately in all aspects of their offspring's growing up, including the choice of college and law school. The term "helicopter parent" was coined as a result of these parents continued involvement in rescuing their children from any and all of life's inconveniences rather than allowing their offspring to learn from their mistakes.

Now, in the workforce, these Generation X and Y members continue to seek the same attention, praise, and direction that they have grown to expect. There is no question that the newest generations to join the work force are exceptionally talented and well qualified. Many senior partners have been heard to quip that they could not get a position at their current law firm, because the standards have become so high. Applicants for entry-level law firm positions speak multiple languages fluently, have traveled extensively, and have a significant interest in furthering justice and dedicating time to social causes.

While their ability is unquestioned, many senior lawyers do not believe that Generation X and Y lawyers have the commitment to grow, strengthen, and maintain the partnerships that they seek.

What has given rise to this mistrust of the generations who are the future of our firms? Some point to the fact that Generations X and Y have not faced many of the challenges faced by their predecessor generations. Generations X and Y have lived through 30 years of unparalleled economic prosperity in America and are inexperienced with the economic hardships that other generations have faced, although this may be changing given the economic downturn that started in the second half of 2008. Some commentators speculate that this gift of bounty actually has translated into two generations unprepared to be mentally tough under difficult circumstances. Other educated observers scoff at the "gain through pain" theory. Unquestionably, the economic boom time gave the Baby Boomers, the parents of Generations X and Y, the time and financial ability to foster their children's many talents. These newest generations were raised substantially differently from their parents, and, as a result, these children have been achievers and super-achievers their whole lives.

WHERE ARE WE GOING?

Now, in the work world, Generations X and Y are told that the next ring to grab is partnership, and they set off on that path. Associates are often so focused on the path to partnership that they often forget that their career at a law firm is longer than a 7–10 year life of an associate. Or they have decided that partnership is unattainable, so they might as well live a more balanced life. More experienced partners, on the other hand, have often forgotten the uncertainties and missteps of the initial years of practice. They are focused on the here and now of adding to the bottom line of law firm profits through their own efforts and those of the associates working for them. The generations find themselves going in different directions.

To ensure that our law firms will continue to be humane, intellectually challenging, and economically viable institutions, however, both sides of the equation need to cross the generational divide. An associate needs to embrace fully the responsibilities of a law firm position that is both highly sought after and lucrative. Incumbent in that challenge is for the associate to take ownership not only of the work that is assigned, but also of her piece in the overall success of the project.

Every member of a trial team has a role to play but thinking beyond the four corners of an assignment is critical. Often the smallest details in a trial can make a monumental difference between success and failure. Finding the unreported case by the same judge ruling on your motion for summary judgment can alter the direction of a brief. Digging out the "deleted" MySpace page of the plaintiff in a personal injury suit, showing him partying the night away while claiming an inability to leave his house, can turn the tide on damages.

By the same token, senior members of the trial team can benefit from sharing the goals and strategy of the litigation with all team members. Moreover, more experienced partners would be well served to be open to good ideas regardless of their source. "Flat" organizations have been shown to be more successful than hierarchical organizations. Anyone on a trial team can have a good idea. More junior members of the team, not burdened by what "usually" happens, can often think creatively in ways that others cannot. In addition, encouraging ideas from all members of the team breeds a sense of ownership that is invaluable to the success of any litigation. Team building ultimately benefits the firm in increased success for clients, low turnover and improved morale.

Associates also need to be educated about the economic realities that law firms face. In many ways, the dramatic increases in the billable hour have been tied to the increases in associate salaries. This escalation in associate salaries has been deemed necessary to attract the best and brightest talent to the top law firms. However, the paradigm may be changing as the commercial climate has changed. Associates should be brought into conversations regarding law firm economics so that they can understand the vision and forces driving their firms. The result will be associates who are more committed to, and more willing to make sacrifices for, their firms.

Naturally, associates' inclination to the short-term view conflicts with senior partners' desire that associates take ownership in the firm and in their careers. To bridge this gap, as a starting point, practitioners both old and new can agree that a career is a 30–40 year commitment and not a 7–10 year path. Closing this gap requires that each party take time to explain her perspective. As partners share more information about the business needs of a law firm with associates, perhaps associates also will show more interest in adding to the bottom line. The goal is to find some period of time in the future when the associate and partner will both be working together as partners and plan for that time.

TELEPHONES V. BLACKBERRIES

The communication necessary to close the gap is challenging, in part, because the electronic nature of practice makes the opportunity for cross-generational interaction rarer than it used to be. Further complicating the effort is that the decrease in interaction conflicts with the needs of the generations.

For example, senior partners value "face time," which remote access does not provide. Young associates want inclusion in decision-making and constant feedback about the value of their contributions. While e-mail potentially could be a tool for more inclusion of associates, as a practical matter, that does not often happen. Understanding these challenges and finding ways to work around them is important to a successful work environment.

Both partners and associates find themselves working remotely at times. Electronic advances clearly have increased the ability to work efficiently from outside the office. Out of sight is out of mind, however, for both partners and associates.

While an associate may feel she is working effectively from home, she may be missing opportunities to hear about new cases, to interact with clients, and to find out about opportunities within the firm. Female associates, in particular, should be wary of working remotely too often because they may already be out of the loop on "hall talk."

Likewise, senior partners do not do the associates any favors by managing from afar. If the associates are the only ones manning the ship at the office, resentment is sure to follow. Therefore, respect the right and necessity of colleagues to work remotely, but remember that, with this ability, comes the responsibility of reaching out to each other in person, too.

Even when everyone is in the office, the tendency to e-mail someone instead of walking down the hall lessens the opportunity for meaningful cross-generational exchange. Moreover, it increases the likelihood of cross-generational misunderstandings. A hastily read-and-replied-to e-mail among the hundreds we receive each day cannot provide the feedback young associates crave. Moreover, e-mail responses that are done quickly and with minimal, if any, editing can lead to misunderstandings. So, get up, take a walk, or at least pick up the phone.

Moving beyond electronic communication has tangible benefits. For an associate wary of being called to a partner's office to report on ongoing research, think of this as practice for the all too seldom court appearance. And, while talking face to face, try to see the partner in a new light. Perhaps you will have an occasion to discuss the pictures of the partner's family on her desk and get some insight into how she juggles her competing responsibilities.

Similarly, a partner walking into an associate's office makes that associate feel valued. If the associate no longer feels like a cog in the firm's production line, her commitment to the firm and her colleagues will grow.

Of course, electronic communication is here to stay. Everyone needs to decide how best to use it.

One example is teaching the older generation the benefits of social networking sites. By spending time on these sites, associates may be investing time in maintaining social connections that will generate business someday. Especially as social networking sites become tailored to business needs, the associate may be able to teach the partner about how to use effectively the services offered.

The younger generation may learn the tough lesson of being cautious about what you say in a public forum. It is not surprising that a generation who blogs or tweets about what they ate for breakfast has a lack of understanding about the need to use a filter in work situations. That filter needs to exist in social networking as well, given anything you say can be a reflection on your firm or clients.

The lesson is to use the electronic avenues to your advantage: connect with potential referral sources; work remotely; and send e-mails any time, day or night. But, remember, there is no substitute for a developing a genuine personal relationship with both your fellow associates and partners. Real teamwork is only developed working side by side, literally.

CHANGING THE PROFESSION

To ensure the success of individual lawyers and law firms, the multiple workplace generations must come together in forums to increase meaningful dialogue. Many firms have embraced diversity and women's initiatives, providing these lawyers an opportunity to network and openly discuss their issues. The vision must now include all members of the firm regardless of their age, gender or ethnicity if law firms are going to be vibrant, economically sound, and significant institutions in the 21st Century.

R U Ready: The Internet for Women Litigators

24

By Sandra A. Jeskie

PRACTICING LAW IN THE Twenty-First Century is more akin to Star Trek than Perry Mason. Rather than pick up the phone, clients often e-mail or text message. Sometimes, they tweet using Twitter. Many clients have virtual presences. In the past, lawyers relied on writing articles and speaking at conferences to showcase their talents. Now, they often participate in webinars, podcasts and blogging. Lawyers often make connections to clients through online social networking and sometimes engage in virtual meetings. The days of sending a letter by mail (or "snail mail," as it is now referred to) are over. Even faxes are considered an inefficient means of communication. Instead, we often prefer to send a .pdf for near warp speed transmittal. The result is that lawyers no longer have the luxury of taking a few days or even a week to respond to a letter. Technology now demands almost instantaneous responses.

While lawyers are traditionally slow to adopt technology, the changes in the Federal Rules of Civil Procedure relating to e-discovery have brought technology into the minds of all lawyers, young and old. Most law firms embrace technology, relying on sophisticated websites, BlackBerrys for every lawyer, and computers in every office.

As a famous song writer once said, "The times they are a-changin'." As lawyers, we have to keep up with our cutting-edge clients or be left behind. We can fight technology or embrace it. Since technology is here to stay and can vastly improve our ability to work more efficiently, I suggest we embrace it. As women lawyers, technology provides us with a wonderful opportunity to multi-task as we have never done before. We simultaneously can keep track of our children, respond to our clients, and market our skills and experience.

E-mail, text messaging, and instant messaging are now so commonplace that almost everyone is using them. Below are some of the more current technology trends that can be adopted to fit your practice. Of course, it is important to consider both the ethical implications and security features of any new technology before you adopt it.

SOCIAL NETWORKING FOR LAWYERS

While online social networking used to be considered a pastime only for our teenage children, the business world has enthusiastically adopted it with great success. Social networking websites function as an online community of Internet users. Such sites provide users with a Web presence by allowing them to create a personalized webpage.

LinkedIn (http://www.linkedin.com) is one of the most popular business-oriented social networking sites for professionals. As of February, 2009, it had more than 35 million registered users in more than 200 countries and territories around the world with executives from all Fortune 500 companies as members.[1]

LinkedIn allows users to create a profile that summarizes both professional expertise and accomplishments. Once you have a profile, you can invite trusted contacts to join LinkedIn and connect to you. Your network consists of your direct connections, your connections' connections, and the people they know, linking you to a vast number of qualified professionals and experts.[2] For example, at present, I have 109 direct connections in LinkedIn. Through those 97 connections, I am connected to more than 21,100 people, whose connections bring my entire network to an astounding 1,926,500 connections. Based on the number of possible connections, it would be hard to argue that LinkedIn does not offer one of the most powerful web-based Rolodexes of its time. LinkedIn also allows you to recommend people, a nice feature that allows you to establish credibility with your connections.

LinkedIn also offers a group feature. Members can join communities of professionals who share a common experience, passion, interest, affiliation, or goal. For example, there are numerous legal groups, including groups focused on a particular practice area or industry, as well as groups focused on women and the law. Some group members actively post questions and answers, thereby allowing them to showcase their talents and experience.

There are numerous other social networking sites, such as Facebook (http://www.facebook.com) and MySpace (http://www.myspace.com), which are widely used. Although they are more generally viewed as non-professional online communities, many lawyers participate in Facebook. While I personally have not felt the need to join Facebook for professional networking, I have heard some success stories, and it certainly offers another free way for lawyers to create a web presence. From all accounts, Facebook allows busy professionals to let their hair down, so to speak. Members can share their personal interests and family life in a way that you would not feel comfortable doing on a more professional social networking site like LinkedIn. As such, these sites allow lawyers to connect with other lawyers, clients and potential clients in a more personal way, enabling them to further their business relationship or establish new business relationships.

Facebook also lays claim to a very notable decision. In December, 2008, the Supreme Court of the Australian Capital Territory ruled that Facebook was a valid protocol to serve court notices to defendants. This ruling is be-

---

1. *LinkedIn About Us.* 2008. LinkedIn. 22 Feb. 2009 <http://press.linkedin.com/about>
2. See *id.*

lieved to be the world's first ruling that gives legal recognition to a summons posted on Facebook.

BLOGGING AND MICRO-BLOGGING

A. Blogs

Generally speaking, blogs are nothing more than a website maintained by one or more persons with up-to-date content. Blogs usually have a number of repeat visitors, and the blog's content can be sent to subscribers. Blogs may allow for interaction by readers who comment on the blogger's posts. At one time, blogs were viewed as a simple journal of life activities or web browsing activity. Now, blogs are quite sophisticated and are often focused around a particular subject or theme, providing readers with a continuous source of news, information and insight about a given topic. Blog readers can opt to receive new blog posts by RSS (Real Simple Syndication) feed or by e-mail.[3]

Lawyers regularly maintain blogs to build and enhance their reputation. Legal blogs are sometimes referred to as "blawgs." There are countless blawgs on the Web today, many of which boast a very strong following.

B. Twitter

Like other social media tools, Twitter (http://www.twitter.com) allows users to connect with other people but limits the feed or "tweet" to a maximum of 140 characters. In the not-so-distant beginnings of Twitter in 2006, it was used to answer basic questions such as, "What are you doing?" Twitter has now evolved into a sophisticated communications tool used by some companies, including eBay and General Motors.

In the recent election, politicians, including Barack Obama, and various news outlets used Twitter with extraordinary results. Twitter is now considered one of the fastest growing social networking tools available. For example, in a recent earnings call, eBay's Richard Brewer-Hay sent approximately 70 tweets giving a blow-by-blow description of the earnings call.[4] Reporters now use Twitter to cover hearings and trials live from the courtroom.

---

3. RSS is a technology that helps you keep track of updates on your favorite blogs or websites. Free RSS Feed Readers include Google Reader and Bloglines. For more information on how to set up an RSS feed, see *Tips & Tricks: What is an RSS feed and what can I do with it?* at http://www.theroadtothehorizon.org/2009/01/tips-tricks-what-is-rss-feed-and-what.html

4. Broc Romanek and Dave Lynn. "How Quickly are Things Changing? eBay Sends 70 Tweets During Its Earnings Call." 23 January 2009. TheCorporateCounsel.net Blog, 22 February 2009 http://www.thecorporatecounsel.net/blog/archive/002000.html.

There are some very interesting blogs that discuss the benefits of microblogging and Twitter. Most relevant for our discussion is the five-part blog series titled, "How to Use Twitter as a Lawyer" by Grant Griffiths.[5] In Part I of this blog series, Griffiths summarized seven ways for lawyers to use Twitter.[6]

1. Follow leaders in the legal field;
2. Conduct research by posting a question;
3. Get breaking news as it happens;
4. Follow trends in the industry;
5. Get noticed by joining in on the conversation;
6. Get up-to-date information by using Twitter as an RSS reader; and
7. Generate conversation around the water cooler.

Kevin O'Keefe's *Real Lawyers Have Blogs* is a leading source of information on the use of blogs and social media for law firm marketing.[7] In one of his posts about Twitter, he shared some interesting stories which can, and should, make every lawyer consider whether she is missing out by not joining in. Kevin reported that, until recently, he thought Twitter was just a distraction. He shared four stories, which I quote below:

1. Working one night last week I was 'tweeting' about the Mariners game while I was listening to it on MLB.com. A lawyer in DC who owns a piece of a minor league team, who had been following me on Twitter, replied back with a direct message about baseball first, which then led to his request to discuss doing some blogs for a number of lawyers back there.
2. I'm regularly exchanging comments via Twitter with a person in IT & Business Development in a top 5 law firm. Very good chance of leading to work with that firm.
3. A week ago Sunday Robert Scoble, one of most widely followed bloggers in the world, 'tweeted' to his 21,000 followers on Twitter that he liked following my blog and following me on Twitter. Robert said he liked what I wrote and said that I was a smart guy (take that for what it's worth). Anyhow, it brought a huge immediate increase in people following me on Twitter. Where that goes I don't know, but

---

5. *See* Grant Griffiths. "How to Use Twitter as a Lawyer—Part I." 11 September 2008. Blog for Profit: Use a Blog to Market Your Business. 22 February 2009. <http://www.blog forprofit.com/twitter/how-to-use-twitter-as-a-lawyer-part-1/>. At the bottom of this blog entry, there are links for the remaining four parts of the series.

6. *Id.*

7. Kevin O'Keefe. "Lawyer Marketing with Twitter Has Arrived." 5 May 2008. Real Lawyers Have Blogs. 22 February 2009. <http://kevin.lexblog.com/2008/05/articles/social-networking-1/lawyer-marketing-with-twitter-has-arrived>.

a lot more people are following me on Twitter, including some reporters and lawyers.

4. I expanded my relationship with high profile PR person via Twitter which led to a speaking engagement at a major national blogging and new media conference.[8]

If this piqued your interest and you want to start tweeting using Twitter, you might consider legal blogger Adrian Lurssen's posting on JD Scoop identifying a list of lawyers and legal professionals worth following on Twitter.[9]

OTHER BUSINESS SOCIAL NETWORKING TOOLS

Yammer (http://www.yammer.com) has been referred to as Twitter for companies. Yammer was launched in September of 2008 and has already gained a huge following. Unlike Twitter, Yammer groups users by e-mail address domain. Hence, people working for the same company are automatically connected through Yammer. It is now used by many companies as a tool for internal organizational communication.

CampfireNow (http://www.campfirenow.com) is another group chat tool for business. It claims to be similar to instant messaging[10] but is designed exclusively for groups rather than one-on-one discussions. It enables real-time communication with two to 60 people, thereby enabling businesses to work collaboratively with clients, customers and colleagues.

PODCASTS, WEBINARS AND YOUTUBE

Lawyers now have the opportunity to target a wider audience with streaming audio and video, rather than focus only on speaking opportunities at a sparsely attended conference. Podcasts, webinars or videos on YouTube (http://www .youtube.com) can be viewed or heard on a computer, iPod or other MP3 player. Incorporating audio or video into your marketing efforts can create an immediate connection between you and your potential clients and provides a great opportunity for busy lawyers to multitask. Simply tape a session and post it on your website, YouTube or somewhere else on the Web for potential clients to view anytime and anywhere.

---

8. *Id.*

9. Adrian Lurssen. "145 Lawyers (and Legal Professionals) to Follow on Twitter." 9 September 2008. JD Supra. 22 February 2009. http://scoop.jdsupra.com/2008/09/articles/law-firm-marketing/145-lawyers-and-legal-professionals-to-follow-on-twitter/.

10. Instant messaging is a text-based real-time conversation over the Internet.

YouTube has become an international phenomenon. Time Magazine rated it one of the best inventions of 2006.[11] It is now considered the largest website for video-sharing online, receiving more than 50 million unique visitors every month. Due to the sheer volume of visitors alone, many lawyers have turned to YouTube to market their practice. Some lawyers use it for video client testimonials or as an online recruiting tool. More enterprising lawyers use YouTube to provide substantive information to enhance their reputation and lead to prospective new clients.

There are also Internet-based radio programs, such as Legal Talk Network (http://www.legaltalknetwork.com), which offer radio programs designed for an audience of lawyers and the legal community nationwide. It also provides an online meeting place for professionals to share ideas, news, information, resources and contacts.[12] It even offers continuing legal education credit for listening to legal news.

VIRTUAL WORLDS—SECOND LIFE

Virtual worlds should not be confused with a virtual law firm, where lawyers work from home. Second Life (http://www.secondlife.com) is a 3D digital world imagined and created by its residents with a population of millions of real people from all walks of life around the world. Second Life has its own economy with users who actually own the intellectual property rights to items they create. Residents can even own virtual real estate. Real estate, items, and/or services can be bought and sold using Second Life's currency, called the Linden dollar. To explore Second Life, users must create their own "avatar," which is a digital representation of yourself. You can then use your computer to navigate Second Life, talk to others, use items and buy and sell goods.

I know it sounds silly to many readers and I, too, have my doubts. I have commented regularly that "I barely have time for my first life, let alone my second life," but many people and lawyers find it fun and profitable. Companies such as BMW, Coca Cola and Calvin Klein exist in Second Life with virtual stores or exhibitions. Even a news agency, Reuters, has a Second Life news bureau and a reporter covering news in Second Life and other virtual worlds.

---

11. http://www.time.com/time/2006/techguide/bestinventions/inventions/youtube.html.
12. "About the Legal Talk Network." 2008. Legal Talk Network. 22 February 2009. http://www.legaltalknetwork.com/modules.php?name=FAQ&myfaq=yes&id_cat=1& categories=About+The+Legal+Talk+Network.

Several law firms have virtual presences in Second Life. Few firms actually attempt to practice law in Second Life, but some foreign firms have tried, claiming that it allows clients who cannot get into their real office to meet at the firm's virtual office. Clearly, there are ethical issues that must be addressed before lawyers can safely practice law using an avatar in a virtual world. There is, however, real revenue being made in the virtual world. Wherever money changes hands, there will be clients with real life needs. Second Life is just a recreation of everything we experience in our daily real lives, including the problems and legal disputes. As such, there are an abundance of intellectual property issues and problems, contract disputes and landlord-tenant concerns.

While virtual worlds have not quite caught up to the legal profession as some expected, you can easily imagine what will happen in the years to come as both the profession and technology advance.

RESEARCH

The Internet has transformed the way we conduct legal and business research. Instead of wiling away the hours in the law library, we research on Lexis (http://www.lexis.com) or Westlaw (http://www.westlaw.com) from the luxury of our office or home. There are, of course, hundreds of other great legal websites that can supplement our research efforts, such as Find Law (http://www.findlaw.com). Many of these websites are free. Depending on your area of interest, there are numerous specialized legal websites that also provide a wealth of relevant information. It is, however, important to double-check all information taken from the Internet and never cite to such information in a brief to the court, unless the circumstances require it.

Since lawyers know how to conduct legal research, this section addresses just a few of the non-legal websites that might benefit your practice.

A. Google

Google (http://www.google.com) has become one of the most powerful internet search engines available. Google's basic search functions allow you to search for any topic or person. In addition, Google Alerts (http://www .google.com/alerts) are a great way to keep up with the activities of your clients or your firm.

Google also offers other search functions that allow you to pinpoint the information most important to you at the time. For example, Google News (http://news.google.com) allows you to limit your search to news reports. Google Scholar (http://www.google.com/scholar) provides a simple way to broadly search for scholarly literature, from many disciplines and sources. Google Reader (http://www.google.com/reader) helps you keep up with all of the information on the Internet by organizing and managing the content that interests you. Google Blog Search (http://blogsearch.google.com) can help you find blogs of interest.

B. Wikipedia

Wikipedia (http://www.wikipedia.org) is a multilingual, web-based, free-content encyclopedia, written collaboratively by volunteers from all around the world. It has grown rapidly into one of the largest reference websites, attracting at least 684 million visitors yearly, with more than 75,000 active contributors working on more than 10,000,000 articles in more than 260 languages.[13]

Because Wikipedia is an ongoing work, and, for the most part, anybody can contribute, it should never be relied upon for research. It is, however, a good starting point to obtain basic information on just about any topic, as long as you recognize that it could contain misinformation. Generally speaking, older articles, which have been extensively edited, tend to be more comprehensive and balanced, while newer articles more frequently contain misinformation.[14]

C. Internet Alerts

As previously mentioned, you can stay apprised of any topic or your clients' activities through Google Alerts. It lets you know when new information on a topic of interest to you has been posted somewhere online and spidered by Google.

A similar service is offered for Twitter, called "TweetBeep" (http://www.tweetbeep.com). The alerts let you keep track of what has been written online about you, your clients or any person or product you are interested in tracking. These alerts can aid in marketing, allow you to better understand various industry trends, and keep you apprised of what is hot in your field. You might also find that they provide helpful ideas for future articles or blog posts.

---

13. "Wikipedia: About." 15 February 2006. Wikipedia. 22 February 2009. http://en.wikipedia.org/wiki/Wikipedia:About
14. *Id.*

D. CEOExpress

CEOExpress (http://www.ceoexpress.com) pares down many of the most used resources on the Web to the 20% that is most critical and useful. It delivers the information in the form of web links in a clear, easy-to-use format. It covers topics as diverse as daily news and business research to office tools and travel.

CONCLUSION

The practice of law has come a long way in a very short time due to advancements in technology. Since the Obama administration is expected to leverage technology and other social media fully in an effort to communicate change and get ideas from a broad range of constituents, there can be little doubt that some of these changes will trickle down to the legal profession.

Technology is a very powerful tool that we can all use to improve our lives and become more efficient. Embrace it, because it is here to stay.

The Next Act 25

By Judge Phyllis W. Beck

As MUCH AS YOU might not like it, when you reach a certain age, you will be shown the door. Some are shown the door because of firm policy; some because their client base has dried up; some because the legislature has set a mandatory retirement age; and some because they want out. Some women will turn off the lights, close the door, and breathe a sigh of relief. Others will try to stay engaged. It is to this latter group that I address my comments.

If you are near retirement age, you will recall that, when you entered the profession of law, you had to overcome sexism. What were you, a female, doing in a traditional man's world? Why weren't you home tending to a husband and children? Would a client have confidence in a woman? Would a woman have stamina to work hard? Could a woman be appropriately aggressive? Would a judge or a jury take a woman seriously?

Now, in the twenty first century, sexism still exists, but it has been attenuated. However, a woman of a certain age faces not only the remnants of sexism, but also ageism. Older folks are frequently marginalized. Especially for women, there may be an assumption that their thoughts and ideas are mired in an earlier era; that physically they cannot keep up with their younger colleagues; that they should quietly move aside and let the next generation take the reins; and that they are probably illiterate in the computer age.

Notice how the media treats the accomplishments of women over 65. The media always reveals her age and then marvels that someone that "old" is still performing at a high level. Articles about actresses Elaine Stritch and Estelle Parsons, each in their eighties, find it astonishing that they are still at the top of their game. In contrast, writings about Warren Buffett, and other men over seventy, assume that they are wiser and more talented the older they get. They do not mention their age, and they do not marvel that anyone so old is so productive.

The woman who has escaped the curse of ageism is Sandra Day O'Connor. After she stepped down from the United States Supreme Court, she has ably served on boards and commissions and is on the national lecturing circuit championing judicial independence. She is a star and, perhaps, an exemplar of how older women will be treated in the future. She also serves as a role model for those who are entering the next phase. She stands tall and looks fit; she speaks forthrightly; she does not discuss her age; and she assumes what she says is relevant and the listener will not pigeonhole her as an older person whose views are unworthy of attention.

In examining your next phase, think carefully about how to proceed. If you do not have sufficient retirement income, then you have no choice. You have to find a paying job. If you are fortunate enough to have sufficient income and good health, then you have to decide whether you want to continue professionally or not. If you choose the leisured life, recognize the draw-backs. You may lose the status you attained as a partner in a law firm or in a government position. For sure, you will lose the support of an assistant. You will be looking up your own phone numbers, stamping your own letters, get-ting your own coffee and doing your own filing.

If you do want to continue on a career path, finding the right niche will take some exploring and adjustment. You will be entering what is now called an "encore career," a "post career "or an "engaged retirement."

Harvard University, recognizing that certain people will seek a second act in a new stage of life, has started an interesting experiment called the Har-vard Advanced Leadership Initiative. For the first class, Harvard University selected 14 high level people who recently retired from responsible corporate or government jobs. Over one year, Harvard will expose the group to courses and experiences that will help them make dramatic shifts from their former jobs to new career ventures. Harvard is preparing them to become social en-trepreneurs; to become leaders in non-profit enterprises dealing with health, poverty, education and the environment. The program is out to show that, in leadership positions, "experience," that is, age, is a plus.

Behind the initiation of this program is the fact that more than 75 million baby boomers, who were born between 1946 and 1964, will soon be retiring from their primary careers. It appears that the traditional idea of leisure and travel in retirement is going by the wayside. Many older people want to be in-volved; want a hand in changing society.

Also, recognizing the need to explore opportunities for baby boomers, a non-profit, Civic Ventures, has become a think tank as well as a "Craig's List" for older folks seeking work in education, health, and social services. It, along with other institutions, is sponsoring programs in community col-leges throughout the country that will turn out second career people who will give back to society. The guiding principal is that engagement later in life does social good for the community and personal good for the participant.

So what should you be thinking about on the cusp of a second career? When you entered the practice of law, you were a path breaker, you fought sexism. Now when you enter the next phase you will encounter ageism as well. From my long career, I learned many lessons, which, I believe, are ap-propriate for the second act as well as for the first.

1. Recognize Discrimination

Most women don't recognize discrimination—whether it is sexism or ageism—when it stares them straight in the face. I graduated from Brown University with a pretty good academic record. My first job was at TIME,

Inc., where I was being trained as a researcher. The magazine stories were pulled together by a researcher, a writer and an editor. The writers and editors were all men. All researchers were women. Certainly, as was shown later, women were perfectly capable of doing the same work as men. It did not occur to me until years later that this hierarchy was discriminatory and sexist.

Later, in the 1970s, a group of women at The New York Times and Newsweek, where a similar situation existed, took legal action. For the first time, I realized that not only had I been in an unfair environment, but I accepted it because that was how it was always done.

So, if you are being excluded, examine the situation to determine if ageism is at its core. If it is, fight it.

2. What You Look Like—What You Wear—Defines You

At TIME, women who were secretaries or in the business department were well groomed. In the editorial section, where I was, women dressed casually and carried dirty raincoats. In an elevator full of people, it was easy to pick out the editorial staff. What they wore told where they worked.

So if you want to stay on the professional side of life, don't slip too deeply into casual. Look the part of someone on the go.

3. Prepare to Achieve Your Goal

After a stint at TIME and a short career at a local newspaper, I stayed at home with my four children. In addition to motherhood, I volunteered at the children's schools and for the Democratic Party. I realized that I would never rise in politics, or any other way, unless I had specialized training. I would be pasting stamps on envelopes for the rest of my life. I decided to take graduate work and prepare for a career. I was encouraged by Betty Friedan's book, "THE FEMININE MYSTIQUE."

So prepare for your next step. If it is to be a sculptor, find an art school; if it is to be a Latin teacher, explore the requirements and begin to fulfill them.

4. Cut Your Losses

I initially enrolled in graduate school at Bryn Mawr College in the Psychology/Child Development department. Try as I might, I could not find a comfortable home in that subject of study. One night, I complained to a friend that I hated my studies. She got tired of my grousing and asked me the crucial question, "What would you do if you were a man?" The question stunned me, and I had no answer, but I thought about it for several days. I realized that

many of the fellows in my class at Brown University who majored in political science had gone on to law school. The idea seemed absurd. It was 1962.
I was responsible for the care of four children and a husband. I knew no other
woman in law school, nor did I know any lawyers. I eventually enrolled in the
night division at Temple Law School in Philadelphia. From the first class at
law school, I knew it was for me. In retrospect, cutting my losses and leaving
Bryn Mawr College for Temple Law School was the right thing to do.

In retirement, explore. If you became Of Counsel to your firm, and it is
not to your liking, do not stay with it. Explore, explore, explore.

5. Pay No Attention to Other People's Opinions

Since I was the only woman anyone knew in law school, social acquaintances felt perfectly free to criticize my decision to attend law school. So-
called friends, and even the children's pediatrician, warned that my children
would come to no good. Without saying it, these people made it clear that, by
breaking the taboo and departing from my expected roles, I and my family
were courting trouble.

Even the organized bar association showed its disapproval. Before taking
the bar exam, a candidate had to be approved by an ethics committee of her
county bar. The first committee I appeared before flunked me. I don't know
for sure, but I imagine their thinking was that someone in my personal position had to be irresponsible and neglectful to pursue a career in law. I got a
second hearing and passed. I took the bar and became a lawyer.

In retirement, if you choose to become an organic farmer or a stand-up
comic, move right ahead. Other people's views of what you are doing should
have no influence on the second act you choose.

6. Go for the Gold

After practicing law and teaching law for about 10 years, I decided to
spend full time in academia, first, at Temple Law School and, then, as Vice
Dean of the University of Pennsylvania Law School. I was in my fifth year at
Penn when I discovered that the Pennsylvania Legislature was adding eight
seats to the intermediate appellate court, the Superior Court. The Superior
Court was established in 1895, and no woman had ever sat on the Court. I
eyed the position as my pot of gold. I applied for the job.

I appeared before a nominating commission that the governor had established. I prepared for the interview in the same way I prepared for law school
exams. I predicted the questions and formulated my answers in advance. The
committee forwarded my name to the governor, and he nominated me. Now,

I needed two thirds of the state Senate to confirm me. Although I had been a Democratic committee person and had twice run for local office in my community, the Senate leadership decided I did not have sufficient political experience or support and refused to bring my name out of committee.

The legislative session ended with no Senate action. The governor renominated me. I lobbied intensely in the state capitol, Harrisburg, but to no avail. Then, I read in the newspaper that a member of the General Assembly, Joe Smith, had been deposed from his leadership position. I went to see him and introduced myself as one loser to another. We had a long chat. His farewell to me was "I support you, and you can tell that to everyone." His endorsement broke the logjam, and I was confirmed. I spent almost 25 happy and productive years on the Pennsylvania Superior Court.

In seeking your second career, keep your eyes and ears open to opportunities. Talk to lots of people about what you would like to do, and let everyone know you are available. Once you see something that interests you, go full steam ahead for it. Second careers are different from first careers. You are a better candidate: more seasoned, more experienced, more knowledgeable about life and more savvy about how to move a case, an organization, or a project forward.

These are the lessons I've learned from my long career that I take into my "Next Act."

Are We There Yet? In Search of Equality in the Legal Profession

26

By Roberta D. Liebenberg

I BEGAN PRACTICING LAW when women were just beginning to enter the legal profession in large numbers. Throughout my career, I have seen enormous changes that have eliminated many of the barriers facing women lawyers. However, although we have made great progress, much work still remains to be done to secure the full and equal participation of women in the profession. While I do not have a crystal ball, I would like to share my ideas about what the future may hold in store for women lawyers.

A. The Work-Life Balancing Act

I had my first child while I was still in law school. After a clerkship on the Fourth Circuit, I began my job search in Richmond, Virginia, where there were very few practicing women lawyers. Prospective employers asked questions that are not only shocking by today's standards, but are also now impermissible. Interviewers routinely asked me whether I intended to have more children; whether I had childcare; and whether I thought I should be given a job when it was likely that I would simply drop out of the legal profession to have more children and raise a family. Having ultimately demonstrated to a firm that I would not morph into the fertile octogenarian, I was offered a job and became the first woman in its antitrust practice area.

When my husband finished his medical residency, my family relocated to Philadelphia, and I had my second child. Defying the expectations of those who had interviewed me in Richmond, I did not drop out of the legal profession. Instead, I joined a large law firm in Philadelphia and continued to work on a full-time basis. Because many of the cases I worked on were major antitrust class actions that required considerable travel, maintaining a balance between my efforts toward achieving partnership and my responsibilities to my family was particularly difficult.

After making partner at my firm, I had my third child. Working part-time but remaining on partnership track had not been a viable option when I had my first two children. By the mid-1980s, however, firms were beginning to recognize that many of the women attorneys that they had hired were dropping out of the profession to raise their families. Therefore, firms realized that they needed to provide alternatives for women lawyers who preferred not to work on a full-time basis while they were raising their children. In light of the considerable time and money that firms were devoting to the recruitment and training of the increasingly large number of women attorneys, it was in their self-interest to retain the services of these women by affording them alternatives to full-time work. These alternatives include part-time, flex-time and telecommuting work, as well as on-ramp and off-ramp programs that enable women who have taken time off to remain connected to their law firms and make a smooth re-entry back into the workforce when they are ready to do so.[1]

Firms now realize that, for many younger attorneys, both men and women, the priority is not always maximizing compensation but instead may be to achieve a desirable work-life balance so they can find satisfaction both at the office and in their personal lives. Indeed, law firms are distinguishing themselves from their competitors by implementing creative policies to attract young lawyers who have shown an increased willingness to accept reduced compensation in exchange for flexibility and reduced hours. For example, a 2007 national survey of the best law firms for women shows that 94 percent of the best firms have written policies for reduced hours; 46 percent of them offer full-time telecommuting; 28 percent have written policies for flex-time; 16 percent have programs to identify and rehire re-entry lawyer mothers; and 8 percent offer job shares.[2] Achieving success with these initiatives requires follow-up efforts, the use of metrics to determine progress, the engagement of both men and women as proponents of the programs, and transparency so that everyone can be made aware of the results.

To attract and retain the most talented attorneys, firms will need to continue to adapt their policies to accommodate the changing cultural values of young lawyers. Creative alternatives include offering different compensation packages based on the number of hours the attorney is willing to work, and offering longer paths to partnership for those who want to work part-time or "off-ramp" for longer periods in order to raise their children.[3] In addition, firms will need to continue to experiment with alternatives to the traditional billable hour model to address clients' concerns about escalating legal fees. These alternative billing arrangements will place a premium on the quality of an associate's work, rather than how many hours she has worked.

B. Achieving Greater Parity in the Number of Female Equity Partners

Since 2002, approximately 50 percent of all law school graduates have been women, and women now account for over 45 percent of all associates.

---

1. *The Opt-In Project Report* (2007), http://www.optinproject.org-a.googlepages.com/Opt-InProjectReport5_22_07_v4cs.pdf.

2. Working Mother and Flex-Time Lawyers LLC, 2007 *Working Mother & Flex-Time Lawyers Best Law Firms for Women: Trends Identified from National Survey*, at 2 (2007), http://www.flextimelawyers.com/best/trends.pdf.

3. Nancy Rankin, Phoebe Taubman, Yolanda Wu, *Seeking a Just Balance: Law Students Weigh In on Work and Family*, at 5 (2008), http://abetterbalance.org/cms/index2.php?option=com_docman&task=doc_view&gid=34&Itemid=99999999.

Women are becoming managing partners of law firms; heading practice groups; are being named general counsel of corporations and deans of their law schools; are being elected as presidents of local, state and national bar associations; and more and more women are serving on the state and federal bench. Women lawyers are now rainmakers and decision-makers and are exercising more power and influence than at any time in the past.

While the attainment of leadership positions by women lawyers is a very positive trend, it cannot mask the disturbing fact that, despite the large number of women entering the pipeline for the past three decades, the number of women equity partners has remained static at below 20 percent. At this glacial pace, it is estimated that women will not achieve parity with men in law firm equity partnerships until 2088.[4]

Equity partners not only have an ownership stake in the law firm, they also enjoy the highest compensation and the most prestige, power and influence. Therefore, achieving this "brass ring" is the true barometer of success at a law firm, and it is imperative that we find a way to increase the percentage of women equity partners in the future. Unfortunately, given the dismal current economic climate, law firms are increasingly resorting to the practice of de-equitizing partners. In addition, firms are making it increasingly difficult to achieve equity partner status in the first place.

At many law firms, the key to achieving equity partner status is having a significant "book" of business. Therefore, it is essential that women receive attribution and full origination credit for the business they help generate for their law firms. For example, if a woman is part of a team that has worked on making a successful proposal to a new client or has played a key role in servicing or growing the relationship with an existing client, she should be given attribution credit commensurate with her contribution. Too often, women are short-changed in this process.

Likewise, women are often disadvantaged in terms of inheriting clients from more senior attorneys, as male attorneys tend to bequeath their clients to their male protegés rather than the female attorneys who have also worked on the clients' matters. In light of the fact that, over the next ten years, 400,000 baby boomer attorneys will retire, firms need to implement more equitable client succession policies so that women are given a fair opportunity to increase their client billings and thereby achieve and retain equity partner status.

---

4. Catalyst, *Women in Law in the U.S.* (2008), http://www.catalyst.org/publication/246/women-in-the-law-in-the-us.

The ABA Commission on Women in the Profession ("Commission"), of which I serve as Chair, is working on various projects to address the long-standing and significant disparity between the percentage of female associates and the percentage of female equity partners. For example, the Commission is working with the Minority Corporate Counsel Association (MCCA) and the Project on Attorney Retention on a research project examining how law firms distribute billing credit and how that distribution impacts compensation and professional advancement of women lawyers to equity partnership status. In addition, the Commission is studying ways to ensure that women are given greater opportunities in the legacy process so that they receive billing credit for clients whose primary partner contacts are retiring.

C. The Salary Gap Between Male and Female Attorneys

In addition to the significant disparity between the percentage of male and female equity partners, the longstanding salary gap between male and female attorneys continues to exist. Indeed, a 2008 U.S. Census Bureau Report revealed that the median income of women lawyers is only 78 percent of their male counterparts.[5] Studies show that the pay disparity increases with seniority. According to the October 2009 National Association of Women Lawyers (NAWL) survey, male associates earn an average median income of approximately $169,000, while female associates earn an average median income of $167,000.[6] On average, male attorneys who are of counsel earn approximately $25,000 more than their female counterparts, while male non-equity partners earn approximately $25,000 more than their female colleagues. Most disturbingly, male equity partners earn $66,000 more on average than women equity partners.[7]

This pay disparity is troubling on a number of different levels. First and foremost, this problem has existed ever since women have entered the legal profession and, despite the passage of time, parity is still a long way off. Second, the fact that women are disadvantaged with respect to their compensation results in greater job dissatisfaction. In fact, a 2005 survey by the Allegheny County Bar Association (ACBA) found that women attorneys were

---

5. http://www.census.gov/prod/2008_pubs/acs-09.pdf at Appendix Table A-2.

6. The Nat'l Ass'n of Women Lawyers ("NAWL") and The NAWL Foundation, *Report of the Fourth Annual National Survey on Retention and Promotion of Women in Law Firms*, at 11 n. 19 (2009), http://www.nawl.org/Assets/Documents/2009+Survey.pdf.

7. *Id.* at 11-12.

twice as likely as men attorneys to be dissatisfied with their employment situation.[8] Not surprisingly, the increased dissatisfaction among women attorneys leads to higher attrition rates, reducing the number of women who will
ultimately be considered for partner.

For the longstanding problem of pay inequality to be ameliorated, women
will need to achieve leadership positions in their law firms, including the all-
important committees devoted to determinations of associate compensation
and partner allocations. Also, as discussed earlier, it is imperative that women
receive full business origination credit for the clients they have helped their
firms to bring in the door and develop, as an attorney's compensation heavily depends on how much business is attributed to her. Pay equality will go a
long way to improving the level of job satisfaction of female attorneys. With
increased job satisfaction, the attrition rate of female attorneys will presumably decline, leading to more women remaining in the pipeline for partner
consideration, and more women partners achieving positions of leadership
and power within their law firms.

D. The "Double Bind" Confronted By Women of Color

The various problems and inequalities experienced by women attorneys
that are discussed above are felt even more acutely by women attorneys of
color. Survey after survey shows that women attorneys of color have distress-
ingly high rates of attrition,[9] resulting in very small percentages of women of
color in the ranks of equity and non-equity partners. Indeed, while women of
color account for about 11 percent of associates, they account for only 3 percent of non-equity partners and about 1.4 percent of equity partners.[10] Thus,
according to the 2008 NAWL survey, "even though there is a greater percentage of female associates of color than male associates of color, the women are
less likely than men to hold the position of non-equity or equity partner."[11]

---

8. *Report & Recommendations of the Gender Equality Task Force of the Allegheny
County Bar Association*, 3 (2008), http://www.acba.org/ACBA/pdf/ACBA_GenderReport_
2008.pdf.

9. Approximately 86% of women of color leave their firms by the end of their seventh
year. Minority Corporate Counsel Association (MCCA), *The Myth of the Meritocracy: A
Report on the Bridges and Barriers to Success in Large Law Firms* at 33 (2007),
http://www.mcca.com/index.cfm?fuseaction=page.viewPage&PageID=614&varuniqueus
erid=29748014318.

10. The NAWL and The NAWL Foundation, *Report of the Third Annual National Survey on Retention and Promotion of Women in Law Firms*, at 8, http://www.nawl.org/Assets/
Documents/2008+Survey.pdf.

11. *Id.*

In addition, women attorneys of color occupy the lowest rung of the compensation ladder; they earn less than white male attorneys, less than male attorneys of color and less than white female attorneys. Indeed, women attorneys of color receive only 47 cents for every dollar paid to their white male attorney counterparts.[12] Further, women attorneys of color experience inferior assignments; unfair performance evaluations; lack of access to clients and networking opportunities; inadequate mentoring; and a working environment permeated with acts and comments that reflect explicit or implicit bias.[13] The challenge of being both a woman and a person of color has proven very daunting and has imposed significant hurdles that are quite difficult to overcome.

To address these troubling statistics, the Commission has published two ground-breaking reports that have provided concrete strategies and tips for women of color to succeed in law firms.[14] The Commission's most recent publication on this subject reflects the insights of a number of women of color who have managed to achieve partnership status in their firms despite encountering numerous obstacles along the way. The experiences and sage advice that these accomplished women offer provide a roadmap for success that can be utilized by law firms to help ensure that their respective women attorneys of color have a full and fair opportunity to succeed as well.

An increasing number of corporations are requiring that their law firms demonstrate a meaningful commitment to diversity by including female attorneys and attorneys of color on the teams handling their matters. Therefore, it is in the firms' own economic self-interest to hire, train and retain women attorneys of color. To reverse the very high attrition rates, firms must continue to focus increased attention and resources on creating a working environment that is hospitable to and supportive of women attorneys of color. These efforts will not only redound to the benefit of those attorneys, but to their firms as well.

E. Conclusion

Although the glass ceiling has been slowly cracking over time, it still looms over us. All of us, men and women, must re-double our efforts to elim-

---

12. MCCA, *supra* note 10, at 25.
13. ABA Commission on Women in the Profession, *Visible Invisibility: Women of Color in Law Firms* (2006).
14. ABA Commission on Women in the Profession, *supra* note 14; ABA Commission on Women in the Profession, *From Visible Invisibility to Visibly Successful: Strategies for Law Firms and Women of Color in Law Firms* (2007).

inate that ceiling once and for all so that the legal profession provides equal opportunity for women attorneys. I have seen first-hand during the course of my career how the profession has been so greatly enriched by the increased participation and leadership of women attorneys.

None of us can succeed on our own. It is incumbent upon everyone, particularly women lawyers, to use our experience and networking relationships to mentor younger women lawyers who are confronting many of the same challenges we faced earlier in our own careers. We each stand on the shoulders of those who came before us, and we must all reach out to help those behind us to climb the pathway to success. I am confident that the future holds great promise for succeeding generations of women attorneys who are following in our footsteps.

Resources

By Alexis Arena

BOOKS:

Brooks, Donna, *Seven Secrets of Successful Women: Success Strategies of the Women Who Have Made It—And How You Can Follow Their Lead* (1999).

Clanton, Karen, *Dear Sisters, Dear Daughters: Words of Wisdom from Multicultural Women Attorneys Who've Been There and Done That* (American Bar Association) (2000).

English, Holly, *Gender on Trial: Sexual Stereotypes and Work/Life Balance in the Legal Workplace* (2003).

Epstein, Phyllis H., *Women-at-Law: Lessons Learned Along the Pathways to Success* (ABA Law Practice Management Section's Practice-Building Series) (2004).

Hatfield Weishar, Hollis and Joyce K. Smiley, *Marketing Success Stories: Conversations with Leading Lawyers*, 2nd Ed. (ABA Law Practice Management Section's Practice-Building Series) (2004).

Hoff, Joan, *Law, Gender and Injustice: A Legal History of U.S. Women* (New York University Press) (1991).

Holtz, Sarah, *Bringin' in the Rain: A Woman Lawyer's Guide to Business Development* (2008).

Kellerman, Barbara, and Deborah Rhode, *Women & Leadership* (2007).

O'Connor, Sandra Day, *The Majesty of the Law* (New York, Random House) (2003).

Riveira, Ashley and Lindsay Blohm, *Presumed Equal: What America's Top Women Lawyers Really Think About Their Firms* (2006).

Slotkin, Jacquelyn and Samantha Slotkin Goodman, *It's Harder in Heels: Essays by Women Lawyers Achieving Work-Life Balance* (2007).

Snyder, Theda C., *Women Rainmakers' Best Marketing Tips,* 2nd Ed. (ABA Law Practice Management Section's Practice-Building Series) (2003).

Stiller Rikleen, Lauren, *Ending the Gauntlet: Removing Barriers to Women's Success in the Law* (2006)

ARTICLES:

Angel, Marina, *Women Lawyers of All Colors Steered to Contingent Positions in Law Schools and Law Firms*, 26 CHICANO-LATINO L. REV. 169 (Spring 2006).

Beiner, Theresa M., *Not All Lawyers are Equal: Difficulties that Plague Women Lawyers and Women of Color*, 58 SYRACUSE L. REV. 317 (November 2008).

Boyle, Kim M., *Best Practices to Achieve Diversity*, 53 LA BAR J 122 (August/ September 2005).

Brouse, Angela, *Comment: The Latest Call for Diversity in Law Firms: Is It Legal?*, 75 UMKC L. REV. 847 (Spring 2007).

Clark, Mary L., *One Man's Token Is Another Woman's Breakthrough?: The Appointment Of The First Women Federal Judges*, 49 VILLA. L. REV. 487 (2004).

Delossantos, Lea E., *A Tangled Situation of Gender Discrimination: In the Face of an Ineffective Antidiscrimination Rule and Challenges for Women in Law Firms—What is the Next Step to Promote Gender Diversity in the Legal Profession?*, 44 CAL. W. L. REV. 295 (Fall 2007).

Epstein, Cynthia Fuchs, *Women in the Legal Profession at the Turn of the Twenty-First Century: Assessing Glass Ceilings and Open Doors*, 49 KAN. L. REV. 733 (May 2001).

Evans, Danielle M., *The Non-Equity Partner: A Flawed Approach to the Disproportionate Advancement of Women in Private Law Firms*, 28 WOMEN'S RTS. L. REP. 93 (Spring/Summer 2007).

Francis Ward, Stephanie, *What Women Lawyers Really Think of Each Other*, ABA JOURNAL (2008).

French, Steve, *Of Problems, Pitfalls and Possibilities: A Comprehensive Look at Female Attorneys and Law Firm Partnership*, 21 WOMEN'S RIGHTS L. REP. 189 (Summer 2000).

Ginsburg, Ruth Bader, *Women In The Federal Judiciary: Three Way Pavers And The Exhilarating Change President Carter Wrought*, 64 FORDHAM L. REV. 281 (1995).

Ginsburg, Ruth Bader, *Remarks For California Women Lawyers*, 22 PEPP. L. REV. 1 (1994).

Kravitch, Phyllis A., *Women in the Legal Profession: The Past 100 Years*, 69 MISS. L.J. 57 (1999).

Lopez, Maria Pabon, *The Future of Women in the Legal Profession: Recognizing the Challenges Ahead by Reviewing Current Trends*, 19 HASTINGS WOMEN'S L.J. 53 (Winter 2008).

Marchman, Judy L., *Focus on Diversity: Retaining and Mentoring Women and Minority Lawyers,* 71 TEX. B. J. 310 (April 2008).

Maurer, Elizabeth K, *The Sphere of Carrie Burnham Kilgore*, 65 TEMPLE L. R. 827 (1992).

Molvig, Dianne, *Retaining Minority Lawyers: Diminishing Departures*, 80 WIS. LAW 6 (September 2007).

Nicholson, Lisa H., *Symposium: Women and the "New" Corporate Governance: Making In-Roads to Corporate General Counsel Positions: It's Only a Matter of Time?,* 65 MD. L. REV. 625 (2006).

O'Connor, Sandra Day, *The Legal Status of Women: The Journey Toward Equality*, 15 J.L. AND RELIGION 29 (2000).

O'Neill, LeeAnn, *Hitting the Legal Diversity Market Home: Minority Women Strike Out,* 3 AM. U. MODERN AM. 7 (Spring 2007).

Patton, Paula A., *Women Lawyers. their Status, Influence, and Retention in the Legal Profession*, 11 WM. & MARY J. OF WOMEN & L. 173 (Winter 2005).

Peters, Eunice Chwenyen, *Making It to the Brochure but Not to Partnership*, 45 WASHBURN LAW J 625 (Spring 2006).

Reeves, Arin N., *Five Principles for Creating Diversity in Law Firms,* 48 PRACT LAWYER 41 (October 2002).

Rhode, Deborah L., *Gender and the Profession: The No-Problem Problem*, 30 HOFSTRA L. REV. 1001 (Spring 2002).

Schafran, Lynn Hecht, *Women of the Courts Symposium: Not From Central Casting: The Amazing Rise of Women in the American Judiciary*, 36 U. TOL. L. REV. 953 (2005).

Sherry, Suzanna, *Civic Virtue And The Feminine Voice In Constitutional Adjudication*, 72 VA. L. REV. 543 (1986).

Vaughn, Karen Jackson, *Special Report: Diversity: Fostering Diversity in Law Firms is an Evolutionary Process*, 28 PENNSYLVANIA LAWYER 17 (March/April 2006).

Wu, Kathleen J., *Focus on Diversity: Diversity is a Journey, Not a Destination: Creating a Sustained Effort to Make the Legal Profession More Inclusive*, 71 TEX. B. J. 142 (February 2008).

ONLINE RESOURCES:

ABA Commission on Women in the Profession
http://www.abanet.org/women/home.html

ABA Guide to Diversity Resources:
http://www.abanet.org/legresource/minority.html

ABA Law Practice Management Section: Women Rainmakers
http://www.abanet.org/lpm/wr/

The Corporette
http://www.corporette.com

Equal Employment Opportunity Commission, "Diversity in Law Firms"
(2003).
http://www.eeoc.gov/stats/reports/diversitylaw/index.html

Holtz, Sarah, Women Rainmakers bLAWg
http://womenrainmakers.blogspot.com

Lawyers Life Coach
http://www.lawyerslifecoach.com

Ms. JD
http://ms-jd.org/

National Association of Women Lawyers
http://www.nawl.org

Report of the 2008 NAWL Survey on the Status of Women in Law Firms
http://www.nawl.org/Assets/Documents/2008+Survey.pdf

Rowland, Cynthia, Women Lawyer Leaders
http://womenlawyerleaders.blogspot.com

Sloan Work and Family Research Blog
http://wfnetwork.bc.edu/blog/

The Glass Hammer: Women Executive Blog
www.theglasshammer.com

The Woman Advocate Committee Website
http://www.abanet.org/litigation/committees/womanadvocate/home.html

Biographies

ABBE F. FLETMAN

 Abbe F. Fletman is the head of the Litigation Section of the Intellectual Property Practice Group, a member of the Commercial Litigation Practice Group and co-chair of The Government Relations and Regulatory Law Practice Group in Flaster/Greenberg's Philadelphia office. She concentrates her practice in complex litigation involving intellectual property, commercial disputes and government entities.

As lead litigator in a variety of forums including federal court, Pennsylvania Courts of Common Pleas, Orphan's Court and Delaware Chancery Court, Ms. Fletman has successfully handled notable cases representing private and publicly held companies, non-profit and for-profit organizations and government entities in jury and non-jury trials, and in numerous appeals.

A recognized leader in the legal community, Ms. Fletman is a past chair of the Federal Courts Committee of the Philadelphia Bar Association and is a fellow at The Academy of Advocacy of Temple University Beasley School of Law, where she serves as an instructor for the L.L.M. in Trial Advocacy and is a barrister in the school's American Inn of Court. She is a frequent presenter at legal conferences, including the American Bar Association Litigation Section annual meetings, the Pennsylvania Bar Institute, and the Philadelphia Bar Association's Federal Bench-Bar Conference. She was co-chair of the Woman Advocate Committee of the American Bar Association's Litigation Section for two years and was named a 2007 Woman of Distinction by the Philadelphia Business Journal and the National Association of Women Business Owners. She was named one of The 50 Top Women Lawyers in Pennsylvania in 2009 and has been named a Pennsylvania "Super Lawyer" in 2005, 2007, 2008 and 2009.

Among her published works, Ms. Fletman is co-author of "Government Entity Litigation" *Business and Commercial Litigation in Federal Courts* (2nd Ed. West, Nov. 2005).

EVELYN R. STORCH

Evelyn, Counsel to Harwood Lloyd, LLC in Hackensack, New Jersey, is a trial attorney specializing in complex commercial, real estate based, construction and employment litigation, professional liability claims, and insurance defense and coverage disputes. She brings to her clients the wisdom of her twenty eight years of trial and appellate court experience in both the state and federal courts. She has litigated intricate matters involving partnership dissolutions, shareholder and securities disputes, restrictive covenant suits, real estate brokerage claims (on behalf of both brokers and developers/owners), and civil rights violations. Her clients include individuals, small businesses, medium and closely held companies and the occasional multi-national corporation. Her diverse experience enables her to adapt her services to the particular needs of each client.

Ms. Storch graduated cum laude from Rutgers School of Law Camden in 1981. While in law school, she was Associate Editor of the Rutgers Law Journal. She was a semi-finalist and won the Best Brief Award in the school's Moot Court Competition. She served as a legal intern to the Hon. Dolores K. Sloviter, United States Court of Appeals for the Third Circuit, Philadelphia, Pennsylvania. She is a member of the New Jersey State and American Bar Associations. She serves on the Amicus Committee of the New Jersey State Bar Association for which she was chair in 2006–08. Evelyn is part of the leadership of the Woman Advocate Committee of the Litigation Section of the American Bar Association. She served as co-editor of this book and is now co-chair of the Corporate Counsel Interview Program for the 2009–10 year. On behalf of the New Jersey State Bar Association, Ms. Storch wrote the *amicus* brief to the New Jersey Supreme Court in *Jerista v. Murray*, 185 N.J. 175 (2005), which upheld the proximate cause requirement in legal malpractice cases.

In addition to serving as co-editor of this book and writing one of its chapters, Evelyn has authored or co-authored numerous articles: American Bar Association, LITIGATION, *Admissibility of Electronically Stored Information: It's Still the Same Old Story* (May, 2008); American Bar Association, Section of Litigation, Corporate Counsel Committee Annual Meeting, *Electronically Stored Information: Are You Ready?* (February, 2008); American Bar Association, LITIGATION, *Spoliation, or Please Don't Leave the Cake Out in the Rain* (July, 2006); and American Bar Association, Section of Litigation, The Woman Advocate Committee Newsletter, *If You've Got It, Flaunt It: Persuasive Brief Writing* (Fall, 2005). Evelyn has served as a panelist and presenter, both locally and nationally, on electronic discovery, bad faith insurance claims, brief writing, and taking and defending depositions.

ALEXIS ARENA

 Alexis Arena is an attorney at Flaster/Greenberg P.C. in the litigation practice group. She concentrates her practice on intellectual property disputes involving trademarks, employment disputes, and commercial litigation matters. Alexis also serves on the Executive Board of the Young Lawyers Division of the Philadelphia Bar Association, the Young Friends Board of the University of Pennsylvania Museum of Anthropology and Archaeology, and is an active member of the Philadelphia Chamber of Commerce.

ALANA K. BASSIN

 Alana Bassin is a partner at the law firm Bowman and Brooke LLP. She practices primarily in products liability. Most recently, her work includes defending high exposure chemical/toxic tort cases, nursing homes and hospitals, and construction products. No stranger to the courtroom, Alana's trial practice has taken her to at least 20 different states defending high exposure, personal injury, and wrongful death cases.

Alana has been selected by Minnesota Law & Politics as a Rising Star for eight years in a row. She is frequently requested to lecture at seminars and called upon by local and national publications. She was featured in the May 2005 New York Times' article, "The Pacifier Isn't for the Client," the February 2005 MSP Business Journal article, "You've Come a Long Way Baby" and was an April 2007 guest on the Minnesota Public Radio "Women on the Move" radio program. Alana also was an adjunct law professor in legal writing at William Mitchell College of Law from 2001 through 2006.

Alana is very active with her firm's diversity efforts and mentoring young associates. She currently acts as the hiring partner for the Minneapolis office and recently authored Gender and Generational Issues Across Borders and Marketing and Business Development for Senior Associates, both of which appeared in *The Woman Advocate.*

In her prior life, Alana spent her free time running marathons and doing triathlons. Now, Alana and her significant other, David Lissauer, spend their time (and get their exercise) chasing their three children: Talia (5), Solomon (3) and Ari (1).

HONORABLE PHYLLIS BECK

Phyllis W. Beck is a magna cum laude graduate of Brown University. She earned a J.D. from Temple Law School night division in 1967 where she was first in her class. After practicing law, she taught at Temple Law School and then was Vice Dean at the University of Pennsylvania Law School.

From 1981 to 2005, she was a judge of the Superior Court, the intermediate appellate court in Pennsylvania. Initially appointed by Governor Thornburgh in 1981, she was elected statewide to a ten-year term in November 1983, and retained in office in 1993. She was the first woman to serve as a judge on the court, which was formed in 1895. She is presently chair of the Independence Foundation, the ninth largest foundation in the Delaware Valley. She also serves as its chief financial officer. Until May 2009, she was general counsel of the Barnes Foundation.

Her scholarly articles, published in a variety of law reviews, reflect her interest in the criminal law, issues relating to women, the family and equality, among others. She is a contributing author to a book on the Pennsylvania Constitution.

She is a trustee and treasurer of the Free Library of Philadelphia. Judge Beck was a founding member and president of Philadelphia Futures, an organization devoted to mentoring children. She is currently on the board of Philadelphia READS, the local initiative of the national program of America READS, and is chair of the board of the After School Activities Partnerships (ASAP).

Judge Beck is a member of the American Law Institute, the Committee on Judicial Ethics of the Philadelphia Bar Association, a member of the Board of Visitors of Temple Law School, and a member of the President's Advisory Board of Temple University. She is a Pennsylvania Supreme Court appointee to the Board of Continuing Legal Education. She also serves on the board of the Mann Center for the Performing Arts. She is an overseer of the University of Pennsylvania School of Nursing, a board member of the Museum of American Jewish History, and president of the Foundation for Cognitive Therapy and Research.

She is the recipient of two honorary degrees, the Judicial Award of the Pennsylvania Bar Association, the Anne X. Alpern Award of the Pennsylvania Bar Association's Commission on Women, the Brennan Award of the Philadelphia Bar Association, and the Florence Murray Award of National Association of Women Judges, the Outstanding Alumni Award from Temple Law School, the Pennsylvania Legal Services Excellence Award, and the Sandra Day O'Connor Award.

Judge Beck is married to Dr. Aaron T. Beck. They have four children and eight grandchildren.

LAURA BRILL

Laura Brill is a founding partner of Kendall Brill & Klieger. Her practice focuses on complex litigation, including intellectual property, first amendment, and appellate matters.

The *Los Angeles Daily Journal* and the *San Francisco Daily Journal* have named Ms. Brill as one of the 75 top women litigators in California. Ms. Brill has been selected for inclusion in *The Best Lawyers in America* for 2007, 2008 and again for 2009 in appellate as well as intellectual property law. Also, *Los Angeles Magazine* selected Ms. Brill for inclusion in Southern California "Super Lawyers" in 2006 through 2009 and named her one of the "Top 50 Women Lawyers" in Southern California in 2008.

Ms. Brill is the recipient of the People for the American Way Foundation's Defenders of Democracy Award in honor of her leadership in protecting free speech and equal rights.

Ms. Brill is a frequent speaker at bar association and industry conferences and has appeared as a commentator on legal affairs on national television and as a guest lecturer at Yale Law School and UCLA School of Law.

From 1997–2009, Laura W. Brill worked first as an associate and then as a partner at Irell & Manella LLP in Los Angeles. In May 2009, she started her own firm, Kendall Brill & Klieger LLP.

PAULETTE BROWN

Paulette Brown is a partner in the New Jersey office of Edwards Angell Palmer & Dodge LLP and is a member of the firm's Labor & Employment Group and the firm's first Chief Diversity Officer. Throughout her career of practicing in excess of 30 years, Paulette has held a number of positions, including in-house counsel to a number of fortune 500 companies and as a Municipal Court Judge. For the past 20 years, she has focused her practice on labor and employment matters. She has litigated a variety of employment matters, including, but not limited to, class actions, sexual harassment, marital status, WARN, race and age discrimination and issues pertaining to FMLA. Paulette is also experienced in all aspects of workplace training and collective bargaining.

Paulette litigates in both federal and state courts and arbitration forums for both unionized and non-union employees. Paulette is a certified mediator for the United States District Court, District of New Jersey and a AAA panel member. She is a frequent lecturer on labor and employment issues and issues related to electronic discovery and serves as Secretary of Committee of the Labor and Employment Section of the New Jersey State Bar Association. Paulette has been recognized by the New Jersey Law Journal as one of the prominent women and minority attorneys in the State of New Jersey.

Paulette is immediate past President of the YWCA of Central New Jersey, which, in the Fall of 2006, opened a twenty-four hour a day, seven day a week, early childhood learning center. One of Paulette's proudest moments was when she led a delegation to monitor the first free and democratic elections in South Africa in 1994. Paulette is a past President of the National Bar Association and the Association of Black Women Lawyers of New Jersey. She serves on the American Bar Association's Commission on Women in the Profession and co-chaired the report, "Visible Invisibility: Women of Color In Law Firms."

As a result of her charitable efforts and work with various bar associations, Paulette has received numerous awards, including the Medal of Honor Award from the New Jersey Bar Foundation and the Equal Justice Award from the National Bar Association. She has also received from the New Jersey Commission on Professionalism, its Professional Lawyer of the Year Award. In February, 2007, she received the American Bar Association's Spirit of Excellence Award, and in May, 2007, Paulette received the NJ NAACP's Trailblazer Award. In May, 2008, she was identified by the National Law Journal as one of The 50 Most Influential Minority Lawyers in America.

Paulette speaks extensively on diversity issues, particularly those related to women and women of color in law firms.

LUCIA COYOCA

 Lucia E. Coyoca is a partner in the Los Angeles office of Mitchell Silberberg & Knupp, LLP. She specializes in litigation, particularly in the entertainment industry, and has extensive jury and bench trial, arbitration, and mediation experience. She was selected as one of the top five percent of lawyers in Southern California by Southern California *Super Lawyers* magazine (2005-2010). Lucia graduated from the University of California Davis School of Law in 1986.

Lucia serves or has served on the board of Legal Momentum (formerly known as the NOW Legal Defense and Education Fund); the Diversity Committee for the Managing Partnerrs Roundtable; the Los Angeles County Bar Association's Fair Judicial Elections Practices Committee; and the California State Bar Committee on Status of Diversity in the Profession.

SANDRA GIANNONE EZELL

 Sandra Giannone Ezell is the managing partner at the Richmond office of Bowman and Brooke LLP. She is also a national trial counsel who spends as much time as possible picking juries. She has tried numerous cases to verdict, always on behalf of defendants and/or corporations, and focuses her practice primarily in the products liability realm. Sandra routinely defends wrongful death and catastrophic injury product liability cases, often involving children. She has leveraged her work in child injury cases into forming the firm's Children and Product Liability Group. She was honored last year with the Burton Award for her seminal work entitled "Round Up the Usual Suspects: Traditional Methods of Selecting First-Chair Trial Counsel in Products Liability Cases Exclude Women and Weaken the Defense," which focuses on the lack of first-chair women trial lawyers in complex litigation. She is a leader in her firm's diversity initiative, which received the 2008 DRI Law Firm Diversity Award. She is a frequent author and speaker in the areas of diversity, women in leadership and trial practice. She balances a trial practice and office management and a fulsome family life with her husband, Shawn, and their four children.

PAULA W. HINTON

Paula W. Hinton is a senior partner in Vinson & Elkins' litigation and regulatory section in Vinson & Elkins' Houston office. Her practice has focused on representing businesses in complex civil trial proceedings and arbitrations across the United States and in international arbitrations for almost 30 years. Ms. Hinton's experience has involved a wide variety of disputes, including those concerning contracts and general business issues, fraud investigations, trademark and trade secret issues, telecommunications and technical litigation, and numerous consumer fraud and other class actions across the country.

Ms. Hinton is a graduate of the University of Alabama School of Law, as well as having earned a Masters in Public Administration. She was a Rotary Fellow at the Universidad de Sevilla, where she studied international comparative law. Among other professional honors, Ms. Hinton is listed in Best Lawyers in America and is a member of the American Law Institute. She has served the bar in many ways, including her service as Chair of the Texas Supreme Court's Gender Bias Task Force and as a board director of the State Bar of Texas. In addition, she has served the ABA in a number of capacities, including as a member of the Woman Advocate Committee and as a 2007 Texas Delegate to the ABA House of Delegates. Ms. Hinton's civic participation includes, in part, serving on the Haverford College Parents' Executive Council, the Advisory Board of the Houston Zoo, and as Chair of the United Way's Women's Initiative. Ms. Hinton has been a recipient of the State Bar of Texas' Women and the Law Section's MA'AT Justice Award, the Houston Chronicle's Texas Executive Women's Woman on the Move Award in 2004, and she was recognized in 2008 as one of the "50 Most Influential Women in Houston" by Houston Woman Magazine.

GILLIAN HOBSON

Gillian is a partner at Vinson & Elkins LLP where she focuses her practice in corporate finance and securities law. She has represented both issuers and underwriters in public and private debt and equity securities offerings totaling more than $7 billion, including offerings of limited partner interests of publicly traded partnerships, also known as MLPs. Gillian also has represented both public and private companies in complex mergers and acquisitions, asset and stock dispositions and venture capital financings. She regularly counsels clients on general corporate matters, including compliance with periodic reporting requirements and has significant experience with proxy disclosure issues, corporate governance, executive compensation and Section 16 reporting obligations. Gillian has been recognized as a "Texas Rising Star" in securities and corporate finance by *Texas Monthly* in 2007, 2008 and 2009.

In addition to client work, Gillian is a member of V&E's Women's Career Development Council, leads a mentoring circle for a group of eight women attorneys, coordinates training programs for junior associates, actively participates in the Firm's recruiting efforts, and is a co-team lead for the University of Houston Law Center. Gillian also serves on the Board of Directors of the Houston Area Women's Center and is a member of the Greater Houston Partnership's Emerging Women Leaders group.

Born in Christiansted, St. Croix, Gillian holds a law degree from the University of Houston and an undergraduate degree from Harvard University. She and her husband, Don, are the parents of two children, Brittany, 21 and Keaon, 16.

DINITA L. JAMES

 Dinita L. James is a partner in the Phoenix office of Ford & Harrison LLP, a national law firm with 18 offices throughout the country that represents management in all aspects of labor and employment law. Ms. James relocated her practice to Phoenix in 2008, after 20 years practicing in Tampa, FL, including seven years with Ford & Harrison. Her first 11 years of practice was the Tampa, FL firm of Trenam Kemker Scharf Barkin Frye O'Neill & Mullis, P.A.

Ms. James has extensive experience litigating complex matters in state and federal courts, including large employment discrimination class actions and collective actions. She has represented employers in defense of individual cases arising under anti-discrimination, whistleblower protection and anti-retaliation laws and in litigation relating to noncompetition agreements and trade secrets laws. She also has an active appellate practice and, in 2009, already has argued cases before the Nevada Supreme Court and the Ninth and Tenth Circuit U.S. Courts of Appeal.

For three years, Ms. James co-chaired the ABA Section of Litigation's Committee on Class Actions and Derivative Suits and, thereafter, served a three-year term on the Governing Council of the ABA Section of Litigation. She also was appointed to chair the Council's CLE Committee after being honored for two consecutive years with the Section's Award of Excellence for CLE Programming. Thereafter, she chaired the Council's Diversity Committee for two years. She will become Managing Director of volunteer efforts for the Section of Litigation, the ABA's largest membership section, in August 2009.

She is a Past President of the Florida Association for Women Lawyers, the Hillsborough (FL) Association for Women Lawyers, and the Ferguson-White American Inn of Court. Ms. James was also recognized by *Florida Trend* magazine as one of "Florida's Legal Elite" (2004–2006). She is AV® Peer Review Rated by Martindale-Hubbell.

Prior to attending law school, Ms. James worked for more than seven years as a reporter and editor for the *Greensboro News & Record* and the *Tampa Tribune* and now advises clients on dealing with the media in high-profile cases. Ms. James earned a bachelor degree in journalism from the University of North Carolina at Chapel Hill in 1980, and returned to UNC-CH in 1987 to attend the School of Law, graduating first in her law school class in 1990. She served as Executive Articles Editor for the *North Carolina Law Review* and was a member of the Order of the Coif.

Dinita is admitted to practice in Arizona, Florida, three federal District Courts in Florida, the federal District Court in Arizona, and the Ninth, Tenth, and Eleventh Circuit U.S. Courts of Appeals.

KOURTNEY L. JAMES

 Kourtney L. James is an associate in the Houston office of Vinson & Elkins LLP, a leading energy law firm. Ms. James has engaged in a domestic and international business transactions practice that focuses on energy, project finance and development, and mergers and acquisitions (including joint ventures). Her experience covers a broad spectrum of energy-related matters within the upstream, midstream and downstream sectors. She has particular experience in the electric power area of wind project development. Ms. James also has represented clients on a variety of transactions involving aircraft financings.

Ms. James earned a bachelor degree in History of Science from Harvard University in 2002. She earned her law degree from Stanford University Law School in 2005, where she served as Features Articles Editor for the Stanford Law & Policy Review.

Outside of the law, Kourtney spends her free time mentoring high school students on college application procedures and planning her next foray to an exotic country.

SANDRA A. JESKIE

Sandra A. Jeskie is a partner at Duane Morris, LLP. She has a diverse national practice focused on commercial and technology-based litigation, including commercial litigation, intellectual property litigation, software litigation, e-commerce, privacy, security and Internet or computer law. Ms. Jeskie has litigated complex commercial disputes in state and federal courts and before arbitrators. Leveraging her more than 16 years experience as a computer scientist, Ms. Jeskie also negotiates and drafts service agreements and content Internet-related agreements. She also counsels clients on a wide range of matters, including privacy, security policies and practices, software licensing, systems development projects, e-discovery, and document retention.

She has appeared on the faculties of dozens of professional education conferences in a number of U.S. cities and around the world, has appeared on the CN8 morning program, and has been quoted in several publications, including the *National Journal's Technology Daily*, *Compliance Reporter*, *Computer World* and the *Philadelphia Business Journal*. She also co-authored a "Contracts" chapter in an acclaimed treatise, *Business and Commercial Litigation in Federal Courts*. In 2007, she was named BTI Client Service All-Star for "delivering the absolute best client service." She was appointed to serve as Special Master to two courts in the Eastern District of Pennsylvania on cases involving e-discovery disputes, and she has served as an adjunct Professor at Rutgers School of Law, Camden, New Jersey. She is vice-president of the International Technology Law Association (ITechLaw), an officer of the Business Law section of the Philadelphia Bar Association, and past chair of its Cyberspace and E-Commerce Committee. She is also member of the Litigation, Intellectual Property and Science and Technology sections of the American Bar Association. At Duane Morris, Ms. Jeskie is co-chair of the firm's Information Technologies and Telecom interdisciplinary practice group, co-chair of the firm's Women's Initiative and chair of the firm's e-discovery committee. She can be reached at jeskie@duanemorris.com or 215-979-1395.

NAN JOESTEN

Nan E. Joesten is a partner at the firm of Farella Braun & Martel in San Francisco, where she is a member of the firm's Intellectual Property and Business Litigation groups. Her diverse complex litigation practice focuses on a wide variety of commercial disputes, including patent and trademark infringement, trade secret misappropriation, and technology-related litigation. She is a founder of the firm's Women's Initiative, and currently serves as the partner co-chair of the firm's Professional Development Committee.

Nan received her B.S. in Chemical Engineering from the University of Colorado and her J.D. from Boalt Hall at the University of California at Berkeley where she is the immediate past president of the board of directors of the Boalt Hall Alumni Association. She was awarded the UC Berkeley Foundation 2007 Trustee's Citation Award for outstanding service to the law school, and she is also a member of the Engineering Advisory Council for the College of Engineering at the University of Colorado. Nan is a co-chair of the Woman Advocate Committee of the ABA's Litigation Section, and regularly has fun at ABA gatherings throughout the year. When not working or attending board meetings, Nan has fun backpacking with her husband and their two dogs in the mountains of California.

MARGARET LAMBE JUROW

 Margaret Lambe Jurow is a litigator with 20 years of experience in New Jersey commercial and bankruptcy practice. She is currently a senior attorney at Legal Services of New Jersey working on an anti-predatory lending and a statewide foreclosure defense initiative. Margaret represents low income homeowners in state court and in bankruptcy court in connection with home mortgage foreclosure defense and consumer fraud claims. Margaret initiated the Pro Bono Foreclosure Defense Initiative recruiting over 200 private attorneys to assist low income families in foreclosure defense. Margaret is a frequent lecturer and trainer with regard to predatory lending issues. She has testified before the state legislature with regard to foreclosure and predatory lending issues.

BETH KAUFMAN

Beth L. Kaufman, a partner at Schoeman Updike & Kaufman, LLP, concentrates her practice in the defense of complex litigation in the federal and state courts and in ADR forums. She was elected by her peers as a New York SuperLawyer and a Best Lawyer in New York, New Jersey and Connecticut in 2006, 2007 and 2008. Member, Council of the ABA Section of Litigation and Board of Directors of the National Association of Women Lawyers and former member of the Executive Committee of the Association of the Bar of the City of New York and former Chair of that Association's Committee on the Judiciary. Ms. Kaufman was appointed by New York City Mayor Michael R. Bloomberg to serve on the Mayor's Advisory Committee on the Judiciary and currently serves on that Committee.

JANET KOLE

Janet S. Kole has been a litigator since 1980, concentrating in environmental law. She has most recently been a shareholder at Flaster Greenberg PC.

She has written numerous articles and books on litigation strategies, most recently "Chasing Paper: Paper Discovery for Young Lawyers," ABA (Section of Litigation 2009). She has been an instructor for NITA programs, for the ABA's Woman Advocate seminars, and for the Philadelphia Bar Association. She was one of the original editors of the first Woman Advocate book.

She is a fellow of the American Bar Foundation and a fellow of the Academy of Advocacy. She is a member of the bars of Pennsylvania, New Jersey and New York.

Although she loves the practice of law, Janet would always prefer to do it on a boat.

ROBERTA LIEBENBERG

 Ms. Liebenberg is a member of Fine, Kaplan and Black. She is a 1970 graduate of the University of Michigan and a 1975 graduate of the Catholic University Columbus School of Law, *magna cum laude*, where she was the Notes Editor of the Law Review. Thereafter, she served as a law clerk for the United States Court of Appeals for the Fourth Circuit.

In May, 2007, Ms. Liebenberg was named as one of The National Law Journal's "50 Most Influential Women Lawyers in America." In June, 2008, she was named as one of the "Top Ten Super Lawyers in Pennsylvania" in Philadelphia Magazine. In October, 2006, Ms. Liebenberg was named by Pennsylvania Governor Ed Rendell as a "Distinguished Daughter of Pennsylvania." In April, 2003, she was named as the first recipient of the Lynette Norton Award by the Pennsylvania Bar Association's Commission on Women in the Profession. That award was given to her in recognition of her outstanding litigation skills and mentoring of women attorneys. In December, 2003, she was named as one of the "Women of Distinction" by the Philadelphia Business Journal and the National Association of Women Business Owners, based on her commitment to professional excellence and community involvement. Every year since 2004, she has been recognized by Philadelphia Magazine as one of the "Top 50 Female Super Lawyers in Pennsylvania" and one of the "Top 100 Super Lawyers in Pennsylvania." Ms. Liebenberg was named one of the "Women Leaders in the Profession" by The Legal Intelligencer. She was recognized as a leader in the field of Class Actions.

Ms. Liebenberg served as Chair of the American Bar Association's Standing Committee on the Federal Judiciary from 2006-2007. In 2008, Ms. Liebenberg was appointed as Chair of the American Bar Association's Commission on Women in the Profession, whose first Chair was Senator Hillary Clinton. In addition, she chaired the Pennsylvania Bar Association's Commission on Women in the Profession from 1995 to 1997. She was appointed by the Pennsylvania Supreme Court to the Interbranch Commission for Gender, Racial and Ethnic Fairness, and serves as Chair of its Domestic Violence and Sexual Assault Victims Committee. Previously, she was appointed by the Pennsylvania Supreme Court to its Committee on Racial and Gender Bias in the Justice System, where she was Co-Chair of the Gender Bias Committee. She also served as Co-Chair of the Philadelphia Bar Association's Women in the Profession Committee.

AMY B. MESSIGIAN

 Amy B. Messigian is a recent graduate of Georgetown University Law Center in Washington D.C., where she was the articles editor of the American Criminal Law Review, editor-in-chief of the Georgetown Law Weekly, and a member of the International Women's Human Rights Clinic. She currently practices labor and employment law and litigation in Los Angeles, with a special emphasis on employment discrimination and on entertainment industry transactions. She has been a member of the ABA Woman Advocate Committee since she was appointed Law Student Liaison to the committee in 2005. In her spare time, Amy loves expanding her culinary skills and creating unbeatable fantasy sports teams. She dedicates this chapter to her grandmothers—Louise Messigian and Anne Polkowski—two inspirational women who cultivated her sense of integrity, self-worth, humility and grace.

LINDA A. MONICA

 Linda A. Monica is a litigation lawyer with more than 30 years in private practice. She focuses her practice in the areas of products liability and toxic tort litigation and has represented several Fortune 500 companies in mass tort litigation throughout the country. She has tried numerous cases in state and federal courts in New England. She is the principal of Monica & Associates, P.C., a law firm she founded in 2004. She is AV rated by Martindale-Hubbell.

Linda has extensive practice management experience in major New England law firms with a primary focus on developing and implementing marketing strategies for practice groups and individual lawyers. In conjunction with her litigation practice, she works with women lawyers and law firms on business development strategies and the implementation of "Women Initiatives." She speaks regularly at national seminars on strategies for effective business development.

Linda developed and chaired the first national conferences devoted solely to the topic of "Business Development for Women Attorneys." In that venue, she presented her "Niche Marketing" approach, which has helped many women lawyers successfully launch their business development efforts. Her strategies on focusing, prioritizing, and leveraging time and efforts enable women lawyers to become more strategic and deliberate as they maintain and sustain their networking and marketing efforts.

She serves on the Executive Board of the ABA's "Women Rainmakers" that has as its primary goals to educate professional women about marketing and business development and to provide networking opportunities. She also serves as co-chair of the "Rainmaking" Subcommittee of the Woman Advocate Committee.

BARBARA A. MOORE

Barbara A. Moore is a native of Morristown, NJ. Ms. Moore earned a B.A. in English from Iowa State University in 1978, with distinction, and was elected to membership in Phi Beta Kappa. In 1981, she graduated from the University of Pennsylvania Law School. Since then, Ms. Moore has practiced law in New Jersey. She began her career as a litigation associate for Pitney Hardin Kipp & Szuch in Morristown. For the past 21 years, she has been employed by Rhodia Inc., a French based chemicals manufacturer with its US headquarters in Cranbury, NJ, where she serves as Assistant General Counsel and Chief Litigation Counsel and manages the company's litigation portfolio, including litigation having an international and global impact for the parent company.

Ms. Moore's various professional affiliations include membership in the American Bar Association, the New Jersey State Bar Association, and the American and New Jersey Corporate Counsel Associations. Among a long list of distinguished career achievements, in 1993, Ms. Moore received the Princeton YWCA's Tribute to Women in Industry ("TWIN") award upon the coveted recommendation of her employer. The prestigious TWIN award is bestowed upon business and professional women in recognition of their many accomplishments and contributions to commerce. Ms. Moore and her husband, Stan Prater, reside in Basking Ridge, NJ and are the proud parents of 15-year-old Victoria.

BEATRICE O'DONNELL

Beatrice O'Donnell is a senior litigation partner at Duane Morris LLP, one of the 100 largest firms in the country. Ms. O'Donnell maintains an active trial practice in the areas of commercial, mass tort, products liability, and patent litigation as well as healthcare-related litigation. Ms. O'Donnell has tried to verdict more than 80 major civil jury trials in both the state and federal courts and has experience in handling hundreds of arbitration and mediations. She served as coordinating counsel in mass tort litigation for multiple clients in the areas of asbestos, pharmaceuticals and food supplements. Recently, Ms. O'Donnell defended a Fortune 500 Company in a complex patent infringement cases and a related contract action involving a life-saving bio-pharmaceutical product.

In 2008 through 2010, Ms. O'Donnell was identified in *Best Lawyers* in America for Product Liability Law and Professional Malpractice Law. Ms. O'Donnell was designated in 2004 through 2010 as among Pennsylvania's *Super Lawyers* in a statewide survey and as one of the *Top 50 Women* in 2009.

Ms. O'Donnell is member of the Litigation section of the American Bar Association and the executive committee of the ABA Woman Advocate Committee. She is a two-term past co-chair of the Pennsylvania Bar Association's Commission on Women in the Profession, and a member of the Philadelphia Bar Association's Women in the Profession Committee. Ms. O'Donnell is a Master and two-term Executive Committee member of the Temple American Inn of Court. Ms. O'Donnell has been serving on her firm's management committee, the Duane Morris Partners Board for the last three years. Ms. O'Donnell is co-chair of their senior women associate mentoring effort through the firm's Women's Initiative.

Ms. O'Donnell has served as a Board Member and Executive Committee member of Living Beyond Breast Cancer for over 12 years and currently is on the Board of Observers of Muhlenberg College and Co-Chair of their Parents Council.

ELLEN OSTROW, PH.D.

 Dr. Ellen Ostrow is founding principal of Lawyers Life Coach, Inc., a firm specializing in leadership, business development and career coaching for lawyers and consultation to legal employers. Ellen's practice is focused on helping women overcome barriers to their career advancement without compromising the quality of their lives. Ellen's email newsletter, *Beyond the Billable Hour*, has been reprinted by bar and women's bar associations throughout the U.S., and she has been invited by the ABA, NAWL, NALP and numerous other legal industry groups to address their members about ways in which women lawyers can succeed professionally while achieving work-life integration. Ellen has been quoted by the *NY Times*, the *Washington Post*, the *Legal Times*, the *ABA Journal, Lawyers USA, NY Law Journal, The Complete Lawyer* and *PINK Magazine*. She is a contributing author for *NY Law Journal Magazine*, NAWL's *Women Lawyers' Journal*, the ABA Commission on Women in the Profession's Perspectives, *The Complete Lawyer*, and other legal publications. Ellen earned her Ph.D. in psychology in 1980 from the University of Rochester and is a Certified MentorCoach.™

HONORABLE GENE E. K. PRATTER

Judge Pratter became a federal district court judge in the Eastern District of Pennsylvania on June 18, 2004. Previously, Judge Pratter was a partner in and General Counsel of the law firm of Duane Morris LLP, having started her career there in 1975. In practice she represented clients in commercial litigation, ethics matters and professional liability and licensing disputes.

A 1975 graduate of the University of Pennsylvania Law School following receipt of her A.B. from Stanford University, she is a member of the American Law Institute and the American Bar Association's Litigation Section and the Philadelphia Bar Association's Committees on Professional Responsibility and Professional Guidance which she chaired from 2000 through 2001. She is a member of the National Association of Women Judges and serves on various committees within the federal judiciary, and represents the judiciary in many community outreach activities. Judge Pratter served as the co-chair of the ABA Litigation Section's Committee on Ethics and Professionalism and of the Section's Task Force on the Independent Lawyer. A member and current President of the University of Pennsylvania's American Inns of Court, she is the author of a number of articles concerning ethics and professional conduct and has presented many programs for practitioners on those and other subjects, including litigation practice and procedures. Judge Pratter is a member of the Adjunct Faculty in Law at the University of Pennsylvania Law School where she teaches Trial Advocacy. Judge Pratter was an Overseer of the University of Pennsylvania Law School from 1993 to 1999.

She has been and remains active in a host of community, church and educational activities and is the recipient of various professional organizations' awards and honors. She and her husband, Robert L. Pratter, Esq., have two children and one grandson.

DEBORAH RHODE

 Deborah L. Rhode is the Ernest W. McFarland Professor of Law and the Director of the Center on the Legal Profession at Stanford University. Her teaching and research focuses on gender inequality and legal ethics. She is the former president of the Association of American Law Schools, the former chair of the American Bar Association's Commission on Women in the Profession, the former founding director of Stanford's Center on Ethics, a former trustee of Yale University, and the former director of Stanford's Institute for Research on Women and Gender. She also served as senior counsel to the Minority members of the Judiciary Committee, the United States House of Representatives, on presidential impeachment issues during the Clinton administration. She is the most frequently cited scholar on legal ethics and writes for general as well as scholarly audiences in leading academic journals and in newspapers and magazines including The New York Times and Ms. She is a regular columnist for the National Law Journal.

Professor Rhode graduated Phi Beta Kappa and summa cum laude from Yale College and received her legal training from Yale Law School. After clerking for Supreme Court Justice Thurgood Marshall, she joined the Stanford faculty. She is the author or coauthor of twenty books and over 200 articles.

Her recent books concerning gender include *Women and Leadership: The State of Play and Strategies for Change* (with Barbara Kellerman, 2007); *Gender and Law: Theory, Doctrine, Commentary* (with Katharine T. Bartlett, 2006); *The Difference "Difference" Makes: Women and Leadership* (2003), and *Speaking of Sex* (1997). Her book on appearance discrimination, *The Injustice of Appearance*, is forthcoming from Oxford University Press.

ANNE MARIE SEIBEL

 Anne Marie Seibel is a partner in the Litigation Practice Group of Bradley Arant Boult Cummings LLP. Since joining the firm in 1998, Anne Marie has been involved in a wide range of complex litigation work, ranging from pharmaceutical tort defense, medical malpractice defense, and significant commercial disputes, including federal, state, and arbitration proceedings relating to the aftermath of a significant corporate fraud. She has been on the trial teams for the first Vioxx defense verdict in Alabama and claims against Richard Scrushy.

Anne Marie is co-chair of the firm's Litigation Life Sciences Practice Group, co-chair of the firm's Women's Initiative, and a member of the Associate Committee.

After receiving a degree in Foreign Affairs from the University of Virginia and before attending Vanderbilt Law School, Anne Marie spent a year in Bonn, Germany on a graduate fellowship. She resides in Birmingham, Alabama with her husband and two children.

Anne Marie has been active in the Woman Advocate Committee of the ABA's Section of Litigation as co-chair of the Mentoring and Membership Subcommittees.

KIMBERLY TALLEY

 Kimberly Talley is a partner at Mitchell, Silberberg and Knupp LLP. She has devoted the last fifteen years of her practice to counseling and defending employers and individual business professionals in all aspects of labor and employment law and litigation.

Ms. Talley has successfully represented employers in wrongful termination litigation, discrimination claims, wage and hour matters, grievances, arbitrations, and alternative dispute resolution proceedings. She provides day-to-day counseling on employee-related issues, including employer-employee rights and obligations under state and federal labor and employment-related laws. She has been named a Southern California Super Lawyer by Key Professional Media, Inc. for 2006–2009. In 2009, she was also named one of the Top 50 Women Attorneys in Southern California by the same publication.

Ms. Talley is a Phi Beta Kappa and *magna cum laude* graduate of the University of South Carolina. She graduated from Harvard Law School in 1989. She is a member of several civic and professional organizations, including the Black Women Lawyers Association of Los Angeles, Inc., Los Angeles County Bar Foundation (Director), Los Angeles County Bar Association, and the Southern California Association of Defense Counsel. She also currently writes a column for Bender's California Labor & Employment Bulletin entitled "Eye on the Supreme Court" which features a discussion of legal issues pending before the United States Supreme Court.

TARA TRASK

 Tara Trask is President and Founder of Tara Trask and Associates, a full service litigation strategy, jury research and trial consulting practice with offices in San Francisco and Dallas. She has 15 years of experience in the field of jury research and has debriefed thousands of jurors, both mock and actual.

Ms. Trask has been involved in over 300 jury trials across the country, including assisting Oprah Winfrey in *Texas Beef Group v. Winfrey* and ABC in *Food Lion v. ABC*. She developed the juror profile used by Exxon in the *Exxon v. Lloyd's* excess case involving the Valdez spill. In an 11 to 1 decision, that jury found that the underwriters should honor the policy and the resulting $250 million dollar verdict was one of the largest in Texas that year. "Your involvement helped us win" summed up Schreiber Foods President Larry Ferguson's views after a jury returned a verdict of $26 million in a complex patent case.

Ms. Trask's practice includes all types of complex litigation, including intellectual property, contract disputes, oil and gas, products liability, medical and legal malpractice, employment, and securities. She is a frequent author and lecturer on juror psychology and other trial science topics. She serves as Treasurer for the Board of Directors of the American Society of Trial Consultants and is a member of the American Bar Association, and the APA Psychology-Law Society.

Ms. Trask is an avid fundraiser, serving on the Board of Directors for Raphael House, San Francisco's first family shelter, and committees for Global Green San Francisco, and Care Through Action. She has competed in over 125 triathlons in the last 18 years, most recently Ironman New Zealand. She lives in Marin County, California with her husband and two children.

TIFFANY M. WILLIAMS

 Tiffany M. Williams is the Deputy Chief Counsel to New Jersey Governor Jon S. Corzine. She is formerly the chief legal counsel to the Speaker of the General Assembly and the Democratic majority caucus. She is a former Assistant United States Attorney for the District of New Jersey and was formerly a senior associate at Riker, Danzig, Scherer, Hyland & Perretti in Morristown, New Jersey. She is admitted to practice in New Jersey, Massachusetts and the District of Columbia.

Index